THE WIND BLEW FROM THE EAST

THE WIND BLEW
FROM THE EAST

*A Study in the Orientation
of American Culture*

By

FERNER NUHN

---

*With a New Foreword by the Author
and
With a New Introduction by
Ellis Allen Johnson*

KENNIKAT PRESS, INC./PORT WASHINGTON, N. Y.

THE WIND BLEW FROM THE EAST

Copyright 1940, 1942 by Ferner Rall Nuhn
Reissued in 1967 by Kennikat Press by arrangement with Harper
and Row, Publishers, Incorporated.

Library of Congress Catalog Card No: 67-27631

Manufactured in the United States of America

Analyzed in the ESSAY & GENERAL LITERATURE INDEX

CONTENTS

[v]

NOTE

THIS book is one of a group of three which I hope to be able to complete, dealing with different strands in our American culture. As the title suggests, this first volume is concerned with the cultural effects of the great current of migration, east to west, which produced the New World out of the Old. In approaching the puzzling question of our European inheritance and our American experience, I have tried to make certain distinctions: between racial memory and working ideas, between nostalgia and true tradition. Working ideas, in such a distinction, would go along with American experience, and make up together what might be called a living tradition. Racial memory alone, however, would produce a nostalgic tradition, the desire to retrace the racial steps; and it is mainly with this strand in our culture that I have dealt in this book. It might also be called our minor "aristocratic tradition," for in effect it is the ever-present pullback toward modes of culture that lie in our past. For the sake of orientation, I have sketched a general framework in the early chapters of this book, and blocked in other main elements. In the other volumes I hope to fill out a conception of our main democratic tradition as part of the world stream of culture, and to deal, too, with a certain tragic strand that I find in our literature.

F. N.

Cedar Falls, Iowa, January, 1942.

FOREWORD TO 1967 REISSUE

The second edition of this book, a quarter of a century after its first release, is presented without change in the original text, except for a few minor corrections. For this reason, I would remind the reader of the time in which the book was written. It appeared in 1942, just at the beginning of the Second World War. As a study in "the orientation of American culture," it must be read with that point in our American experience in mind.

In the words of the original fore-note, the volume "is concerned with the cultural effects of the great migration, east to west, which produced the New World out of the Old. In approaching the puzzling question of our European inheritance and our American experience, I have tried to make certain distinctions: between the racial memory and working ideas, between nostaglia and true tradition. Working ideas, in such a distinction, would go along with American experience and make up altogether what might be called a living tradition. Racial memory alone, however, would produce a nostalgic tradition, the desire to retrace the racial steps; and it is mainly with this strand in our culture that I have dealt in this book . . . For the sake of orientation, I have sketched a general framework in the early chapters . . . and blocked in other main elements."

The book was originally projected as one of a series of three. For various reasons, the other volumes have not materialized, though it is possible that a volume centering upon Emerson, Lincoln, and Whitman as types of American greatness may in time appear.

However this may be, I hope the reader will approach this book as a self-contained unit. As I look at it again, I am struck by the degree to which, in fact, it does present a rounded view of American culture. Six of its nine chapters are concerned with such a general view. The last chapter particularly, "On New

FOREWORD TO 1967 REISSUE

World Grounds," develops certain ideas about American conditions and experience which are meant to characterize our culture as a whole.

Since 1942, tremendous changes have occurred in American and world civilization. The relationship of the United States to the rest of the world has altered greatly. It is commonplace to note that two new foci of world power and influence have emerged in place of Europe, which was the center of world civilization for so long: America and Russia (with China perhaps a third focus, whose meaning is not yet clear.) Europe is no longer, consciously or unconsciously, the seat of spiritual and cultural authority for America, as I suggested it still was in America's naive intervention in World War I and her naive withdrawal from Europe afterwards. It took the Second World War to break the European mother-image in the American psyche—break the Golden Bowl for good.

Now, a whole new Pandora's box of forces and mysteries, internal and external, have been opened up for America to try to understand and meet. With its wealth, technology, and all the rest—and back of these, its political and cultural evolution—America, more than any other society, has been the producer of these new conditions and forces. This book, of course, does not consider this new phase of American experience. Yet I believe this study contains certain germinal ideas which are pertinent to this new period, which indeed may throw some lights upon it.

As for American cultural nostalgia, which is the specific theme of this book, no doubt some form of this nostalgia will continue to appear. This study tells the story of one form of American nostalgia which has run its course.

I must leave the three main studies, of Henry James, Henry Adams, and T. S. Eliot, as they are. However, I am glad for this chance to make a few comments upon them, particularly on the last two, from the perspective of more than two decades.

I would like to add a foot-note to the study of Henry Adams, confirming his brilliant talent for prophecy in certain areas of history. The awesome event of the release of nuclear energy in 1945, three years after this book was written, fits in almost perfectly with Adams' projection of the "acceleration of energy," as part of his theory of the "Rule of Phase in History." This foot-note, of course, leaves unchanged Adams' conclusions about the meaning of power in modern society, and my own conclusions about the conflict in Adams' life between power and love.

The chapter on T. S. Eliot is left as it is, too, even though it can not take into account the long and significant period of his life between 1942 and the poet's death in January of 1965. I am glad, however, for this opportunity to add some comments and reflections in view of this later period.

In my study of *The Waste Land,* I made some effort (pp. 221-226) to follow out the skein of allusions to other literature woven into that work. The margins of various books I own, such as the Bible, continue to be marked with new notations ("see T.S.E." etc.) about these allusions, so dense and elaborate is that web! Many scholars, however, have been at work in this area, so that I need not try to trace these lines further.

I wrote of Eliot's life (page 203), that he had "sought to make, apparently, a complete break with his American background, and pick up as it were the very threads of the tradition that his ancestors had dropped three centuries ago, when they left old England." The poet's choice of a burial place, revealed at the time of his death, bears out this observation in a curiously literal way. He had asked to be, and was buried in the little church-yard at East Coker, the village in which his paternal ancestors had lived up to the time the founder of the New England line left there for Massachusetts. Except for brief visits which enabled him, apparently, to arrange for the interment, and to write the poem, "East Coker," the poet seems to have had no personal involvement with this village. Its chief significance, for him it seems clear, lay in its being the spot of earth in which the St. Louis-born author might unite his ashes with the dust of his English forebears.

Mainly, however, I want to note the development which took place in the poet's later life and work. However the later work, from the "Four Quartets" on, compares with the earlier work in sheer poetic force, it shows the author emerging into a freer, more fulfilled phase of his life and thought than the one dealt with in this book, which I have called "Orpheus in Hell."

The earlier work, for example, contains nothing like the open, warm-hearted quality of the poem celebrating his love for his second wife called "A Dedication to My Wife" (Collected Poems, 1909-1962.) What I have written herein of the alienation of the life of the senses from the life of the mind in the earlier poetry (e.g., p. 218) obviously could not be applied to this poem. One rejoices in what this difference reflects concerning the poet's own life and experience. I would like to make clear my admiration for the character of Eliot as it emerges over the years: the moral and intellectual as well as aesthetic integrity to which it witnesses.

Finally, as to the style of this book, I hope new readers, with one of its first readers, Alfred Kazin (in *Books* of the Herald-Tribune, June 7, 1942), will be able to "get used to a certain orphic looseness" in it. The writer has lived to wince at places where, in its "studious informality" (to quote Mr. Kazin again), the manner becomes a little *too* loose, even jaunty. I would judiciously tighten it in such places, if I could. However, generally speaking, the style must continue to be what it is, and I trust readers may find Alfred Kazin not entirely wrong in ob-

FOREWORD TO 1967 REISSUE

serving that "it is the kind of style, to reverse some wit's remark about Macaulay's, in which one *can* say the truth."

Since the above was written, I have had the pleasure of reading the evocative introduction to this second edition by Dr. Ellis Johnson. I am grateful to Dr. Johnson for his catching so well the spirit of this book and suggesting so vividly what it is trying to say.

Ferner Nuhn

Claremont, California
August, 1967

ACKNOWLEDGMENTS

"Henry Adams and the Hand of the Fathers" was published in shortened form in *American Prefaces*: *A Journal of Critical and Imaginative Writing*, Iowa City. Acknowledgment is also made to Charles Scribner's Sons for permission to quote certain passages from the writings and letters of Henry James; to Houghton, Mifflin Company for Henry James and Henry Adams; to Harcourt, Brace and Company for T. S. Eliot; and to Robinson Jeffers and The Macmillan Company for verses quoted from "Invocation," *Californians*.

INTRODUCTION TO THE 1967 REISSUE

There was never any doubt about the nature of the glitter seen in the western sky—

> gold in the east looked like reassurance and promise of return, while gold in the west looked like opportunity, and could make a family leave home and altar and kindred to try a hazard of new hope.

The New World is the most fabulous example of this movement. It emerged late in time and the great fact about the New World was that it *existed*. With all due courtesy to Europe, the style of arms, loot, and alarms was played at its height by the Old World making a stage of the New. A directing hand thousands of miles across the sea gave it character, but it was biologically, culturally wrong and the offspring evidenced sufficient readiness to try fortune on their own.[1]

Fortunate in variety as well as in common qualities, the North American colonies complimented each other and were much more effective working together than any could be working alone. Massachusetts liked to appeal to conscience, Virginia to reason, and it took both rational and spiritual elements to produce *democracy*—our light and our pride. Equally fortunate was the strong middle ground in every sense of the term; Illinois and Lincoln seems a superlative example—

> It would be hard to mention someone else with quite as much right to mix high with broad, and put in the same sentence charity toward all and firmness in the right as God gives us to see the right.

We might have had something very big and found that it was only *Rome* all over again. There "class" was narrow and meant to be; some of the nobles were really fine and noble, but others were not, and there was no check on them. Here "class" was a balance between the "natural aristocracy" of John Adams and

INTRODUCTION TO THE 1967 REISSUE

Jefferson's "common man," Lincoln and his "people." Theirs was the best statement thus far of a democratic Plato's *Republic,* an everyman's version of Castiglione's *Perfect Courtier.* It would take many impulses and efforts at approximation before our society would begin to catch up with them, but if much Emersonian self reliance would be required of Whitman's universal men and women

> Let no one sneer at size and wish it smaller just for the sake of neatness. That would only postpone our problem and the world's.

The trick in trying to fix American character, itself at least half unconscious, is in recognizing its *multiplicity;* the successful seeker of some single strain or determining line of culture would soon pass outside it altogether.[2]

FORM is the burden of the East Wind's message: order, tradition, style—form! T. S. Eliot once remarked that "the spirit killeth but the letter giveth life," but *The Waste Land,* the height of complicated cross-reference—is a picture of what is dying in the present as it is of what is dead in the past. "Sweet Thames," our author says in recalling true nuptial song of Spenser's day, "run softly till our poet ends his dirge, for he sings not loud or long." As the poem turns from prophecy into confession the form turns from epic to mock-epic; "Orpheus in Hell" does not deem this modern world important enough to deserve serious treatment.[3]

If anything like a half conscious international character emerges Americans will have done much to create it: "They were always falling out of themselves into the empty spaces between nations!" But the air there was too thin to sustain life, and the war that looked like Wilson's opportunity was only the stroke of doom for Henry James' world.

INTRODUCTION TO THE 1967 REISSUE

... you cannot imagine Woodrow Wilson coming from anywhere else but America. The mixed innocence and idealism, boldness and inexperience—

There is no real happiness in a drama and the clock cannot be turned back; death, not life, awaits the human heart bewitched by the enchanted past (but James himself remained unscathed). Is this, then, the lesson of the master?[4]

The real turn of the screw comes with Henry Adams.

Westward the star of empire takes its way— and the closed circle looked like the doom of this "pennon-flying star" on this earth, at least. "The Virgin and the Dynamo"?— THE LADY AND THE TIGER!—and science was leading the world to the worship of pure force.

If energy seemed to him to be running downhill, then it was necessary to show that the universe was running downhill. At last he found a generation to listen to him, the disillusioned generation after the War.

Which War? Henry was a clairvoyant child of CIVIL WAR ("again, after terrible conflict, and with whatever ill grace in part, the country risked return to its principle of common choice, South with North") who clearly foresaw promised confusions ("the risks were real, the strength of the country in the twentieth century lay more than anywhere else in the good will that had been created in the nineteenth"). The United States could be glad the risk was run, still now (1942) we of the New World *are* in peculiar position to observe the enigma of the closed circle.[5]

Perhaps there is saving grace in a "new American unconsciousness" which must be studied "shallow in historical time" or not at all.

Its density is in the *space* dimension, a product of movement rather than status, and of interrelation rather than single line heredity.

Today, as Winds blow from the East and from the West, a new generation may well profit from the wonderful work which follows—

> you have to live in a present, and to dig yourself out of the American present is only to come up in some other national present, or some "past present," or the vague international present or a kind of *nowhere* present.[6]

Ellis Allen Johnson

State University of New York
College at Cortland
July, 1967

---

[1] Is it just an accident of geography and the beginnings of human life that migration has been generally westward, and memory eastward? Does it have something to do with the movements of the globe? "The sun is of course our earth's own star, and there might be good solar reasons why mankind tended to look to the rising sun for its faith and the setting sun for its hope." Flying west on American at 20,000 feet was ideal for considering "Space in America"; the four subsequent chapters, specific references from which are from pp. 24, 26, 29, 34-36, 38, 57, 76 and 78 below, similarly soared. Many things popped into the mind of this student of cultural history as they were pondered, more would certainly follow as Chapters II-V were re-read and thoroughly enjoyed.

[2] The reader inclined to pursue this personal flight of fancy will be welcomed in reviews of such relevant studies as Daniel Joseph Boorstin, *The Americans: The Colonial Experience (New York History*, XL, January, 1959, pp. 78-81) and *The Americans: The National Experience (New York History*, XLVII, July, 1966, pp. 318-21); and Paul M. Angle (ed.), *Created Equal? The Complete Lincoln-Douglas Debates of 1858 (The Annals of*

INTRODUCTION TO THE 1967 REISSUE

the *American Academy*, 320, November, 1958, pp. 151-52); Mary A. Wyman, *The Lure for Feeling (The Social Studies*, LII, November, 1961, pp. 235-36), and peripheral points posed in Ernest Barker, *Greek Political Theory: Plato and His Predecessors (Social Education*, XXV, November, 1961, p. 382); Lily Ross Taylor, *Party Politics in the Age of Caesar (Social Education*, XXVI, May, 1962, pp. 277-78); and John S. White, *Renaissance Cavalier (The Social Studies*, L, December, 1959, pp. 271-72.)

[3]Ferner Nuhn's nuance suggests, somewhat inversely to be sure, the "sweet Thames, flow gently till I end my song" of Thomas Wolfe— "Kronos and Rhea: The Dream of Time," *Of Time and The River* (pp. 866-70) which *is* loud and long. Abstrusities epitomized in *The Waste Land*, brilliantly presented in the "Orpheus" below, were perceptively delineated on Thursday, April 27, 1967 in Chicago as Loren Baritz commented on encoding creative work, codes, and decoders—"Cultural History," *Sixtieth Annual Meeting, Organization of American Historians* (my immediate objective on the astrojet high-lighted in note 1 above).

[4]"The Enchanted Kingdom of Henry James," entered by a one-time English major turned to Clio, underscored certain observations of H. G. Wells (the hippopotamus searching for a pea with his nose and civilization running a race between education and catastrophe). James' muse, pursued in what Walter Lord deemed *The Good Years* before the First World War (1960), seemed to point toward *The Coming Caesars*, Amaury de Riencourt's challenging interpretation of New and Old Worlds in the light of *Weltgeschichte* (1957). This thorough dissertation on the author of *The Ambassadors* recalled a modest one on *The Ordeal of Woodrow Wilson (The Social Studies*, LI, October, 1960, pp. 190-92; that flaw in *The Golden Bowl*, surely smashed by World War One, seemed realized in the fate of *Titanic*.

[5]1914-1918, while appalling in virtually every respect, is still insufficient solely to explain the audience appeal of "a postwar mind that had somehow developed in the prewar period"—or the heavy "Hand of the Fathers." This short chapter was published at the same time Quincy Wright released *A Study of War* (University of Chicago Press, Two Volumes, 1942) and both were immediately followed by the first sustained nuclear reaction. "Dear Henry, speak for yourself!" Mr. Nuhn admonishes. Ultimately he must: "The New York Gold Conspiracy, *Chapters of Erie* by Charles Francis Adams, Jr. and Henry Adams (Cornell, 1956); *Democracy: A Novel by Henry Adams* and *The Selected Letters of Henry Adams* (Farrar, Straus and Young, n.d.); *The Education of Henry Adams* (Random House, 1931); *Mont-Saint-Michel and Chartres* (Doubleday, 1959); and "Introduction" to Brooks Adams, *The Law of Civilization and Decay* (Vintage, 1955).

[6]The italics in the quotations from pp. 76-77 are mine; by p. 258 I was back east, thoroughly grounded and happy to join our author "On New World Grounds." History is safe only as history; "Security lies in knowing both the repetitions and the variations, for there is never life without both. Then the past comes to the present, the present leads into the future, and there is no gap to stare across with longing or fear."

THE WIND BLEW FROM THE EAST

CHAPTER I

Space in America

~~~~~~

AMERICA is the country that was born in historical daylight. We brought the printing press with us; there was a printing press ready to bring. Word-of-mouth tradition has had only a limited play with us. Our first immigrants were mostly reading and writing men and women, and were interested quite from the first in reproducing their kind. Our last immigrants and those in between have either been of the same sort, or notably anxious to make up for lost time—for their offspring where they themselves came too late.

This has meant with us an absence of historical shadow, a thing which has curiously troubled many of our cultural historians. Where is, not our past, but our *dark* past? Where is the mythic, the oral, the half-lost and half-lit? Where is the incredible and terrible?

Well, we have had our own terror and darkness, and perhaps will be capable of producing more of it. Our artists have not escaped the universal shadow. Hawthorne worked in some of it; Melville more; Robinson Jeffers has been exploring the cold white and the empty black. There will be others.

[1]

We are not wholly without the strand of word-of-mouth tradition. With us still, in spite of our best efforts to get rid of them, are our own aboriginals, our American Indians. Ever since we got here, and I think to more and more effect, we have been picking up that red-earth strand, for what it may mean to our common life using the same earth these predecessors of ours have known so much longer.

Then there was the frontier, a fresh-green sort of shadow that pushed always ahead of the printing press, all the way across the continent. It gave us another mythic strand, unquestionably our liveliest one. The oral flowered there and produced, as a devoted band of scholars has been showing for some time, a little family of oversized folk. There grew Paul Bunyan, John Henry, Mike Fink; a well-above-life-sized pioneer couple, with babies to match; assorted Western heroes and heroines proliferating to this day. With the heroes, grew a spirit—an intangible new sense of human possibility. Invaluable to us is the language, spirit, and character we got and have from our great epic period.

Only, we cannot put too heavy a weight on obscurity—not on our side of the ocean. Printing press and letter box were always close on the heels of the hunters. We have not been able to lose many of our documents, and the great bulk we have saved are all too clear in their import. It was and is a world of human-sized people. The biggest do not sit well for portraits as grandees or demigods. We have a Thomas Eakins, not a Joshua Reynolds. Our romancers have been well advised to choose vaguer and more distant scenes for the fancier type of gods and goddesses. You might draw a man Lincoln-tall, Franklin-wide. You would have a hard time deifying George Washington.

True enough, there is the great world strand, the one we came from and brought with us. It is the deepest back, the largest root. The mythic in it is ours too.

Nevertheless, the break, the long mother cord thrown across the empty water and knotted off on this side, is of the greatest importance to us. We are Old World children, with a difference. We have been given a new heaven and a new earth, something to bring to its own strength and fruit, before we can be sure we are ready to merge strands again with our ancestors.

Our chance is selection. All the gods come down to us, elder and younger, but we can do some choosing. Some of the elder and even middle-aged gods and goddesses might well perhaps be waved a kind farewell. Helen and Mars, Tristan and Isolde, even St. George, or the Lady Beatrice: how much are we to form ourselves in their images? The question is how they prosper us on our own grounds. Which ones have had the better feeling for the nurture of our New World garden?

This book is going to deal with the pilgrimages some of our more romantic children have made to the shrines of the elder gods and goddesses. But for the first few chapters, let us look at our New World home, and how we came by it.

We are peculiarly the children of world space, both by division and extension. The Atlantic Ocean marks the division. A three-thousand-mile wide continent measures the extension. Our life of course is in space and time together, or does not exist at all, and we do not lack time. But we have had an unusual concern with space. We might almost say that space has been our time; at least it was until we filled up the space. It is a matter to consider, whoever wants to understand where we are now.

I think a good many of our cultural historians and critics have been too much time-thinkers so far as America is concerned. Theories have been made which minimized or left out place-changes and evolution through space, and somehow failed to catch life in the United States. Our biggest fish escaped these nets.

One such theory is a kind of one-piece revelationism: as if culture were revealed somehow all at once, at some far-off point, and then was either purely transmitted to other places, or weakened and lost where it became much different. I believe this, or something like it, is called "diffusionism" by anthropologists.

A school of literary criticism has held, I think, a similar view: that American literature is at best a "copy" of transatlantic originals, and that we on this side have frequently corrupted the text. Even worse, we have often chosen to copy texts that were corrupt to begin with, for instance, that of Rousseau. His was already not a true original, but came from some other source.

I would not care to defend Rousseau at all points; in fact, I would be glad to agree with many points made by anti-Rousseauans. I think some of Rousseau's self-pity and wishfulness may have got into modern thought about society and progress, and has not helped it where it has.

Still, the big movement of which Rousseau was only a part, and of which Jefferson and Washington and Emerson and Daniel Boone were in some respects other parts, is not to be described merely as sentimentalism. This New Nature that the world embraced proved herself one of the truer and more fruitful goddesses, even though some of her followers have always confused her with the Old Nature.

As for the "natural man" or "common man," I believe Jefferson's or, say, Cooper's image of him is much less sentimental than Rousseau's. Tears and hysterics are certainly not associated with our strong silent heroes of the forest; though there has always been a good dash of manly feeling, not to say posing for the profile, in our Leatherstockings, down to Gary Cooper.

But we would have had to invent the natural man if Rousseau or someone else had not. The place called for him. Did Daniel Boone ever hear of Rousseau?

I am sure, however, that the literary "American Farmer," J. Hector St. John Crevecoeur, must have read his Rousseau, to judge from his introduction to the little collection of letters from the American Eden which he wrote for the benefit of intellectual ears in effete Europe. "Behold, Sir, an humble American Planter, a simple cultivator of the earth, addressing you from the far side of the Atlantic; and presuming to fix your name at the head of his trifling lucubrations . . ." Life is seeing itself, quite obviously, in the slightly synthetic image of art.

And when our simple countryman again and again protests that he is "neither philosopher, politician, divine, nor naturalist"; when he admits that his wife is worried lest it become known among the neighbors that "here liveth a scribbling farmer" and that she had rather they "be as we are, neither better nor worse than the rest of our country folks"; when he declares himself a perfect stranger to scientific rules of writing and asserts that such value as his "trifling lucubrations" may have, must come from "the spontaneous impressions each subject may inspire"; we are not only sure that our American *ingénu* has learned well his lesson from Rousseau, but that he is one of a long line of self-admitted American "naturals," down to Will Rogers.

Nevertheless, you would be well warned against that pose of simplicity and rustic naïveté. You are not to take it at face value, any more than the British Parliament was to take Franklin's slightly ostentatious informality for lack of authority, or London audiences take Artemus Ward's dead-pan style of humor for stupidity. This ostentation of innocence was, as Henry James might have put it, and indeed did put it, the American's little "secret, his joke."

Henry James, of course, saw it as a poor joke. He assumed it could only be protective coloration for the "terrible denudation," the comprehensive lack of all those items of high civilization, from thatched cottages to cathedrals and crowns and miters to ivied ruins, which he detailed in a famous paragraph in his biography of "poor Hawthorne."

Actually, it was much more than a defensive measure. It was a new mode of expression. It was only natural for a natural man to find his own mode, in answering the other mode, the very civilized one so often assumed by foreign visitors, which stooped down to say a good word while it had no trouble finding twenty bad ones standing up very straight for a raw, plebeian, backwoods civilization. The backwoodsman might well make capital of his disabilities. The mode of simplicity, not to say simple-mindedness, had its advantages, and was to enjoy a long and on the whole successful run.

Eventually, in fact, it captured the other side. The American natural, having crossed his own continent, and found impressive additions to his stage property in Western scenery and talk, took his little joke back to Europe and exploded it on the mother continent. Like a troupe of Marx Brothers, he swarmed over and wise-cracked his way among the shrines and temples which his more refined compatriots approached only in shoe-removing awe. He removed the shoes the other way. He was a success, only too much of a success. But his laughter cleared the air.

If Rousseau had fathered these questionable American innocents of "Innocents Abroad," he would hardly have recognized them on their return to Europe, or cared to admit it if he did. He might have owned Crevecoeur's stilted agrarian simplicity, but what would he have made, finally, of Josh Billings? In the strict following out of the theme, the gentleman was to be stripped down to the man. What now if he posed as a rube, a dub?

Well, the answer might be illuminating to the purer idealist of nature and the common man, or any other abstraction for that matter. Give a man a chance to talk, and he will use roughly the language he knows. The cracker box, the spittoon, and the double negative might not be the choicest idiom, but it was his own, and the common man recognized it. He could develop in and from that glass.

This was strictly "folk," on this level, this oversized image. But then, if you are looking for gods or goddesses, the place is among the folks, either at home or somewhere else. There is no question; this was a new image. Where had there risen a laughing god before? one especially without the satyr smirk, for it was definitely not that. He might have started out as a lone woodsman and re-emerged as a bad small boy, but from the first he made a great point of chivalry, and he ended up a good family man. In that and other respects he was a *novum*, quite different from any visible predecessor, including the Far Eastern jolly round Buddha. He was not fat; he was inclined to be thin, and he certainly was not quietistic, either for the belly's sake or the soul's.

The laugh sometimes came from the wrong side of the mouth; there was a tendency to financial grandeur that went oddly with the rustic idea; and there was a strange streak of melancholy. I do not propose here a complete appraisal. Not to be left out, however, is the purest flower of this line, an imaginative character with more of the dawn freshness of myth about him than any other we have made, and more of its universality—Huckleberry Finn. This urchin Odysseus, coming deep as he did from the waters of the middle of the country, floating its picaresque highway, glimpsed always through green leaves; this young river god would be equally at home and as much equal to any occasion, you could think, on the Nile of ancient Egypt or the Yangtze of modern China.

Finally you might add that, if we must have oversized figures in human form, we could get a worse one than this agile, sober, joking folk god of ours. You might get, for example, a really scowling oversized man, and no joke, on horseback. Against such a contingency, I think our hero would prove one of our ablest defenders, as he has proved himself able in difficult situations before.

The "natural man" is folk and more than folk, and my main point here is simply to show how different an idea might look—

if indeed that was the idea—after a long dive through salt water and a long journey over new country. How much resemblance was there in the end between a French sentimentalist and an American humorist? You could show much the same for a dozen other ideas taken as given in Old World terms, and their reality after New World experience.

My point has to do with moving and stopping in space, and it is not hard to see two streams verging off always from a central current. In one stream move the figures that responded to the new space, and mostly they had good reason: they remembered worse conditions where they had come from, and liked the new freedom and the chance to grow. On the far edge of this stream are the folks that always moved on, whether to something better or not. The western sky always looked rosy. Closer center are the ones that picked and chose and stayed, but still rose to the occasion.

Then there is the other stream, and the figures in it are those that mostly felt they had come down, coming across, and saw the new space as empty and flat, the "terrible denudation" that James talked about. They kept their faces turned back over their shoulders, and sometimes turned around and went back where their faces were turned, whether it was really better there or not. These figures are the subject of this book.

The figures in the center current are various in place and calling, and show a certain natural progression through the years from ecclesiastical, political, and practical toward social, philosophical, and aesthetic. Yet they have a recognizable family likeness.

Here is an example of the way the extreme divergence announced itself in the early years of the nation. First from far right, in Popian couplets, by one William Cliffton, a young Philadelphian of well-to-do family, though of frail health:

> In these cold shades, beneath the shifting skies,
> Where Fancy sickens, and where Genius dies,
> Where few and feeble are the muses strains,
> And no fine frenzy riots in the veins,
> There still are found a few to whom belong
> The fire of virtue and the soul of song. . . .

You can see how early began this frost, denudation, degradation, and deliquescence which Henry James, Henry Adams, and Irving Babbitt each in his time were to find far advanced, in a large flat democratic land that hardly ever treated the superior few as superior enough, by their own account. There will be others.

Next from well to the left, about the same time, Philip Freneau:

> Now shall the adventurous muse attempt a theme
> More new, more noble, and more flush of fame
> Than all that went before. . . .

This also, you will notice, is in Popian couplets, or not intentionally far off, and only shows how far the American muse had to go after 1800 before becoming adventurous at all, three thousand miles away from Pope. Freneau's own muse did journeyman's service for Jefferson and what Jefferson stood for, but she was quite clearly, or mostly, a political muse. But this loud beat for an American prodigy, with a full-blown song at once utterly strange and immediately recognizable, was to be heard late and soon in the land, wherever two or three young people were gathered together near a printshop.

It was not all one way, even on the same side. Who, for

instance, but our own Henry James, after piling his precious items of high civilization on one side of the scale and taking his place there himself, was sure to put some innocent young American girl on the other, and find the two pans just about at a balance, or even tipped her way? James, you might say, had his own little joke, it is hard to say on whom.

Romanticists both, these horizon people, west or east, all ahead or all return. At the risk of running against Irving Babbitt again, and also the standard nomenclature of the schools, I am going to insist that the character of our main tradition is not "romantic," in any useful meaning of the word. Whether religious, political, or aesthetic; bred in town or country; appearing in Virginia, Massachusetts, Illinois, or Camden, New Jersey; I believe you must call this central strand of our culture whatever you call integrated and lasting.

The men in this main stream saw the new space given us to use. Washington surveyed the Western Reserve. Jefferson saw to the Rockies and beyond. Franklin was our first intercolonist and even internationalist. Lincoln stood at a point where the whole continent could move up and around him if it would. Whitman and Emerson could let the world come to their doors.

The new space did not mysteriously produce, by itself, the ideas that these men found and used. The ideas came from everywhere, and many of the best came from far back in the Old World. Ideas are universal.

Nor is there something special and peculiar about nature in the New World. The laws of physics and life are the same everywhere too.

But the chance to apply ideas afresh to nature—that is the

chance the new space gave. This is the classic New World tradition: to make the best use of the chance.

This New World tradition is the great world tradition too. For what can mean more to the world as a whole than the best use of some part of it? What means more to the future than the best use of the present? Those who saw life as forever ahead or forever behind would make little of life. Those who worked with the space, in the day, were also working with time.

East Wind—Western Star

~~~~~~

TITLE to a certain piece of earth is one of our more or less useful human fictions. Leave in enough time, and we are all natives and all interlopers. The only true title to things is use, and good use in the long run is good title, while bad use is bad title. We will soon lose what we cannot use well, no matter how sure we are that we own it.

Still, the fiction persists that ownership is somehow superior to use, and that the greatest dignity possible is to have everything without doing anything. Own something, and you can patronize the man who made it. This conception of grace in living has I think been particularly held by the ruling classes of our mother island, England. You can even find it in Adam Smith, if you look for the image of felicity behind the economics of wealth. It is the leisure-class ideal. Real work, according to *The Wealth of Nations*, is a necessary indignity; consumption of the fruits is style, and the more you can have fruits without work, the better. Even the worker is to despise his hours of labor as time lost, and expect no comfort or consideration there; while afterward he is to join the English gentleman in so far as he can from his place and pay envelope, and be a lord of the pub in his off hours.

But everywhere, we have yet to even up the balance of grace and work, to the improvement of both, and put more grace in our work and work in our grace. Grace without work remains the would-be goal for most people, even in a democracy. And it is roughly nothing other than the aristocratic dream of doing nothing, coming down from all history.

This, anyway, is the message of the East Wind, as it has come to our shores, and then blown across the country. West for work and money, back East for ease and grace. West for profanity, East for piety. West for action, East for status. West for function, East for ornament. West for democratic color, East for aristocratic form. That is what the East Wind says. The wind may be dying down; I think it is; but it has worked with us a good while and made currents and eddies that may last out a long while still.

This East Wind is also of course the current of memory, and gets its selective force from memory. Massachusetts, hardly through fighting off the redcoats, is worried about the ragged coats of Jefferson's mob, and begins to think much better of British full dress. Ohio remembers Massachusetts; Oregon in turn Ohio. Kentucky soon leaves off the coonskin cap, and almost outdoes Virginia for elegance in the drawing room; while Virginia is restoring everything she can of the Old Dominion style, short of rejoining the Empire. The lost heritage looks all the brighter for distance, and we happily fix on some one shiny ancestral name while we easily forget the other sixty-three dull or tarnished ones.

This memory current is naturally only from one direction, and that is what gives it its eccentricity. It is always easier to think back; but thinking ahead of one's memory terminus, in the great east to west migration, takes imagination. Often the imagination is too lively, often too dull.

Boston has no trouble believing in the solid fact of London, but Springfield, Illinois, looks hazy, or garish, not to mention even Springfield, Massachusetts. Richmond is sure of Oxford, England, but has doubts of any good thing coming out of Oxford, Mississippi. Rumors of buffalo and massacres satisfy Maryland for a long time in thinking of Nebraska; while Iowa and Idaho are roughly interchangeable to Pittsburgh. Charleston would question you strictly whether civilized man had ever set foot west of tidewater.

One could make an interesting sheaf of maps on this order: the United States at various moments charted from various points along the east-west trails. Each map would have the landmarks put in with a fair accuracy in the eastward area; while to the west the country would have to be labeled *terra incognita*, with rumored rivers, faint trails, rude outposts, and fabulous beasts.

A certain moral theory has gone along with this memory current. For memory tells one thing to the moral sense, while imagination tells another thing. Anyone could easily recall the good and sufficient reasons why he had got to where he was, and why he had pulled up stakes farther back, but it was harder to imagine good reasons for someone's pulling out from one's own home town. Instead you could think of very dubious reasons, and point to cases to prove your point.

Who would want to leave Vermont for Iowa, or Iowa for Colorado, unless he had failed to make good, somehow, in Iowa or Vermont? And there could be worse kinds of failure to leave behind even than debts and mortgages. But who would want to leave New Freedom, Independence, Happy Valley, New Eden, or Zenith, anyway?

Well, of course it was in order to arrive at New New Freedom, New New Eden, and so on, and it was never hard to find the real substance of the debate. It came up every time Congress met and every time the party chieftains tried to make a vote-getting platform. Money might be made in the West, but it flowed back to the banks in the East, and then could be loaned back to the West. Titles might be proved in the West, but they were granted in the East, at least as far east as Washington. Money was power, and so was title-granting, but votes were power too, and votes had a tendency to flow west with the titles, willy-nilly. There was no question but that the real core of the matter revolved around this interesting center of finance power, patent power, and vote power.

Nevertheless, the moral tone was conspicuous on both sides, and rarely failed to be lofty. And the loftiness took a characteristic turn from the peculiar fact of east-to-west movement, west-to-east memory.

For the east-looking-west tone, you might listen to almost any representative from New England almost any day up to 1900, or later, speaking on the subject of Western lands. Here is an example as early as the debates on the Constitution, even before there was a government in Washington. The question is the question of voting rights for new states that might be carved out of the Western Reserve, and Gouverneur Morris of Connecticut has arisen to call attention to the fact that the West "would not be able to furnish men equally enlightened to share in the administration of our common interests." Why? The answer is quite clear. Who were these possible Western voters except ne'er-do-wells and renegades from the East? Had they not always left behind them debts and decency, if not wife, church, and child, when they left the land of their fathers for the godless West?

The rest of this whole moral argument easily follows: it should not be arranged that inland states, or territories, should have quite the same voting power as the enlightened maritime states. And title to land should not come too easy: it should be paid for at the usual Boston or New York rates. Virtue, in short—Eastern virtue!—should be protected so that it could legislate for and lend to the unvirtuous in both these departments, and thus save the whole country from falling into the pit.

From the other side of the hall, you can be sure there was an answer, and there always was, from Patrick Henry of Virginia to Senator Benton of Missouri, and from Senator Benton to Senator Borah of Idaho. It was not unknown that the answer came from someone holding warrants, options, or other interest in tracts of Western territory, though this was not always the case, any more than the other voice always belonged to a holder of bank paper. Andrew Jackson would do as well as any (not to weight the scale too heavily with, say, Abraham Lincoln!) to state the other sentiment. The United States government, said Andrew Jackson, had a high duty to perform in this whole question of the disposal of Western lands. It was "to afford to every American citizen of enterprise the opportunity of securing an independent foothold."

And the rest of this argument easily follows: give the people the easiest access to the land, not the hardest; let them prove their title simply by living on it and working it; keep the whole finance power over the land as weak as possible; and let the new territory become a state with equal voting power as soon as titles, improvement, and votes made a reasonable showing, at least on paper.

This is American history, and our interest is only to illustrate a two-way pull in American culture. But Henry Adams, who stood just between history and aesthetics as he stood uneasily between a number of other poles, was to write a famous culture history from just this divided ground. He hardly knew which pole attracted him most: the land power or the money power; the virtue of the "superior few," or the energy and votes of the many; Thomas Jefferson or his great-grandfather John Adams; Andrew Jackson or his grandfather John Quincy Adams (but I think he would have answered that one quickly enough); Abraham Lincoln or Robert E. Lee; Bryan or McKinley. And involved with these questions were perhaps even deeper questions for Henry Adams, such as Love versus Power, and Mother Nature versus Father God.

Adams put the East-versus-West argument in these words, and I think, with a little attention, you can detect the moral note in it: that whereas "Virginia had been founded by a great liberal movement aimed at the spread of English liberty and empire," and while "the Pilgrims of Plymouth, the Puritans of

Boston, the Quakers of Pennsylvania, all avowed a moral purpose," Adams was sorry to record that "no such character belonged to the colonization of 1800" and later. It was purely
materialistic: "From Lake Erie to Florida, in long unbroken line,
pioneers were at work, cutting into the forests with the energy
of beavers, and with no more express moral purpose than the
beavers they drove away."

Henry Adams, we must conclude, had never attended a Fourth-
of-July celebration west of the Alleghanies, for if he had he
would surely have heard the pioneers or their posterity state the
most express moral purposes in having driven away the beavers—
and the Indians. In fact, to reconstruct what the pioneers on
various occasions said for Illinois, or Arkansas, or Oregon, one
need only make the appropriate substitutions in what Adams
said for Virginia, to wit: "Illinois (Arkansas, Oregon) was
founded by a great liberal movement aimed at the spread of
American liberty and democracy."

This sounds I imagine sufficiently familiar, and is I think as
valid as Adams's original statement. Not that it shows, any
more than Adams's statement does, a necessary connection between virtue and geography. There are too many variables; you
cannot control the experiment. It does illustrate roughly the
way the east-to-west rule actually worked. It might indicate,
too, one of the difficulties of American history, and why Henry
Adams in particular found his own history made so little sense.

So far as this particular debate was concerned, it never came
to blows: not between East and West. Blows were given and
blood was spilled, alas, across another line. Still the debate
went on, the taunts and countertaunts, and it kept its character

from the different standpoints provided by status and memory on the one side, and mobility and new claims on the other.

Only the assurance given by status could have made Josiah Quincy so sure of his epithets in referring to "the wild men on the Missouri" and the "race of Anglo-Hispano-Gallo-Americans who bask on the sands in the mouth of the Mississippi"; or George Moses a hundred years later in shaking his finger at the Western "sons of the wild jackass."

Conversely, your Western voice always felt the weight of status against it, and had to shout as it were into the teeth of civilization. The prevailing winds and waves ran against that quarter, and bucking them always had the look of insurgence. The Western tone was sometimes shrill and scream-eagle, sometimes loud and windy. Again, it was deceptively quiet in the style of the simple-minded backwoodsman.

Every state had its East, every state had its West: that is one reason the East-West affair ended as amicably as it did. Or almost every state. There is California at the far edge, and she is a special case; just as Massachusetts and Virginia are special cases at the near end. Massachusetts and Virginia, it is true, had had their West, their bright Western stars. They had practically discovered the Western star. But then, after they had settled down and grown pious, there was only the Atlantic Ocean to look back east over and remember back across with nostalgia. One had to leave the country if he wanted to follow his ancestors back from the Atlantic seaboard. Some filial Americans in every period did just that.

California had the whole eastward circle of civilization to look

back over, if she cared to; but ahead there was only the pale
Pacific for the star to set into, unless one wanted to start over
again, and swallow his Chinese tail. It would be a long time before anyone knew just what to say about California. Everything
ended there, or everything began again there; you could not tell
which.

The country in between could take what satisfaction it could
in being more or less two-directional and unexceptional; and I
suppose if one were to look for the most exceptionally normal
it would be close to the middle. Every section to its own pecu-
liarities.

But the special character of the memory pull was not its giving
the new settler a memory; no one was without his memory. It
was a matter of identifying the good of inheritance itself with
another place—a place further east. All the connotations of
memory, the selective connotations, one might fix on some point
where the fathers and mothers had once been. It was a long
backward vista that thus opened up, if you took it too seriously.
Generally, some certain point had the most color—Boston, London, Rome—for piety sake, for "the best that has been thought
and said in the world," for the golden bowl of leisure or the
golden day of glory, for shrines and temples, lamps, incense, and
images.

The child of the East Wind would be off at the first good
opportunity. He had heard the song of the nightingale on the
East Wind, and so he could not hear the meadow lark. The Hudson or Ohio or Mississippi looked wet, ordinary, and not at all
likely to catch fire, while everyone knew that the Thames, or
the Seine, had been set afire again and again. He was quickly

alight with recognitions as he went back, and often he did ignite some new or partly new lamps.

Frequently he found that the priests of the old temples had grown dull in the service. His fresh senses could serve him well in the old places, and bring a new enthusiasm to old forms. At any rate, that was his role. If one followed the memory trail, he would have to make the best use of his imagination on his best memories.

One other characteristic of the East Wind was to remain for a long time, which had nothing to do with going back or going on. The East Wind was the general purveyor of the "idea," be it new or old. The current of the idea was east to west, no matter where the idea really started. Sometimes it started in the West— some discovery of folk myth or of politics, or art. But it took the East Wind to give it good standing, and send it back with authority. Sometimes it had to go back as far as London or Paris to get such standing.

There was a priesthood of this movement too. There were circles which made it their interest to pick up any new idea from anywhere, and put it in the regular way of circulation. The Eastern centers were in a position to render this good office. They had the machinery, the printing presses, the gathering and exchanging and sifting faculties.

It looked every now and then as if a center of this sort were forming in the Middle or the Far West, or the South, or Southwest. They formed, hung together for longer or shorter periods, or hung on with stubborn and somewhat obscure tenacity indefinitely. Something came of them, often a great deal. But generally they broke up again, or went underground, and had to leave it to the East again to distribute their products. You could not tell how long it might take for New York to move to Chicago.

This priesthood gyrated rather rapidly and offered in general a quicksilver type of authority. But that had been its nature everywhere and in all times. Ours appeared a lively and able order, with more and better facilities as time went on.

The other current, the one that drew westward and stirred the imagination rather than the memory, was on the whole much the stronger force with us. If you are betting as between the past and the future, a wind or a star, bet on the star.

There is no need to be mysterious as to what the star signified. It signified fortune, wealth, opportunity.

That started from the Old World too, looking west for wealth, who knows how far back in time. Robinson Jeffers, at the California far end of the circle, might be watching the star either setting for good, or leading on to something not very good in the big Pacific, but in any case, he has written vividly about it. He calls it the "evening star," and names the poem, "Invocation."

> My fathers looked from unremembered ways,
> Up to thy guiding light; and swore at dawn
> To turn their shoulders downward, and still gaze
>
> The whole day toward thy setting; and were drawn
> Out of huge Asia, past the Euxine sea,
> Northward of cloudy Caucasus, and on

THE WIND BLEW FROM THE EAST

Westward, free wanderers. They would look for thee
At fire-lighting each night; but when thy face
Was hidden, there they halted, eagerly

Awaiting thy new birth, and in that place
Built huts and plowed the field. Thy light renewed,
They rose, and tracked the westward wilderness.

Now I, the latest, in this solitude
Invoke thee from the verge extreme, and shoal
Of sand that ends the west, O long-pursued.

It is interesting to speculate why it should always have been a Western star that meant adventure of the wild, not an Eastern one. Is it just an accident of geography and the beginnings of human life that migration has been generally westward, and memory eastward, or does it have to do more intimately with the movements of the globe? The sun is of course our earth's own star, and there might be good solar reasons why mankind tended to look to the rising sun for its faith and the setting sun for its hope.

So at least it has been, and gold in the east looked like reassurance and promise of return, while gold in the west looked like opportunity, and could make a family leave home and altar and kindred to try a hazard of new hope.

The New World, if not the only example of this movement, is certainly the most fabulous example of it. Moreover, with the hazard of it over, and the last segment covered, we in the New World are in a peculiar position to observe the enigma of the closed circle.

We are all too vividly aware of the effects of this long-pursued end, the eddies and whirlpools set up as the current is blocked at its western outlet. Waters have risen, the returning tide is felt all around the globe. Gates once opened are closed, or old gates forced. Dykes are raised, and Robinson Jeffers, among others, has been singing a dark song of humanity treading on itself.

There might be other frontiers than free land. Scientists and inventors were apparently opening up certain kinds of new frontiers even faster than they could be used to advantage. Nature is not, perhaps, just a matter of virgin cover. The answer seemed to lie, or could lie, not with nature's limits but with man's. The further hazard of fortune could well lie along the lines of man's own self-development and self-order. That would be, perhaps, a wild enough nature left for him to conquer.

Robinson Jeffers, as I take it, staring from his verge extreme, is not hopeful of any such human way out of the closed circle. The wilderness inside man looks wilder to him apparently than the one he conquered outside. Or its tameness might prove even unhealthier than its wildness. Hence the dark song of humanity doomed without its perennial baths of fresh earth and blood. Somewhere Mr. Jeffers has queried, When Alaska is peopled, will Venus lack plowland? That would be an evening star indeed!—one to be reached over an ocean thinner than salt water. But if men cannot arrive at that new frontier, Jeffers seems to suggest that nature on this earth may well be through with the trial of man and his picture-making consciousness. Rock and ice and the subforms of rapacious life are only waiting for the light to go out. Men would not be able to stand it, or so I read Robinson Jeffers: themselves living with themselves.

It could be so. Evidence is not wanting to support the darkest kind of view. Lights have been going out on every hand, and the capacity of man to live with himself has not been demonstrated clearly anywhere, either with much or little of nature's resources given him to begin with.

Still, it would seem even less demonstrated that the effort has seriously been made. Until tried, it seemed premature to say whether the clearing of his own wild nature is a less wholesome exercise for a man than clearing away trees, wolves, and so-called savages.

Westward the star of empire takes its way

One conclusion we might risk concerning this glittering platitude, with evidence from all directions to support it. The closed circle, late or early, looked like the doom of this panoplied, pennon-flying star of empire—on this earth at least. Men would take their bearings from some other quarter, or find their fate also in the star's blazing setting.

In such garish colors you might paint the primitive aspects of our Western star. It repays however a closer view. After all, it was a mild and homely light for most of us. How large a percentage of us, when you add everybody up who came to America, down to the last refugee, carried a gun westward? The expression and style was in the manner of movement—the manner of "seeking new fortune"—and this manner changed. In time, there was no place on earth where movement was so free and secure over so wide a space. There was no place on earth where new homes were offered to so many on such generous terms.

How did the change come about?

Let us not forget the lodestar of fortune—new fortune. No lesser force would have been strong enough to create the current westward. Everything possible was in that current, good and bad, outlaws and homemakers, pirates and patriots. But none of them would have been in it if crude fortune had not been in it. The great fact about the New World was that it existed.

But there were conditions and forces working on the current which would help to fashion its character. Here are two great ones:

The late emergence of the New World in time, in terms of Western civilization.

The logic of immigration and settlement, namely, that certain classes of people would be drawn across, and not others, bringing the ideas that were of their class, and not other ideas.

What do they make in combination, the great delayed gift of matter, the selection in terms of people and ideas to use the matter? The answer is the parturition of America out of Europe.

The current begins at a certain time and not earlier—that is, for the great modern stream of immigration out of Europe. There had been the faraway Asiatic migrations, with their independent cultural evolutions. In time, elements from these amazing early cultures might re-enter the modern New World stream, with great effect. But the overwhelming current from Europe, with its great power and continuity, comes at a certain late stage of history. It is delayed far past Fire, and Cereals, and Animal Husbandry; past language and writing; with centuries of history since Moses and Jesus and Greece and Rome. It comes in the day of the Renaissance, out of scientific theory, out of a certain new confidence in the natural world; in the day or influence of

Luther, Calvin, Fox; the Jesuits, the Franciscans; Copernicus, Galileo; Erasmus, Bacon, Locke.

Then, there is the stream of people that came from the Old World at this stage of civilization—another selective factor. It is not evenly drawn from all types and classes. It is drawn more from the propertyless class than the propertied, more from the managed than the managing, more from the disestablished than the established. The masters, generally, do not leave. The well-fixed of Europe stayed, the more comfortable, the ruling class of Church, State, and business. The too-fatalistic stayed, too, and perhaps the very poor. But in between were the types that went: dissenting, Separatist, adventurous, the dispossessed but ambitious, younger sons—some ejected rather than choosing—members of minority or outlawed parties, missionary priests, restless bloods, seeking spirits. The settlement of America is the unsettledness of Europe.

Theirs will be the European ideas that emigrate to Massachusetts and Missouri and Mexico. Their ideas will be the ones that gradually shape the New World, evolving in time its own styles of fortune.

There is never any doubt about the nature of the glitter seen in the western sky. The glitter is of precious metals lying in the west. Originally misconceived to be the riches of India, the fire was quickly enough perceived to be Peruvian gold, Mexican silver and copper, and in good time the gold of California and Alaska. The glitter toned down as the treasure became less easily removable. It took on a duller if really richer luster as it became the furs of Canada and the Great Lakes, the fisheries of Newfoundland, tobacco in Virginia, grass in Argentina, and pine forests in Minnesota, cotton, sugar cane, rice, Indian corn, thousands of square miles of black virgin loam, and so on down to coal and oil and tin and wheat and coffee and hogs and oranges and sunshine (gold again!) and potatoes. But meanwhile every Danubian peasant had learned that the very streets of the New World were paved with dollars.

We need not stop long with the familiar story of the earliest form of movement, and its accompanying style of fortune. It was heroic, violent, gaudy—the style of Cortes, Pizarro, Drake; and only a little less so the styles of the Hudson Bay and other royal companies. The style of our native adventurers and empire builders was to be gaudy enough too. But with all due courtesy to our mother continent, Europe, it would have to be put down, historically, that this style of arms, loot, and alarms was played at its height by the Old World making a stage of the New. That gave it its character, the management from afar, the directing hand across thousands of miles of seas.

At one end was a bewildered aboriginal—Aztec, Incan, Chippewa—and he had the gold, the furs, or simply the land. At the other end there were kings, queens, and bishops; courts, and counting houses; in Castille, Lisbon, London, and Amsterdam; and they did the accounting, after shipment, on as much goods as arrived. The various royal houses and companies offered their good services, at least, at the usual rates, say ten or even twenty shillings annually on the pound.

But with the change in commodities, there was a natural change in the style of fortune. Gold to tobacco meant adventurer to colonist; furs to lumber meant agent to entrepreneur; lumber to corn meant lumberjack to farmer. Glass beads and rum gradually lost their remarkable exchange value. Extraction generally speaking slowed down, and transfer went through more and slower motions, more of them closer to the point of production. The cut to the home office was reduced, and the adventurer become colonist tended to become native, and find his allegiance to the old home gradually slipping.

He might be accused only of wanting to take the whole profit for himself, if finally he was moved to shake off the mothering hand altogether. Still, a farm has a better chance of keeping its topsoil if worked only to satisfy the operator, and not a landlord as well. And New World culture began to be possible only as it stopped being Old World exploitation.

Yes, North and South America, it had been the same. The mother country held too tight a leading string. England or Spain, she had tried to keep the blood-flow of trade and culture of each of her offspring circling back only through her own veins. It was biologically, culturally wrong, and the offspring at last revolted. From the St. Lawrence to the Plata, there was a throwing off of the Old World hands, and a readiness to try fortune on their own.

Only then, we might begin to see the full effect of that logic of migration that had settled America. Then we might make out the different dream of those folks who had actually followed the Western star, and stayed and built where it had taken them.

CHAPTER III

Energy in Ideas—Styles in Fortune

~~~~~~

I WANT to keep in view the difference between an idea one uses and a memory one cherishes. It showed energy in an idea to cross the Atlantic. It meant it was a working plan that could be used on new material in a new place. Memory suggests that you need to go back to the old situation, the old days, the old manners, to recover the values you read into it.

Science—the new scientific view of the natural world—was an idea with energy, and easily crossed the ocean, ready to apply itself to new material; while royalism, for instance, turned out mostly a memory that stayed behind. The kings stayed where they were, or wherefore kings? But it meant their idea finally did not move, either. Other more mobile and energetic ideas, in this class, swam ahead and took its place. In religion, it was no accident that Christianity, out of all the hundreds of ideas and images in its class which floated in the current of history all the way back to Osiris and Vishnu, was easily the one that had shown the greatest energy to move both down through time and across through space. It was the least local: Jesus had seen farthest around the world. Not that the Christian emissaries, when they got around the world, always illustrated what Jesus had meant! Nevertheless, when it turned out there were two worlds instead of one, and a second chance in space, Christianity was very well prepared. No other religion had nearly as much to say about second chances and new worlds.

Across both the south and north Atlantic, the energy shown by the Christian idea was remarkable. Recently it has been found— see the work of Mr. Hjalmar Holand—that even the early Norse expeditions had as part of their impulse the Christian idea; and Leif Ericson, no other, was the first Christian missionary to the New World. Likewise, it appears that the expedition that carried Norwegians and Swedes as far as Minnesota in the fourteenth century, where they left the famous Kensington rune-stone, had as its main commission a Christianizing purpose.

In our famous colonial period and afterward, it was not only Christian, but resurgent Christian ideas which helped propel boats across the Atlantic.* Thousands of memories and accidental accretions were left behind, clinging to the soil of the Old World: magical rites and formulas, old saws and signs and "warnings," hobgoblins and forest gods, ghosts and "little people." The ideas that had energy to move westward were the ones that least depended on usage and place. Actually, they asked for a new trial and new place. Some of them were strong enough to blow whole ships across the Atlantic.

Commentators have arisen in recent years to correct the impression that it was all Liberty of Conscience and True Faith

---

* For an able treatment of this subject, see Ernest Sutherland Bates: *American Faith.*

which drew our Pilgrims to Plymouth, our Puritans to Boston
Bay, our Friends to Pennsylvania, and so on. They have made
their point. It was very much the main chance again, and likewise Power and Rule—their own hard rule often for the hard
rule they had left behind. Still, all history from Massachusetts
and Pennsylvania to California and Oregon continues to beg the
original and more interesting question. If these first enterprises
and their various successors did not bring certain ideas with
them, and were not pilgrimages to some degree in a different
sense from trade drumming and land promotion, then we are all
well fooled.

I say well, because when you can put across an idea, and
start it operating in more or less earnestness over a country, you
have done the essential thing that can be done with an idea.

True, this main idea, if that was it, of liberty of conscience
and truth to one's own faith—such an idea could be taken up
and used against you, if you were too narrow in your idea of its
use. Our famous forefathers were often just that.

The question always was, whom will you allow this precious
freedom to be true to his belief—everyone, or only those whose
beliefs agree with yours? The Boston and Salem deacons and
magistrates often answered, "Only those who agree with us."
This of course left others, who believed deeply but differently,
nothing to do but depart, and start another community of their
own.

This is what Roger Williams did, leaving Boston and Salem
under just these circumstances, and founding Providence, in
Rhode Island. Williams was one of the few men who saw the
whole logic of this "freedom-of-conscience" matter. If you saw

grounds for demanding it for yourself, the same grounds demanded you allow it to everyone. On these grounds, and no other, your society must be built. It must be one which granted freedom of belief as a right, and whose highest established officers had no jurisdiction over what people thought—though they must have some over what they did. This is what Roger Williams came to see so early in our American experience.

At the same time, Williams saw the principle of liberty from the other side. Unlike some later easy-minded believers in "civil liberties" who liked to patronize Williams as an early forerunner, Williams understood why he valued this liberty so highly. It was because he valued truth so deeply. And when he agreed in everyone's right to their own belief, he did not also agree that everyone's belief would be equally "true." Williams believed in freedom because he believed in truth.

But on either side of the question, Williams was far ahead of his day. Williams and Anne Hutchinson and John Wheelwright did not carry the day for freedom in the new land. In fact, the day might well have been lost had it not been for help from men and ideas farther south than New England, some religious of the school of William Penn, some secular in the rights-of-man tradition of Erasmus, and Voltaire, and Montesquieu, and Tom Paine, and Thomas Jefferson.

The little cluster of former colonies was fortunate in its variety as well as in its common qualities. Massachusetts and Virginia, for example—the two perhaps with the most decided characters—tended to complement each other, and made a much more effective pair working together than either did working separately.

Massachusetts liked to appeal to Conscience, which she took to be divinely inspired and hence indisputable. Virginia, while her piety tended to be somewhat conventional, liked to appeal to Reason, which she took to be natural and unanswerable. Together these great parent states, with some help from the others, it is true, produced our main light and pride, democracy. And it took both elements, the rational and the spiritual, the rights of man and the faith in Right itself, to make the new conception.

The new plan was based on "government by consent of the governed"—a proposition inspired from the underside, so to speak, from our experience of government without such consent. Our founding fathers themselves hardly saw at the time its far-reaching logic, when put in operation from the top side. Yet inevitably, to stand by the principle it was necessary to move with the logic. There could be no reservation or quibbling as to who "the governed" were. They had to be everybody—all "the governed"—or else the proposition was a sham. Nor could there be reservation as to what "government" included. It had to cover vital common concerns, or again the proposition was a sham. There would be trouble, and there was, whenever it became apparent that practice failed to satisfy the essential meaning.

But back of this proposition was the new faith, with its two parts. There had to be, on the one hand, a new confidence in average human beings. That was where the rights of man came in, the rejection of the old idea that only a few people deserve respect, and the acceptance of a belief in the worth of the human type itself. This was a "broadening" movement: it meant a more inclusive conception of "the many." On the other hand, there had to be, and could be, for the individual person actually a

[35]

narrowing movement, or better, perhaps, a centering one. The individual—more individuals than ever before—could have greater single-mindedness toward his own truth, which no power on earth had the right to control or influence, especially when he entered a voting booth.

This is the paradox of democracy which men like Emerson and Whitman were to meditate over later: a truer "individualism" on the one hand, a wider community on the other. A little meditation shows that, far from being opposed, both ideals reach their own greatest development only together.

But this is why we were fortunate in having parents of different types, so to speak, among our founding states. Here, as I have said, was Massachusetts, or the Conscience state. She tended to emphasize the single-minded man, listening alone to God.

Let us be ruled by Conscience, said Massachusetts, with no compromise on worldly considerations (unless those of decent, thrifty folk with money to lend!). At best, a Roger Williams or even John Adams could see the logical extension of this, and say, Give every man freedom of conscience, so all may be single-minded in their choices. But at worst, the Essex-Junto-Deacon-Magistrate type of Massachusetts man tended to conclude: Few people have any consciences! Therefore let the Elect Few rule the Lost Many—for their own good, of course.

The more secular political theorist of Virginia tended to emphasize the common-minded man, acting according to Nature. Let us follow Nature—the common human type which we all are—by the light of Reason, given to our type by God, if you will, but no good unless exercised by the creature to whom He gave it to use. Let us have faith in the nature of the creature, as well as of the Creator. All men are created equal. Give them all the same rights. Give every man a vote on the same terms (at least, those whose natures are far enough developed, i.e., not, perhaps, men of a certain "lower" race! If the Massachusetts type was sometimes self-righteous, the classical-naturalist-rational Southern type was sometimes only rationalistic). But at best a Jefferson followed out this theme to both logical ends, the broad end of the natural rights of all men, and the narrow one of the single-minded Right Rule, or inner test of Virtue, for any one man. There is good reason to think that the author of our Declaration of Independence, like most men of classical training of his time, used Happiness and Virtue interchangeably in his own thinking, and thus had in mind something better than a hedonistic goal for the national energy when he wrote *Pursuit of Happiness.*

But on the whole it looked as if it were fortunate for the country that there was middle ground for it to stand on between Virginia and Massachusetts; even though, curiously enough, Massachusetts and Virginia tended to join in thinking that New York, Pennsylvania, and Illinois made a vulgar and common middle ground indeed! Nevertheless, it would have to be recorded that it was on this ground, roughly speaking, that democracy flourished and grew strong, and was saved from a sad death in early youth.

Going from Massachusetts, or even idyllic Vermont, to New York State, you leave classic white frame houses and tidy, self-contained green valleys, and come upon a more motley scene and architecture—General Grant Gothic, Hudson River Bracketed, or mere nameless, square, carpenter-made houses; wide and loose green and brown valleys, smoke and skyscrapers, and finally almost amorphous plains and plateaus, before more mountains and more valleys. Something the same might be said going from Virginia to Tennessee to Texas.

Starting from fish-shaped Paumonok, taking the Brooklyn ferry, spending many days and nights among the towers of Manhattan watching faces from the ends of the earth, then on to practically all points west and south and north, and east again, and you could get Walt Whitman, with the help of a very wide concave mirror and a strong inner light of the George Fox-William Penn variety, not to mention a spark struck by our own Emerson. With help from various directions, south and north, up and down, a few great books and a great deal of observation of people in a simplified environment, and reflection upon the dubious human instrumentality for any divine purpose; a slowly gathering power of focusing a very deep-reflecting mirror indeed; and you could produce, from this central ground, Abraham Lincoln. It would be hard to mention someone else with quite as much right to mix high with broad, and put in the same sentence charity toward all and firmness in the right as God gives us to see the right.

The interesting thing is how the style was changing as these various energetic ideas crossed the Atlantic and then began to cross the continent, emerging and re-emerging in different human guise out of different situations, social and material. You might trace the ideas back, but however far you went, you could not find any expression of them quite like *Leaves of Grass*, or the "Second Inaugural Address." Whitman and Lincoln offered images, in turn, which had the energy to go much farther, and generate a great many more impulses and efforts at approximation, before our society in any broad sense would begin to catch up with them.

Moreover, it was a long time true that the mere fact of there being more country west helped out these active ideas. If you want to see how much difference open country west could make in the evolution of a new culture, you might compare an American state or even a Canadian province with one of those islands in the Caribbean, such as Jamaica, which were settled by more or less the same stock with more or less similar original reasons for settlement, but which lacked open country west.

It turned out it was not so much a question of some particular separatist idea getting control, as the fact that no one of them was big enough to get control in a big country. There was protection in space, as there was to be protection in numbers— providing you allowed free access to the one as you were to allow free expression to the other. Free land further west was a sort of Bill of Rights in itself. It as much as said, if they will not let you express your beliefs where you are, then go where there is no one to tell you what you can or can't express.

Plymouth and Boston Bay had offered much this sort of opportunity to people who felt censored in Leyden or London, and Providence, in turn, offered it to people censored in Boston. The Separatist from England might well find himself separating from Separatism in Massachusetts, and New York became the supporter of his dissent. Differences might develop either on the right or left, and Vermont could salve the wounds of Church of England heretics driven out of dissident Connecticut. Pennsylvania and North Carolina might have room for Scotch-Irish Presbyterian infidels denied welcome in New England. Quakers and Jews, Catholics and Baptists, all had their difficulties and all, to a degree, had their remedy. The most original and startling sainthood of them all—the Latter-day Saints—probably encountered the greatest difficulties of all, and went the farthest to find their cure.

In other fields of endeavor where social and economic ideals mingled with religious, a similar process of proliferation, secession, and removal took place, and all up and down the green valleys there appeared for shorter and longer periods small shining models of the millennium, as Harmony broke away from Harmony, and Community seceded from Community.

With all this, however, there was progress in first laying the basis for, and then establishing and putting in practice, the great overall ideas that were to distinguish American institutions, namely, the separation of Church and State for the freer breathing of men in both their bodies and souls, the distinction between speech and act in the matter of civil loyalty or disloyalty, and the final sovereignty, in act, of the people making common decisions concerning their own government.

Not that there were no violations of some or all of these principles, in both spirit and letter. Violations were repeated and often glaring, and their end is not in sight. Still, you could get almost any American to affirm his deathless belief in one or the other or all of the above principles, so far at least as some interest of his own was involved, and this was a remarkable gain. For then, one could at least point to his inconsistency in invoking other rules for other people's interests; and anyone with enough command over his own temper had a chance always of confusing the opposition.

If any further proof were needed of the comparative triumph of these general ideas, it lay in the attraction they held, along with New World fortune, for people in the Old World who ran into difficulty in some respect with old country styles in ideas or institutions. The roll of such people's names, obscure or noted, was long and is still being added to, all the way from Jack Smith to Carl Shurz and Isadore Cohen to Albert Einstein. The vitality of the Goddess of Liberty in New York harbor was greater than even Americans had supposed, and the disorder of the Old World continued in some part to make the order of the New. "It's a free country" became just as famous a saying along the Rhine, the Po, and the Danube as that the New World streets were paved with gold.

There seemed to be safety both in space and in numbers, so far as the health and growth of these newer ideas were concerned. For, in spite of those historians and commentators who liked to think differently, defection from them—the ominous phenomena of Hartford Conventions, Kentucky Resolutions, and firings on Fort Sumter—did not take place with increasing frequency and seriousness as you went from east to west with the population center, and as the number of stars in the blue field of the flag increased from the original thirteen. On the contrary, such phenomena diminished in actual seriousness, and while the newer Western states came into the sheepfold with a great deal of bluster, brag, and even gun waving, they really did not question the value of a single sheepfold as their predecessors and progenitors on occasion had questioned it. They took it as natural to belong, and had good use, for their own purposes, for the regulation equipment of guns, uniforms, badges, and flag that went along with belonging.

Moving westward was mostly along the great parallels, as if each of the original colonies threw a long shadow straight west across the country. That was the way many of the original thirteen liked to draw their early maps—extend the state indefinitely westward! It was also like Betsy Ross's flag—thirteen stars and thirteen parallel stripes, the stripes for the original states only. Nevertheless, while this purely parallel movement was the standard form of migration, new effects began to be noticed, and seemed to increase in rate through the whole nineteenth century. These were mixing effects, culturally speaking: crisscrossing, merging, multiplying, and blending. Older domestic stocks and types, as well as a great variety of new exotic stocks and types, went into this process.

The farther west you went, the more blending there was of the original native elements, and one began to detect a southern drawl in the speech of Wyoming and Montana, while in Oklahoma and Texas you could make out, in a slowed-down fashion, the twang of the Yankee horse trader.

The international orchestral effect seemed to reach its highest pitch in the large seaboard centers, where accommodations were most numerous and accessible if not spacious, and from there to spread into the interior. But the railroads, the mines, the fields, and the factories soon drew these new arrivals into almost every corner of the country, and the mingling effect was in some degree continental.

ENERGY IN IDEAS—STYLES IN FORTUNE

There had been nothing like it for variety of color and movement since Cortez entered the court of Montezuma. Searching for a figure, observers of the phenomenon lit upon the melting pot, which perhaps was not too happy a choice either for sentimental or artistic purposes. However, some figure was needed to describe what actually took place, as Spanish hot dishes worked their way north and east from the southwest, along with Navajo silver and turquoise; as the French mackinaw came southward, to be followed later by Swedish blond hair, Danish pastry, and Norwegian ski suits; red Italian wine moved into the interior from both seaboards; Bohemian folk songs met Negro spirituals, and Irish jigs mixed with Kentucky hoedowns; German beer and freethinking from the cities ran into German piety and sauerkraut on the farms; Yiddish jokes joined Negro rhythm on the stage and Jewish light added to Brahmin light on the high court; Welsh, Polish, and Lithuanian strength met in the mines and steel mills and went from there to labor halls and colleges; Fifth Avenue reminded you first of London, then of Paris, and then only of New York; and all over the country impossible Czech, Yugoslavian, Russian, Finnish, Turkish, Greek, and Armenian names began to be spelled in a little less impossible English, in order to be more like American.

English language and its literature, with the American stream taking a larger and larger place, was necessarily the glass into which all elements had now to look to recognize themselves as best they could; and few regretted that the tongue used by Chaucer and Shakespeare and Lewis Carroll was the one, after their fashion, taken over by a hundred and fifty million Americans of various ancestry. It was generally agreed, too, that for a frame for the whole picture, nothing could have been more fortunate than the original English talent for orderly government. It was further agreed, however, that the talent for *self*-government was the best feature of this basic contribution, and there tended to be less and less regret all around at the early date at which it had been asserted.

There was no particular reason for hanging on to the melting-pot figure; in fact it seemed a poor one for its suggestion less of a weaving of many-colored strands into a single cloth, than of running all colors into a dull neutral. Anyone with an artistic eye would prefer a bright and variegated textile, to a putty-colored mass. Nevertheless, there was reason to suspect that some people, who said they had come to dislike the melting-pot figure, actually meant they disliked the significance of it, when they said it suggested something both too heterogeneous and too standardized.

For could there be any figure for the good society that did not somehow involve singleness and community on the one hand and multiplicity and variety on the other?

There is still no getting away from the glitter of fortune. Early or late, it was only that golden color that could draw westward with enough force to make people leave old homes and forget old household gods.

The forgetting was as important as the new experience. A wise man, Pythagoras, stated this proposition a long time ago: When you go abroad, don't turn around at the frontier.

Some turned around, looking back even across the very wide frontier, the Atlantic Ocean. Others did not turn around, at least until they knew their way in the new country; and on the whole they were the ones that expressed the more characteristic new style.

If culture were only a mechanical spread of ideas, it would probably be a loss to forget anything. It so happens, however, that old people die and children are born, and culture like life is always a birth and a forgetting.

There was often real loss and ignorance as a result of moving from older cultures to the wilderness, and building up a new culture from the first stroke of an ax and pierce of a plow. A man learned something about the functions of tools and the ways of materials, but at the cost sometimes of the graces of living which, in the end, the tools and materials were meant to serve.

The truth which pioneer Americans, east and west, were privileged to relearn was the truth of function: how things work, and the order of the more necessary over the less necessary. It is a great truth, and was to distinguish the new country, and American thinking, for a long time. What's the use of it, how does it work, show me, I'm from Missouri. You could look back at almost any older civilization, and see how truths of function had been forgotten, and rote ways of doing things went on and on, with many unnecessary and often oppressive motions.

Americans did not like frills and highfalutin ways, and in general the new things they created—Puritan furniture and Detroit motor cars and Chicago skyscrapers and Hemingway's prose —had a stripped, functional, clean design and efficiency of operation.

Still, there was a functional, or motor type of man developed in America, too, that left something to be desired: he did not know just why he was operating, though he could operate very efficiently. He worked and worked and worked, and when he had nothing to use his hands and head on, he was often at a loss what to do at all. Often he was the very man who woke up somewhere in middle life wondering what he was really after, and what he had been leaving out of his life. Then he might begin a hurried search all over the world to find it.

The older cultures often seemed to have this other thing— grace, composure, peace. Americans were inclined to dislike the fatalism, the resignation, the obscurantism that often seemed to go with graceful living and peaceful dying in the Old World. But too close attention to function and the main chance, as well as an early revulsion from it, led some Americans on these far quests for the elder gods and goddesses.

On the whole, however, the people who felt they were rising in the scale as they came across were glad to forget many things they left behind. They were the ones who coined the phrase "old country ways," which meant certain folkways and habits of mind which they knew had limited their development as human beings, however quaint they might be as customs. This was an old theme too, one on which Americans had discoursed from the first. John Adams and Thomas Jefferson were both eloquent upon it. The letters they wrote home from abroad were caustic with phrases concerning court manners and styles in aristocratic living on the other side of the Atlantic.

Later American immigrants came to much the same conclusion, and while they talked somewhat about bowing and scraping, and ever-present uniforms and official arrogance, they talked more perhaps about old-sod superstitions, stern marriage customs,

tyrannical fathers, money hiding, and other "old country ways."
There were of course new arrivals at all levels who looked behind them after crossing the frontier, and yearned for the altars
and ways of the lost motherland. But your true child of the
Western star, whether late or early, spurned the past as a bucket
of ashes, and generally his instinct was right. The past was a
peasant shawl, a bit of faded lace, an old wives' tale, a younger
son's portion, a broken chain.

The death and forgetting in this emerged after a generation
or so as a birth and an innocence. This growing up again meant
ignorance and infancy, adolescent blundering and agony, sopho-
more brightness and imitation. Much of what was thrown away
had to be brought back, though often in a new form. Much of
what was new was thin, uncertain, overgenteel or overcrude.
It took a while for the new sediment to settle thick enough for
new roots to take hold, and for the plant not be blown over
by every breeze, east or west.

The difference, however, was the difference between growth
and aging, between creation and copying. The best parent, with
the best intentions, could not do what the child on its own had
to do.

There would be time enough for refinement and elaboration;
but only the crude is worth refining anyway. The appeal of
fortune and new space was elemental; it molded mass rather
than sharpened line; drew out the fraternal instinct instead of the
filial; rewarded energy instead of form; and all these are healthy
processes in a young organism. Action and the main chance reduced all kinds to a common denominator, and broadened a

large new base by taking from a great many old narrow heights. In time the new pyramid might be worth anyone's looking at.

Gradually the other current was felt—the one that pushed back, against the East Wind. Memory itself underwent a change as it looked back from points farther and farther west. The newer states, the ones hatched out of the Western Reserve with mingled fear and hope in Washington, remembered their national procreation with pride and piety. There might not be much gain from a Royalist to a D. A. R., but there was some; at least it meant that reaction did not go back technically beyond 1776 and the Atlantic Ocean.

Massachusetts and Virginia began to write fairy tales about their own prodigies of 1776 and 1812, and Missouri and Illinois believed them. It was Rousseau and his noble common man all over again, with a purely New World setting. The situation called for democratic heroes, images, myths, sayings; and Henry Longfellow and Parson Weems obliged.

The founding states found their own platitudes, which they had halfway come to doubt themselves, returned with fire in the mouths of the Clays and Jacksons, the Bryans and La Follettes. Lincoln read *The Life of George Washington.* Carl Sandburg and Vachel Lindsay read Lincoln. Somebody else read Lindsay and Sandburg. What had first been a theory and a hope, then a battle and an experiment, became a faith, a tradition, a song.

The founding states had most of the glory and difficulty of the original conception. In the later periods they took the risk of apotheosis. It is always dangerous when you get to the point of having a past to be proud of; it may seem to take the place of a present. Moreover, it is disconcerting to find that its proudest ornaments have become the commonest property, and its greatest names the most familiar words in everybody's mouth. Virginia and Carter Glass would live to hear Thomas Jefferson being quoted against them by the latest young insurgent from Wisconsin or Washington.

The force of the returning current, whether it moved from west back to east, or from the base of the pyramid upward, was the force of a body, a state of being, an incarnation. This is the way the ideas worked out, not on paper, but in the flesh. Jefferson and Madison and Adams and Franklin finally agreed on the theory that all would join in a single union. Jackson and Lincoln showed what the theory actually meant, and who had to be included, if it meant what it said. Henry Ford, Thomas Edison, Western Union, Union Pacific, the *Saturday Evening Post*, the "St. Louis Blues," Sears-Roebuck, Walt Disney, Standard Oil, Fred Allen, D. W. Griffith, were some of the millions of facts born of the theory. This is what happens when you turn a rich continent with a certain principle of liberality over to the more or less voluntary impulses of a lot of people—let them more or less scramble for it.

It was not all pretty and fine by any means, what Europe was to lump together with a certain mingled admiration and contempt under the name Americanization. For Europe was finally to feel this returning wave too, all up and down the scale from Hollywood to Woodrow Wilson. But the main question had to do with its lasting qualities, its new sources of energy, its new style and form.

One could quite easily trace the evolution in style, certain features going down and disappearing on one side, as it were, while others came up and formed on the other.

On the whole, the feudal style—the proud, narrow, if high forms—disappeared. They did not seem able to throw down roots in a big country with many sorts of social lines erased, or at least well smudged. Function did count, and where there was function there was power. In Tidewater Virginia and South Carolina, for instance, in spite of the feudal forms, there was power as long as there was function. There was greatness as long as a George Washington or a George Mason thought of himself as a man of affairs in a big country and not only as a squire of Mount Vernon or Gunston Hall. But the early decay of Tidewater, with its great fading houses and memories of a feudal grace, was first to prove the essential unreality of the aristocratic style in the New World.

Again, on the Mississippi and the Columbia, as on the James and the Rappahannock, great ornate houses, Victorian rather than Georgian and not to their advantage, melancholy with the memory of quick fortunes in land or furs or lumber, proved again the impermanence of feudal glory under our Western star. These houses glittered for a time with bonanza wealth, then echoed with the ghostly footfalls of children dead by their own hand, or burned in their sudden blaze of fortune; until family line and house together vanished.

True, other forms of wealth than slave labor or grants of forest land continued to promise feudal magnificence, and Saratoga Springs or Bar Harbor or San Simeon thrust up castellated towers, gingerbread gables, or shiny new cubes of concrete and glass. As long as there was function, these remained; but as mere grace they rarely survived a generation. There was function to begin with, in most cases. It would be a great mistake to think that John D. Rockefeller and Andrew Carnegie were not true creators of the new forms that were inherent in the new theories as applied to a new continent. Our question has to do with where the forms lasted, where the style had strength, originality, and endurance; and this tended to be on the highway instead of the private drive; in the million living rooms rather than in the ten or twenty drawing rooms.

The note of destiny sounded in the gaudy superstructure of high finance, as it had sounded three centuries before in the gaudy deeds of the conquistadors. This was the way the act always opened, in the grand-opera style. Yet it tended to steady down to something more simple and colloquial, something, natively speaking, more classic.

The native character of typewriters and radios and Chevrolet cars was unquestionable. It had yet to be decided whether the style of financing and producing and profiting from these native products would become as functional and democratic as the products themselves, and whether we would have a Fordization of banks and bonds and factory politics as we had of transportation and communication themselves. But the signs of the decay of function on this high superstructure were appearing, and it looked as if it were only a matter of time before this feudal style of finance would join the great houses of Tidewater in reflecting a vanished splendor.

There is nothing new in this law of displacement, by which social forms at a certain high level become overblown, and drop off, while functional forms continue to evolve where they can actually serve the needs of those who need services. This law is as old as human society, and the only question is how our main ideas and principles have affected it, and if they can control its eccentricity and violence a little, and put power and resources promptly enough where they are wanted badly enough, and thus keep the whole organism adjusting as it functions, and functioning as it adjusts.

That our new principles had made some effect was evident from the regular dismay of people on higher levels at seeing people below them making use of the same ladder they had used in order to reach the same place. There was regularly the beginning of doubts, on the part of such arrived people, of the soundness of the ladder, and the value of those principles which they themselves had once loudly acclaimed when they had needed them most.

Thus the Federalists had looked askance at the Jeffersonian Democrats using popular sovereignty to climb to power by; and began to doubt popular sovereignty. Thus many of the old Whigs had feared the new Chicago Republicans; and good Republican farmers feared the newly organized Grange, while the Grange lived to suspect the Farm Bureau, and the Farm Bureau the Farmers' Union. Thus the descendants of English farmers in Boston had to be as easy as they could at seeing descendants of Irish farmers using their own steps to climb into the State House; the D. A. R. came to see revolution in the mere use of the Bill of Rights; and the Liberty League as conceived by the National Association of Manufacturers vented its dismay at either liberty or association in any style but its own.

All these were mostly good signs rather than bad. They meant that the principles were actually working—to a dismaying degree at least. One could easily point out where they were not working, because not invoked. Still, as such matters go in history, the success of the original ideas was remarkable. When you could use them to gather into the same national body, on the same terms, thirty-five states whose very existence was hardly imagined by the first thirteen; when you could use them to accommodate tens of millions of new people with almost unpronounceable names, from almost unheard-of places, you had accomplished an extraordinary feat. No feat like it in fact had ever been accomplished before.

Except for the disaster and confusion of the Civil War, the accommodations, the adjustments, the shifting of the center, extension of the circumference, rising of the base, and displacement at the top—all these evolutions had gone on in a remarkably fluid and mild manner. It marked a new style in the history of such evolutions, and one which deserved the most respectful attention from every angle, below, above, left and right.

For as a matter of fact, nothing had so insured safety at the top as mobility at the bottom, or security on the right as freedom on the left. When you no longer felt people crowding you from below, when you were no longer jostled on the sidewalk by people both on your right hand and left hand, that would be the time to worry.

There is no denying that fortune destroyed as well as created life in the New World. Many of the more ardent votaries of the Western star were consumed in her fire, just as many of the children of the East Wind were to lose their way in the back trail toward grace.

Virtue and survival depended on something other than either movement. They depended on keeping faith with the land and life itself, wherever you were. This meant, generally speaking, the less gaudy styles of fortune, the more stable kinds of production—economic or cultural—which put back as much as you took out. It meant the triumph of the kind of ideas and grace which could grow with the land where you were, and did not require a return ticket back, or a new ticket farther on.

Still, the experience of the Western star remains one of the great heritages of the New World. It is part of classic American piety, this sense that men here have been given a new chance, a new hope of "bettering their condition." The heart that has never been lifted up, the spirit that has never felt wonder and gratitude at the great fruit of fortune, so long delayed in the world's slow ripening, can hardly be said to be initiated in the New World mystery.

No credit belongs to the people of the New World for their great piece of fortune. Their only credit lies in their hazard of it, in what they have made of it. It is not luck they have made as much as they have. Let no man say that America is all luck and good fortune! Men labored to make, others fought to save these forms by which a continent has been won to a new style of fortune. It will not be luck, one way or another, what happens in the future. Much more promise lies in the country's star than has ever been realized. All depends on how the promise is met, and how many people continue to feel that they share in its meeting.

CHAPTER IV

The "Elect," the Superior Few, the Saving Remnant

〜〜〜〜〜〜〜〜〜〜〜〜〜〜〜〜〜〜〜〜〜〜

WALT WHITMAN is often thought of as the American who stands for bigness, and sings mere size. I would not say there are no swollen words anywhere in Whitman. Yet it was Whitman who could see a mouse as well as the ocean, and who, for himself, swore he would accept nothing that all cannot have the counterpart of on the same terms.

There is a democratic oath for you.

It was not Whitman, the intellectual democrat, who wrote a book out of near idolatry and envy of the biggest creature on earth, the whale. That was Herman Melville, who was much more the intellectual aristocrat. Whitman said that size is only development, an observation to put mouse and leviathan much more nearly in the same class, and ease the mind of Ishmael.

Few of us may be prepared to take Whitman's democratic oath, and test the reach of our sympathy by rejecting the means of our separation. I want to keep in view, for the purpose of

[55]

orientation, a central, classical American standpoint, reaching toward the broadest inclusiveness on the one hand, while conceiving, on the other, the possibilities of a new individual.

It would be hard to find anyone else so near the center of this two-way evolution as Whitman—unless it is Lincoln. But among our poets, Whitman has taken in the most territory; he has best sensed a new particular, a new type. The two have to go together. Scope is significant only as development. No curly-tusked mammoth ever saved himself and his type simply because of bulk. We have got a continent-large entity called a nation containing a hundred and fifty million people, less or more, for particulars. Let no one sneer at its size, and wish it smaller just for the sake of neatness. That would only be postponing our problem and the world's. At the same time, let us see how it is built up: what our idea of a particular is, and how to add the particulars together.

We might get something very big, and find that it was only the Roman Empire over again, a classical style, if you like, but not one that is worth the trouble of repeating. Look at the particulars. Your Roman particulars are slaves, soldiers, and a "rabble citizenry" for the large part, and a handful of rulers and nobles for the small. Some of the nobles are really fine and noble, but some are not, and there is no "check" on them, as our founding fathers liked to say, to keep them from becoming tyrants and wastrels.

Where is the "class" in this Roman-classical style? The class was of course in the superior few, the true nobles, and so on. It was a narrow class, meant to be narrow. The inferior many were not meant to have class, because they were not supposed to have it in them. They were the common herd, the rabble, the vulgar many, the envious multitude, the turbulent, ignorant, seditious, emotional, unstable mob. I am not making up those terms. Read them in any political or social discussion from Plato's *Republic* down through the debates on our Constitution, and even to the last argument between newspaper columnists. Some of the terms have softened. Some real difference has been made in our idea of people in general. But the argument still goes on to which the terms refer.

Well, we might create something as big, merely in bulk, as the Roman Empire, but with a different setup, and a different styling of the particulars. We might believe in a new sort of class. The two would have to go together, for the kind of organization breeds the type, just as the type makes up the organization.

Where is class in a democracy? That is where Jefferson comes in with his type of the "common man," Whitman with his universal men and women, Lincoln with his "people." All of them want class and mass to approximate more and more the same thing. Unquestionably it is not so in terms only of natural power, or talent. John Adams, in that delightful correspondence between the old men, finally got Jefferson to admit that there is such a thing as a "natural aristocracy" in the sense of people endowed with greater original gifts. Still, Jefferson would not say that the plan of an aristocratic society is better than the plan of a democratic one. The question always is, not whether there are superior people, but whether any people should have superior rights under law. The notion of equality under society might be very important as a plan to work on. Where do you expect these superior people to come from? Where will we look for quality in a democracy? Do you think it is of no importance if the ruling idea is that quality and class is a small affair, a matter of the few born gentry or "quality," or if the idea is that quality might come from anywhere, and any lad aspire to be president?

As for your natural aristocrat, what does he actually look like? It is a little hard to recognize him when he actually appears, but my nomination is Mark Twain, nature's darling surely if there ever was one. He has the true aristocratic flair, and he submits himself to no such democratic discipline as Whitman. He loves luxury with the best of them, impresses everyone with the true regal style, and writes a great book about a penniless waif, Huckleberry Finn. He is born to the purple, in a small town in Missouri. He adores the saintly Joan of Arc, often writes like the village atheist, is fascinated with all the trappings of courts and chivalry and almost savage against feudalism and royalism. There is some discrepancy, apparently, between one idea and another and one instinct and another. Yet there is no doubt, here is your man of lordly natural power, for what that may mean simply as a biological fact. I wonder if John Adams would have recognized him?

There is still the effect of one or another kind of type-ideal in society, and after all, that is what we are concerned with here, since we are not empowered to create new types in nature herself. I only want to suggest that Whitman looks like our best man for knowing what he is about in the logic of democracy, and what new type-person he is looking for to make a new order. Do not imagine that Whitman's type-ideal, the true individual in a true democracy, is somehow a more primitive, rudimentary, less evolved person than the corresponding type-ideals of other styles of society—for example, the "perfect courtier" of the Renaissance. It takes evolution of a part to make it reflect more of the other parts in a given whole. It takes subtlety in a man to see himself as one individual among many in a large populous country, or even, world.

Is there some great subtlety and mental acuteness required to dismiss most of your fellow men under the cover-all type, the vulgar herd? Does it take less or more mentality to try to imagine not only you and your own little circle as living individuals, but everyone alive—individuals all—of a great variety on the one hand, and some essential identity on the other, even with yourself?

This is the task of the imagination in a democracy. You may follow Whitman's conception of it, both as to the general and particulars, in *Leaves of Grass* and *Democratic Vistas*.

There, I think, is our best statement so far of a democratic Plato's *Republic*, or a common man's version of Castiglione's *Perfect Courtier*.

Let us not shirk the contrast or let Plato's name keep us from examining Plato. For as a matter of fact, in this old argument about the superior rights of superior people, it is to Plato, and his *Republic*, that you find yourself led sooner or later for the most influential statement of the aristocratic theory. We may as well meet it at its source.

But there are other terms for this theory of the exclusiveness of virtue. There is the term "saving remnant" which has an ecclesiastical and Old Testament sound. There is the "elect" which sounds like Geneva and John Calvin. You might have a society, a theocracy, made of the "elect" for the superior few, and the lost or the damned, for the vulgar many. But it would still be the same question, whether self-admitted "better" people ought to have special powers under law. This is no academic question in our American history, with its examples of ecclesiastical aristocracy in New England, and dreams of Greek slave-republics, with patriarchal overtones, in the old South.

But to take up Plato first. What is his theory based on, that it should have provided almost the standard language for superior people talking about a superior society, from Cicero to Samuel Johnson, and Plutarch to John Adams?

It is based on an analogy between the make-up of an individual and the make-up of society, and briefly this is the way it goes. There are "good" and "bad" elements in our natures as human beings, and it depends on which we allow the mastery whether we are virtuous or not. The bad elements are many, good is one. In a good man, virtue, or reason, is in control, much as an expert horseman is in control of a fractious horse full of all kinds of wayward impulses. Now, only a few people in any society have learned to master themselves. The great majority are very limited in their powers of reason and self-control, and live simply by following their impulses and desires. They are easy marks for any politician who makes them rosy promises of wealth, liberty, and so on if he is given power to run the government. Who, then, do we want to have the final say in government, these emotional and unmastered many, or the superior and self-controlled few? Naturally, we want wise and self-mastered men to govern us. But these are a small minority in any society. Therefore we will not expect good government in a democracy, for that means giving the final sovereignty to the unwise and unvirtuous, since they are always a large majority in any society.

There is much else in *The Republic* of great interest concerning an ideal state, not to mention an ideal philosophy. I happen to think the philosophy very great indeed. It is the political science we are concerned with here, and especially this bit of reasoning on which Plato rested his theory of "rule by the superior few." The reasoning was so logical and irrefutable to those in every age who acknowledged themselves to be the superior few whom Plato was talking about, that for a couple of thousand of years you might have heard any number of Roman patricians, French nobles, or British lords quote Plato and break into fits of rage at the very idea of being questioned as to their fitness to govern dispassionately without any advice from "the turbulent many"!

And in the twentieth century, in the United States, you might hear a good many captains of industry break into very similar rage when questioned concerning their fitness to rule the economic world without advice from their employees or the public. Here, perhaps, is where the theory of rule by the superior few had come to lodge during this time.

What is wrong with Plato's analogy? It is this, that Plato might address himself to the question of an inner check for the control of the individual organism, or of an inner check for the control of the social organism, but it is a great mistake to confuse the two. An inner check for a man is not an inner check for a government (or industry); nor is an inner check for a government an inner check for a man. With a little reflection, one will see that inner becomes outer, in either case. When the government puts a man in jail, that is an outer check on the man. We call it "authority," and realize it is necessary when a man's inner check has failed. When the Congress overrides the president, or when thirty or forty million men vote a new Congress into office, that is an inner check in society—but an outer act, or power, on the part of the individuals involved, and just the opposite of a check. We call it popular sovereignty.

Democracy, in short, has tried to go just in the opposite direction from Plato's theory of rule by the superior few. The more men that we can trust to rule themselves from inside for as much of their personal lives as possible, the better we like it. This is "freedom," and it saves society acting upon a man from the outside, in the authoritarian manner. But the more men we can get to exercise their power, or vote, publicly, the more we like that too. This is responsibility, or democracy, and it means that society gets the voluntary instead of the involuntary consent of its own citizens. We are sure that voluntary consent in the long run is much stronger than involuntary, as a social force.

But when Plato had worked out his scheme for "rule by the best," it turned out to be simply a self-perpetuating oligarchy, so far as the organism of society is concerned. Not trusting the mass of people to rule themselves, they had to be ruled from outside, in other words, by imposed authority. Trusting the superior few to rule for the many was of course to give them social power without check at all, except their own self-restraint. Plato put this self-restraint in by definition, but this is as it may be. When Plato turned his Republic over to some actual "guardians" to run, they might or might not turn out to have the self-restraint that

Plato read into them. If it happened they did not, there was no help for it. There was no way to get rid of such untrustworthy guardians short of revolution.

George Washington learned the classical rules of conduct, and Thomas Jefferson was a classical scholar in the eighteenth-century manner, and I think both of them knew what Plato meant by self-mastery, the inner check, and so on. Therein lay the Greek, the Platonic, contribution to our American democracy, roughly speaking. It was in the field of individual ethics, and no one would want to underestimate it. Nothing can well take the place of a person's own self-discipline; and some theory of true virtue and individual responsibility is quite a good thing to have current in any society. If Rousseau or Shelley or Marx assumed that the right new kind of society would make individual virtue obsolete, and solve everybody's personal problem, they were badly mistaken. To judge from the number of individuals in the twentieth century who were postponing solving their personal problems, this new kind of society, that would solve such problems for them, was widely believed in and waited for.

Social ideas, social discipline, and social checks are something else, and Plato and Plutarch and Cicero were well abandoned by Jefferson and Madison and Franklin at this point. Our founding fathers did not assume that an inner check in an individual is an inner check in society. They carried out the logic of the analogy and said, very well, if every organization needs an inner check, let us have a social organism with its own internal checks. Society is not moral, like an individual, and let us not trust any ruler or self-perpetuating ruling line to stay just and good with no check upon it but its own self-restraint. Let us not trust even ourselves in that position, and like Plato, wish to play God to our fellow men. But if we are really virtuous and well-intentioned, let us risk having to meet other people's opinion on that matter. That is part of the test of superiority in a democracy.

There was a certain cumbersomeness, perhaps, about the scheme of internal checks and balances that our political philosophers worked out, because they were still thinking of special cases connected with older forms of the state. Still, it has not happened often in the history of the world that so much philosophy, statesmanship, generalship, and political talent came together in a group of men who had an opportunity to put their beliefs into actual practice. Plato is still in little danger from the competition of say Franklin and Jefferson in the realm of pure philosophy, addressed as it must be to the individual mind. In the realm of social philosophy we can be glad we got Jefferson and Franklin instead of Plato.

Plato was not the first or last idealist, very sure of his own disinterestedness, who when he turned to men's institutions read his own virtue into the system by definition. The Church was to do much the same thing: establish itself as a perfect institution (invisibly), by definition, no matter how much its human parts might visibly err; and pass down its ideal absolute authority (by definition) from hand to hand in an unbroken material chain.

Curiously enough, a very different sort of man, Jean Jacques Rousseau, fell into the same sort of reasoning when he came to set up his ideal state, in spite of all his theoretical belief in natural men making their own "social contract." It is very hard for a genius to turn over even the most foolproof formula to the mercies of other minds, which cannot be expected to be as wise as his own! Rousseau was no exception, and in thinking of all the vicissitudes to which a human society was liable, without his counsel, he found it necessary to leave in some sort of absolute touchstone of wisdom. This was the mysterious character he called the Lawgiver. Who was this man, what position in an actual society did he hold, and who put him there? No answer, the reason being that this character was simply Rousseau. He was a sort of Holy Ghost of Rousseau, bequeathed to posterity for all time.

The Church theory of an invisible right backing up, absolutely and without recourse, a visible human authority was not limited to the Roman variety. One of the best examples was our own early New England church rule.

If I am not mistaken, a metaphor, like Plato's, which served to convince ecclesiastical authorities of their own peculiar right to rule in human things was the metaphor of St. Paul and others about the warring members. It goes very much like Plato's analogy of self-mastery in the individual and in society. The members of the body want to follow their own impulses, each member seeking its own desire, or perhaps conspiring with other members in a sort of subversive mutual gratification. They can be ordered and controlled only by the one spiritual member, the head. Society is like this too; a church is like this. The members, especially the lay members, who are like the physical members of the body, must be ruled by the spiritual part. Theoretically this spiritual part is God, or Christ, an invisible presence accessible to anyone, but actually, in cases of church or civil discipline, the ordained representatives of the invisible must act for Christ or God. They are Plato's superior few, or wise guardians, who because they are themselves dedicated to God's truth, make the only safe masters of human society.

Backing up such a theory was the potent idea of the "elect" itself. This is the belief that certain people are chosen to be God's own true children, while others are not so chosen, but instead are predetermined to be "lost." It becomes the responsibility of the chosen, then, to act for God, and it is easy to see what a tremendous potentiality for good or for harm falls upon an individual who feels strongly that he is elect, especially if he is also in a position of power in the human world. John Calvin worked out this theory of the elect in one of its most extreme forms, and unquestionably it was from Calvin and his Institutes that our New England church rulers derived their idea of "election." Calvin in turn had derived his view chiefly from St. Paul, and thence one might trace it, in various forms, back to the Old Testament and the Hebrew conception of "the sons of God," or the "chosen people." In Isaiah it appears vividly as an appeal to "the saving remnant," without whose true devotion to righteousness the world would be lost.

I do not want to deprecate this idea of election, especially in the sense of Isaiah, and indeed in that of all the great prophets, of a high calling to act truthfully and justly. In this sense I believe there is a saving remnant. But the point is, and always has been, whether one who thinks himself elect thinks also he may arrogate arbitrary power to himself, and is not bound by rules by which others are bound. Or, to put it another way, the question is whether the elect can be distinguished by some outward sign, and especially by the signs of office, or institutional authority. Isaiah most certainly did not think so, or confuse material power

in any form with moral power. Like all prophets, he was wary
of institutions, and the saving remnant he appealed to was no
visible elite, but simply men and women through the ages who
would be distinguished by nothing but their own inner virtue.
These—the people of conscience—were Isaiah's saving remnant.

With Calvin, it was somewhat different, for Calvin was setting
up an institution, and here the great problem is always how to
translate "inner virtue" into social regulation. Calvin answered it
much as Plato did, first by assuming that there is a class of the
elect absolutely distinguished from a reprobate, or lost class, and
then assuming that there is some way to find them out and give
them peculiar powers in society. There was a contradiction here,
for no one had insisted more than Calvin that a man's election
is invisible to other men—only God knows his elect. Calvin passed
the contradiction over, and in actual practice the society he set
up was one which gave the minister and a few elders power to
judge others, not only in conduct, but in belief, or in other words,
as to their election—and use the civil authority if necessary to
enforce their judgment.

Roger Williams, as we have already suggested, went to the
heart of the matter with his brilliant division of "the law" into
two kinds, or tables: first, the private laws of conscience, and
second, the public laws of conduct. Let us put truth where it
should be, in the invisible world, and human conduct where it
should be, in the visible one; in other words, let us separate
conscience and conduct, Church and State. If men's actions are
contrary to civil laws, and injurious to the public weal, very well,
let the civil authorities judge and deal. But if it is a matter of
belief, doctrine, conscience, the individual must be allowed to

judge for himself. But in a theocratic society, authorities will and do take it on themselves to decide matters of conscience for others. In that case, as Roger Williams liked to point out in the language of the day, the authorities might actually cause people to sin, by forcing them to affirm what they did not truly believe. So Williams, like the Quakers, was against requiring public oaths, maintaining with much reason that for the state to put people on their oath for special occasions suggests that it condones lying ordinarily.

But the more tangible result of theocracy was that it subjected people to actual physical discipline for spiritual offenses. This discipline could be, and was, quite serious, all the way from a few days in the stocks to exile or execution.

Here the analogy of the head ruling the members runs into its more bizarre possibilities. To cut off a "member" from the actual human body is quite a drastic decision for the "head" to make. Unfortunately the head of a social institution who decides on such a step with regard to a member of the same institution is not faced with any such inconvenience to himself as losing one of his own hands or feet; which only goes to show how comforting an analogy may be when it analogizes one way but not another.

The heads of the Boston theocracy, the Saints in Israel, the superior few, the elect, the ordained instruments of invisible justice in the visible world, did not hesitate to make the necessary sacrifice of an erring member of the community for the good of the whole body of the elect. I need not recite here the list of such actions which the civil-religious authorities of Boston, Salem, and elsewhere, found it their duty to take, all through the seventeenth century. Roger Williams himself, for no cause essentially but the difference of view stated above, was banished from Boston in the middle of winter. John Wheelwright and others suffered a similar fate. One of the more triumphant actions, from the point of view of the Church powers, was the case of Anne Hutchinson, the most influential woman of her time in the colonies—much too influential for the comfort of the ruling ministry.

Mrs. Hutchinson's exile from Boston fell upon her, as it happened, in the final month of pregnancy, and required her to make her way on foot in this condition to Roger Williams's new colony at Providence. The Boston church, using the proper ecclesiastical-judicial form, had given up this woman to Satan, and nothing could have been surer proof that Satan had received her than the fact that she suffered a miscarriage shortly after arriving in Rhode Island. Governor Winthrop, on receipt of this news, was quick to draw the obvious lesson and publish it abroad with all the graphic details. He only thought he was carrying out, as indeed he was, the unpleasant duty of an elect of God who claimed the power to decide on other people's election.

One might look at other examples in our history of the spirit of the elect, when they assume their own peculiar election. There was, for example, the righteous indignation of the New England Federalists at Jefferson's brazen appeal during his campaign for president to the votes of the people as a whole, the "vulgar many." Jefferson, it seems, would not recognize the superiority of the superior on their own testimony. These New England Federalist leaders were largely the descendants of the old church rulers, and the interesting thing is that they saw Jefferson's movement in the light of sacrilege to the communion table. Letting "the rabble" into the voting booth was like letting unrepentant sinners into the church.

That was the form the idea of rule by the superior few tended to keep in New England and the North. It was an outgrowth of the sense of correct church standing, and intended to make, as it were, a religious test for civil and social standing. The South, needless to say, kept its own idea of the elect, or ruling class, though not I believe in the true tradition of Jefferson. The Southern style was less ecclesiastical than social, and tended to make this sort of equation: those people are right whom we meet socially, even when they are wrong; while those people we do not meet socially are wrong even when they are right. The latter class tended to include of course not only Negroes, but strangers.

Once again, here is the trouble with the theory of the better rule of the better people—how can you recognize them? Anyone would admit there must be superior people, absolutely and abstractly speaking. But might they not be strangers as well as acquaintances, people living north, or south, or east, or west of you; dark of skin as well as light, poor, or rich, or Whig, or farmers, or women, or Catholics, or immigrants, or even bankers? God himself, it seems, had failed to put a special mark on the forehead of the righteous, so that anyone could pick them out in a crowd. It always came down to some customary sign, and this usually turned out to be simply respectability, or family, or wealth—"the wise, the rich, the good," as the best people of New England were soon putting it. These were recognizable signs; the invisible thing—wisdom or goodness—went with the visible—wealth and social position, and saved one a great deal of trouble deciding whether people you hadn't met might be virtuous even though strangers.

In the end, I think one may see this idea of the exclusiveness of virtue as simply a form of personal and family pride. What is faith in a hereditary class, anyway, except the idea that our particular family line—our little blood cluster and type—is the only one we can trust to rule the roost? Follow this out a little, and you can see many interesting effects. Jesus could speak of a single spiritual origin, or God, for all men, and hence of all men as brothers; but if we fix on a single hereditary line as the medium of God's blessing, then those we feel to be our "brothers" become a very small group indeed, while most people alive become distant cousins, or total strangers; while curiously enough, we ourselves become not the direct children of God, but only the grandchildren. I am not being playful. When we come to look at the case of Henry Adams we shall see how much this sort of genealogical refinement appears to have taken place, psychologically and emotionally.

Meanwhile, let me return to my insistence that the democratic view of humanity takes not less, but more imagination than the aristocratic view. It takes more imagination say for an employer to see the men in his shop as fellow workers than as deserving "sons" toward whom he is a father: and vice versa. It takes more imagination for a government official to think of "the people" as fellow citizens than it does to think of them as childlike beneficiaries of his good works. It takes more imagination, and not less, for a writer to conceive of an unknown audience of varied people as worthy of his best thoughts, than to write with a few chosen friends in mind.

[71]

THE WIND BLEW FROM THE EAST

For an extreme example of writing for a few friends, let me quote this verse by Ezra Pound, called "Causa":

> I join these words for four people,
> Some others may overhear them,
> O world, I am sorry for you,
> You do not know these four people.

Here, as you see, the elect, the worthy type, the people like ourselves, have dwindled to four individuals out of all mankind—five counting the author. This represents close to the minimum of imagination concerning people one has not met.

CHAPTER V

Pure Lines and Poor Relations

HENRY ADAMS, like many of the rest of us, was fascinated with the question of the American character. Here was the big new country started under certain special conditions; the delayed start in time, the great rich virgin space, the new ideas chosen for trial and certain old ones thrown in the discard. What would be the result? The first six chapters of Adams's history of the United States in Jefferson's and Madison's administrations make such fascinating reading just because of their vivid sense of this old and ever new American question. The potentiality of the country! When the American character began to show its own nature, what would it be like? "Of all historical problems," Adams wrote, "the nature of a national character is the most difficult and the most important."

The unsatisfactoriness of Adams's effort to solve this "most difficult" of problems was as striking as its brilliancy of approach. Adams could not put the two parts together, democracy and freedom on the one hand and righteousness and law on the other. There is no doubt, Adams was fascinated with the new idea, democracy. He was fascinated with the new American character, especially in women. You will always find in Adams's writings— in the two novels he wrote clandestinely, in the autobiography, in the letters, even in *Chartres*—you will always find hints of the new, delightful type, the American woman, just as you always find her in the novels of Henry James. The freedom, the freshness, the straightforwardness of the new American woman! Our puzzled and somewhat precious intellectuals, drawn as James and Adams are to the old European forms, are nevertheless drawn to the new American character, too, where they can see it and be delighted with it without being confronted at the same time with the logic of a new principle. That would be—to Adams or James —in the case of pretty American women, like James's Isabel Archer of *The Portrait of a Lady* or Adams's Catherine Brooks of *Esther*.

It is a matter for consideration, why Henry James and Henry Adams liked to paint the American woman as a new type, and would paint her in the most admiring light, but did not like as well to paint the American man as a new type. The American man was likely to be a boor in the pages of Adams or James, while if a man was not a boor he was almost sure to be, not a new-type American, but an old type, a little weak, precious, and slightly pathetic, like Strether of the *Ambassadors*, or Wharton in Adams's *Esther*.

Adams was enamored of democracy where he did not have to consider it intellectually. When it came to the intellectual principle, he was always disturbed, as in dealing with Jefferson. He instinctively felt that John Adams and not Jefferson was right in morals, character, and principles. And yet, the course of democracy, the course of the American character, seemed to be away from John Adams toward Jefferson; away from John Quincy Adams toward Jackson; away from Charles Francis Adams or Charles Sumner toward Lincoln. Worst of all, to Henry Adams, it might even be toward Ulysses S. Grant. No wonder Henry Adams could make nothing of the "sequences of men,", as he said concerning his own history. The sequences of women might have been different! But it was hard for Adams, or anyone else, to equate the old-style gentleman, of the Adams breed, and the American character. These two figures did not seem to be traveling the same road, and Henry Adams could keep company with one or the other, but not with both. He finally decided, apparently, to abandon them both in favor of the thirteenth-century Lady; but that is another story.

The difficulty in trying to fix the American character lies in its mingling of cultural strains. Anyone who starts looking for some single, pure old strain, or line of culture, is soon outside of the American character altogether.

Yet it is just some one pure strain that is likely to appeal to the more literal type of aesthetic mind. Hence the long journeys of our intellectuals, back to the thirteenth century, back to the Pueblo Indians, back to Greece or Florence or Canterbury.

Character is at least half unconscious. The unconsciousness of Isabel Archer, or even Daisy Miller, was what attracted Henry James to them, himself so overconscious. It was the sign of their new type. They did not *see* as much, perhaps, as one of James's internationalized observers, Fanny Assingham for example, but they *stood* for more. They suggested a fresh pattern, identity, something in themselves—and the identity was somehow American.

But where did it come from, this new unconsciousness? Henry James never inquired, in fact he instinctively turned away from the new conditions, in America, that had it in them to breed the new type. The type interested him—but against another background. If only you could have your cake—the fresh simple American type—and eat it too, that is, take it out of crude America and set it in an old, cunning, finished environment! Henry James fed the new American unconsciousness to old overconscious Europe, halfway realizing there was something a little ghoulish about the transaction, which you get from the strange undertone of a typical Jamesian novel. It was a one-cycle operation; it could not be repeated. You cannot imagine second generations of Henry James's characters, for they do not exist. But this, too, is another story, that we will go into later.

The point here is the nature of the new American unconsciousness, which must be studied shallow in historical time, or not at all. Its density is in the space dimension, a product of movement rather than status, and of interrelation rather than some single-line heredity. If you do not care to look for the American character where it is—in these new interrelations—you will not find it at all. If you are looking for it in some "deeper" background back of the American background, you will only find something else—the old colonial character, or some other national character, or no character at all.

This is just what has happened in the case of many of our more conscious intellectual types. Looking for depth in the wrong place, they easily dig themselves quite out of earth. The tendency is to follow some one supposed taproot, which, curiously, instead of taking you deeper into the ground, soon has you in the air, rootless. After all, you have to live in a present, and to dig yourself out of the American present is only to come up in some other national present, or some "past present," or the vague international present, or a kind of nowhere present.

This explains why America, in the Western Hemisphere and three or four thousand miles from Europe, has nevertheless been such a factor in internationalism. Someday there may be such a thing as an international character, an international unconsciousness. If and when that day comes, Americans will have done much to create it. They were always falling out of themselves into the empty spaces between nations!

The air there was too thin to sustain life. Woodrow Wilson found that out, or rather, did not find it out in time. Henry James had counted on a density of international atmosphere which did not exist, and so he fell back more and more into the British climate, which where it was thickest was not international at all, but most insular. The war that looked like Wilson's opportunity came as a stroke of doom to Henry James's international world, as he himself halfway saw and expressed in that black letter to a friend, at the opening of the war, concerning "the treacherous years" on which he had built his faith.

The new international ground was not ready, and you could not say that Wilson's seeding of it was seasonable. The intended seed never came up; the actual harvest was quite a different grain. Only the bare intention remained as a seed, for a possible far, faraway harvest. But it would take someone with much more unconscious feeling for many more nations, to cultivate the true international soil.

The point is that you cannot imagine Woodrow Wilson coming from anywhere else but America. The mixed innocence and idealism, boldness and inexperience were peculiarly American—along with a certain personal vanity that I think you would have to call purely Wilsonian. But the confidence that inspired the extraordinary effort in the international field was precisely the thinness in the man of the national character, the uncongealed nature of our national mold. This was Wilson's strength and his weakness. Only a character more sure in the first place of his national footing could have trod with the necessary realism and fortitude the still uncharted, anarchic international terrain. But only a character so nationally unfixed would have risked treading the international field at all.

The American, with his shallow unconsciousness—shallow that is in time—is thus quite easily drawn off his base, blown over, like a plant without a strong taproot. Even the more "typical" American, say George F. Babbitt, is not so sure of himself as he likes to make out. Take him out of his setting, the apparent fortune of his immediate environment, confront him with something of the old, obdurate stuff of the world, that he would call "ancient history," and he is likely to be quite helpless. George F. Babbitt and Woodrow Wilson and Daisy Miller are alike in being easily confused by time and evil. It is their strength and their weakness.

This situation, of the time-innocent American confronted with the evils of history, is one of the standard situations of our cultural drama. It is surprising how large a part of our literature in some way deals with it. And not merely literature. Real life, biography, history often take the same turn, from Jefferson's unhappy experiment with "peaceful economic weapons" in the international field (the embargo) to Henry Ford's grandly irrelevant peace ship. Henry James, in the novel, called it "the international situation" and became its most practiced and famous exponent. Yet how little the "international situation" was James's invention is evident when we remember that one of the first works of artistic merit written by an American—Royall Tyler's *The Contrast* —was of the same material. Here, as in Henry James, is the simplehearted American, a little crude in manner, but good in heart, pitted against the finished but more selfish European, and making his case on sincerity. The subtlety of *The Contrast* is somewhat less than Jamesian, but the situation is not different in kind.

Nor is the situation international only. Again and again the same elements compose themselves within the national boundary, with only lesser variations in type, for contrast. Let New England, New York, Virginia stand for the more finished and self-conscious; let Ohio, Missouri, or California, in turn, stand for the more rudimentary, naïve, yet in a sense, the further differentiated in terms of unconscious character; and the same dramatic pattern repeats itself, the same interaction between different levels of history and different fixations of type.

We might call this the "interregional situation," and for a suggestive example of it, in the sphere of literary consciousness, consider the case of young Hamlin Garland. Here it is plain that no sense of international contrast, no "prefiguration of Europe," was needed for the interaction of innocence and history to take place. Contrasts within the country were sufficient.

Garland's "middle border" had been little treated in literature before, as deliberately chosen subject matter. Here it appeared, simple, humble—oh, so humble!—but with a certain candor, a direct view of life, that was to be its own hallmark, and a new note in American culture. The country boy born in Wisconsin, who had declaimed the standard pieces of eloquence in a two-by-four village academy in Iowa, who had seen what the pioneer was up against on the burning plains of Dakota, and who in good time had the chance to orient himself amidst the world's store of knowledge in Boston, swore to tell what he knew, without dressing or palliation. Young Garland in the first fresh tide of self-consciousness is almost the very type of intellectual young America, so eager, so serious, so full of his new truth.

The wind blew the wheat in waves of marvelous golds and greens across the prairie seas; the life of the toilers was full of the human warmths of barn-raisings and husking bees and country festivals. But there were the hard, crooked fingers of the old: the bowed and bent backs of women who had been beautiful lithe young girls, mothers depleted by too many children, withered and querulous spinsters. These were the simple facts, too, and why lie about them? A proper portion of the sweat, flies, heat, and drudgery must go into any honest picture of "main-travelled" American roads.

New England, with its high moral philosophy, had not looked at life in the face quite in this fashion. Certain things were better not dwelt on. The underside of life was the underside, and the soul ought to turn away from what was ugly to what was beautiful. That was New England, even at its best. Garland's roots were in another soil, a soil that could perhaps stand a closer and more literal working. The flat simple statement, with nothing of the "transcendental" in it, was a new thing in American literature. It was the voice and perception of the interior, and young Garland, humble, half afraid at his own daring, but with a first dogged will and clear-sightedness, gave it utterance.

And then to think that Howells praised him, and Hale, Miss Wilkins, Higginson, Warner, Stedman, the elite of Eastern culture, appreciated his "drab little volume"! To the country boy, the son of the humble Garlands and McClintocks, it was almost too much. The honor of being invited to afternoons and evenings on Beacon Street, even to be asked to speak before assemblies of learned Boston women!

Yes, after a time the sharply-lensed pictures of "main-travelled roads," with their heart-reaching truths and fine overtones of beauty, became a "drab little volume" to their own creator. It is the story of Henry James's Roderick Hudson on an interregional instead of international scale. Roderick Hudson, the promising young American artist, went to Italy and soon lost what native promise he had, for he lost his own character. Garland needed to go only as far east as Boston. The older, more finished society upset the new uncertain character, and the artistic impulse evaporated when the feeling for traditional conformity came in. The youth who had touched center when he was a son of the people gradually drifted to the periphery as he became the "gentleman of letters."

There was irony in it, for Garland's fame in Boston was because of the early vigorous books. The irony was, as it always is, that the author in his later propriety actually became the provincial which he only feared he was earlier, for propriety—that is, somebody else's standards of good taste—is always the standard of the provincial.

My point of course is not that character in one place is truer or better than character in another, but that one can be true only to his own character. Garland dug himself out of his own layer of life, thinking he was digging deeper, and, as usual, it was the time-root that led him astray. That looked pure; it happened to be the New England root. It could have been any other, but in the Middle West, it was usually the New England strand that had the fixed, finished look.

The other dimension, the spatial, was mixed, raw, hybrid; and in Garland's autobiography, *A Son of the Middle Border,* one can easily make out these two distinct forces pulling Garland in different directions.

It is a vivid book, and the picture of the one influence, the immediate one of place and present life, is vividly drawn. Garland put in it the vigor of the raftsmen and the mill hands, and the gay hopes of the land-seekers singing "over the hills in legions, boys." And there is also the disillusion, the overwork, the sweat and heat and difficult living. But here was Garland's layer of experience and unconscious feeling, set in this whole inarticulate epic of the search for the promised land.

But there was the other influence too, and we must recognize it as the "literary" one: Garland's sense of a New England heredity. Son of the middle border though he was, we must not forget that Garland was the grandson of New England—for Garland could not forget it either. It seems to have been Grandmother Garland who impressed this fact on the boy's mind. Her home, says Garland, set though it was "in the midst of the tumult, surrounded by this coarse, unthinking life" stood "a serene sanctuary of lofty womanhood and New England virtue." And from her, as he testifies, Garland received his first literary instruction. He was already aware that Grandmother Garland stood for something far-off and finer, opposed to what was near and crude—a "partial set-off to the vulgar yet heroic influence of the raftsmen and mill hands."

The Grandmother Garlands *were*, indeed, the literary influence in the pioneer West, these intelligent, capable, genteel, bluestocking daughters of New England who had followed some rougher male to a home by the "western waters," or who had come to preside with competence over unruly conglomerate classes in the little red schoolhouses. And the small "sanctuaries of New England virtue" which they set up were undoubtedly setoffs to the vulgar West—the Huckleberry Finn West, the raftsman West, the tobacco-chewing West, the hired-hand West, the new German and Dutch and Scandinavian immigrant West, the Bohunk section-gang West.

The Middle Border could be grateful to New England, and her schoolteachers, that it received a literary stimulus—and sorry only that it came so often undistinguished from a second-hand gentility. A budding author, like young Garland, could not for long be true to his "vulgar but heroic" literary material and to the overgenteel literary mode. For a time he held the two in a precarious balance—then the one, the gentility, won out.

Grandmother Garland, who may have started the grandson on his way, just as surely called him back. Her image in Garland finally could not countenance *Main-Travelled Roads*, which while it did not leave out moral insight, left in the sweat, flies, heat, and drudgery. Ladies, according to Grandmother Garland's code, did not sweat, they perspired. Her niceties, all the more nice because remembered at a remove from New England society itself, at last ruled the grandson and ruled out the son of the Middle Border. The honest-eyed country boy was lost in a dress-coated figure that had the anxious, apologetic air of a sort of second cousin to a Boston Brahmin—a country cousin, for all his moving, now, in all propriety, in the proper circles.

One could look for his own character in the living relations that made it, or be content with being a sort of poor relation to another character. The new conditions were "mixed" only in terms of old lines of culture; the new character was pure only in its own terms! That is the distinction which Garland and many other literary young Americans found it so hard to see, and which led them so easily to write "good-bye Wisconsin," etc. Garland's story illustrates the "interregional" form of the difficulty.

Fortunately, the Garland of the early books lived on, whom Whitman had hailed as one of the "literary pioneers of the West for whom he had been waiting." Other sons and daughters of the Middle Border could go on, gratefully, from where the early books left off. The direct view of life, the close hold on factual reality, the sense of the new mingled relations—these were more and more to appear as the character of the region.

There was some advantage in the fact that cultural lines *did* become more and more mixed, and Grandmother Garland, so to speak, lost her dominant position as literary mentor to the

Middle West. Dreiser, Sandburg, Anderson, along with Masters and Lindsay, were names that told of the crossing of more strands to make it less likely that some single strand would draw back and away. Looking back, for these later Middle Western Americans, was not like looking up, as it had been to Grandmother Garland, and looking around was not to look down.

It was possible anywhere along the route that space had opened to make a new orientation that went as deep at the center and as wide at the circumference as you could wish. A very remarkable discovery was possible, that life is life everywhere. It was even possible to go, and mean not simply to go back—"you can go now yes go now," as Sandburg wrote. Or you could stay, even in Chicago.

History with its grace and glitter and knowledge and evil had nothing necessarily to upset the new American character. It all depended on whether one started with his own—and knew what was his when he started. Starting with one's own, from Paumanok or Concord or Kansas or Kokomo, assimilation was boundless; whether one went anywhere or not. This was the very simple truth that nevertheless had taken a couple of centuries and a war or two in America to bring home to the Eastern seaboard, and which every point of longitude west had painfully to discover for itself.

This book has mostly to do with this truth not being discovered. It is about the Americans who started and did not start with their own, or did not know, when they started, what their own was.

I think this is the case, in one respect or other, with the three men I have chosen to illustrate my story, Henry James, Henry

Adams, and T. S. Eliot. The interesting thing in all the cases is not the fact of going back for a point of orientation—to Mother England, to Mother Church, to twelfth-century France—but of going back half-unwittingly. It is not clear in what character they start out. There is a kind of enchantment about these pilgrimages, a witchery of the time and place dimensions. I hope the proper chapters will bring out what I mean.

CHAPTER VI

The Enchanted Kingdom of Henry James

THE familiar does not enchant us, though it may move us in other ways, even to wonder when it reveals some unsuspected depth. But enchantment involves strangeness as such. The fascination is between two different orders of consciousness—rabbit and snake, or the orphan girl and the prince. Similarly, there is always a foreign element in the legends of enchantment. Not only is the spell itself cast by some alien power, but often it takes a stranger from another kingdom to arrive and perceive the spell. The inhabitants are too close to it; they are all infected; they are enclosed within the element itself. Revelation has to come from outside if the spell is to be broken.

But suppose the stranger does not want to break the enchantment, which he finds altogether delightful? The stranger may be the last person, in fact, to want to disturb anything and remove the spell. It is the scene transfixed which fascinates him, the unconscious beauty, the lovely arm stopped in mid-motion toward the antique loom, the head bowed in charming naïveté before the beautifully carved if dust-covered image. So he withholds his other knowledge, or even denies it. He succumbs himself, perhaps, to the enchantment.

Yet, so long as it remains enchantment, it remains fixed at the point of the strange, and so fixed there is something life-stopping about it. The fascination excites but does not fulfill. Fulfilled it would be something else: union, or perhaps disillusion and separation. But remaining fascination it is in some sense a constraint upon life. The stranger must either break through—blow his trumpet, say his word of truth—or break away to find life again.

That our Henry James was a man who came under a spell will hardly I think be disputed. He came under the spell of the "wonderful otherness" of Europe. Just in what way he responded is another matter. We do not see the young American quite in the role of the fairy prince who awakened the sleeping beauty, or the hero who blew the trumpet. The fully revealing stroke was not in the James manner. The truth gleamed still, as it were, under glass; the enchantment was nurtured even as it was exposed. At the same time, we know that the knight from the other kingdom had his own knowledge, which served him for his own purposes. He came with a fresh vision, from a different world. He managed somehow to stand off from the enchantment, to see it with new eyes, even as it held him for its old charm.

"You Americans are incredibly romantic."
"Of course we are. That's just what makes everything so nice for us."
"Everything?"
"Well, everything that's nice at all. The world, the beautiful world—or everything in it that *is* beautiful. I mean we see so much."

James saw so much, though it did not turn out to be all so nice
—the world, the beautiful world! Life itself, in the end, had
something to add in the way of knowledge and to the peril of
enchantment. Yet the enchantment had certain qualities of its own:
this confronting of two strangenesses, with flashes, hints, gleams,
passing between.

But there is no question about the principle involved. It is
the principle of otherness as opposed to sameness; it is a fascination with difference. And who was more fascinated with differences than Henry James? Social differences, place differences,
racial, national, cultural differences were his meat and drink.
The common, conversely, was his poison. It was almost his only
swear word.

The very impulse of a cultural pilgrimage is a sense of the
importance of differences. A feeling for universal life might be
satisfied, presumably, wherever life exists. People would be people, nature nature, life life, on the Hudson as on the Thames.
But the common denominator of the human was not Henry
James's theme, nor life or nature as constants modified by variables. No, the variables, with James, were primary; the constants
were secondary.

His rule of otherness guided him to the last. Even America,
the native land, could take on interest when it appeared to have
grown strange, yet not until the foreign seemed to have become
familiar. "It was American civilization," the expatriate wrote
concerning a late visit home, "that had begun to spread itself
thick and pile itself high as the other, the foreign exhibition
had taken to writing itself plain . . . Nothing could be of a

[89]

simpler and straighter logic: Europe had been romantic because she was so different from America; wherefore America would be romantic because she was different from Europe."

The logic is simple and straight enough—if you take it as the logic of exoticism. How can one explain such a lifelong passion for otherness?

That we cannot explain it wholly in terms of environment is clear from the fact that Henry's brother William, from virtually a common starting point and common upbringing, arrived at an almost opposite mode of feeling. Europe and America, to the older brother, were equally part of an interesting if possibly multifarious cosmos, and his net was thrown to catch any fish of reality, common or uncommon, just so long as it was a lively one. Life stood above charm for William, as charm stood almost above life for Henry. From the start provided by the remarkable elder James, either course was apparently possible, and the difference must have depended virtually on temperament alone.

How else than by an astonishing trait of temperament can you explain the almost ludicrously precocious response of the infant Henry to his other world, to "Europe"? So far as exposure is concerned, the older brother was exposed quite as much as the younger. The exposure took with Henry as it did not with William. Henry's response—like a definite sort of tropism—seemed to be set from the first toward that glamorous distant light.

If we are to trust Henry's own testimony, which there is no reason to doubt, the first registering of the wonderful "abroad" was made on the mind, literally, of a babe in arms. The story became a family marvel, how Henry, "a baby in long clothes," seated opposite his parents in a carriage "on the lap of another person" (I am quoting the novelist's own words), formed the impression through the clear window "of a great stately square surrounded with high-roofed houses and having at its centre a tall and glorious column."

It was the *Place* and *Colonne Vendome*, in Paris, whose "admirable aspect," the novelist insists, he thus took in for all time. And, as if to test our credulity still further, he adds, "while I waggled my small feet, as I definitely remember doing, under my flowing robe."

Europe, Paris, a stately square, and Henry James, infant feet dangling under infant robe, "forming the impression"—the first in what a series! Such was the minute exposure needed, apparently, for Henry's fixation on his "other world."

From then on, back in America, the other world loomed, glimmered, gleamed—in the Jamesian idiom. English place names on his parent's lips were large with import—Green Park, Windsor, Richmond, Piccadilly, Sudbrook. It was as if knowing what they signified in the way of a particular manner of life—English life—desperately mattered to the small American boy. If his parents would not talk of Europe, it was always possible to draw out a maternal aunt "who had imbibed betimes in Europe the seeds of a long nostalgia." Books and magazines that had been manufactured in England and could be fondled and sniffed at a stationer's counter in New York had a particular smell to the precocious Jamesian nostril, an unmistakable *London* one, much more exciting than any native odor.

What it all came down to was Henry's feeling that to be living in America was not to be living at all, but only preparing to live. The best one could do, under such circumstances, was to treasure up every hint of what life on the other side, the right side of the railroad tracks, so to speak, might be. And in fact, no one was ever to charge up his mind to the point that James did for picking up the vibrations of another continent. But with so much of reality sensed as "otherness," how much of it was left for the sense of sameness, of identity? This is the philosophical question that continually stands before us in considering Henry James.

Meanwhile, from the record of the small boy's life, we have an almost bizarre instance of the extent to which his precocious fancy was ready to go in reading significance into what was other than himself, simply because it was other. "I seem to have been constantly eager to exchange my lot for that of somebody else," the novelist recalled, "on the assumed certainty of gaining thereby in the bargain." So that, on a visit to the penitentiary at Sing Sing, arranged by the insatiably curious elder James, the small boy actually envied the lot of the convicts behind the bars. "They were so *other*" from himself! And "to be other," he confessed, "other almost anyhow, seemed as good as the probable taste of the bright compound wistfully watched in the confectioner's window."

On the wrong side of the confectioner's glass, on the wrong side of the railroad tracks: such was the situation which our young novelist apparently felt himself to be in. And when being on the wrong side figured even jailbirds on the right, the wrongness must have been wrong indeed. How can you explain it?

The first conjecture might be that there was something about the little boy's own circumstances—social, financial, hereditary—which aroused a feeling of shame. Was the poor lad's breeding and background so disgraceful, somehow, as to make any alternative look desirable?

By almost every accepted standard, his circumstances were exceptionally favorable. Financially, for example, the grandfather, the first William James, had established a large family fortune, in the classic American manner of arriving as a poor if not penniless immigrant and through his own efforts and character making himself one of New York State's most respected and substantial citizens. So substantial, indeed, that the fortune he left, amounting to some three million dollars, had been enough to make his numerous posterity comfortably independent well through the generation of Henry, Junior. And if it might be supposed that inherited wealth is itself a bad thing, because it leads to idleness, luxury, conservatism, or whatever, there was the father, Henry James, Senior, who put no value on wealth as such, and was himself neither reactionary, idle, nor materialistic, but quite the opposite on all counts.

Incidentally, this situation might help to explain the novelist's own rather curious attitude toward money, which made the possession of worldly means—and a considerable amount of it!—virtually a prerequisite for the good life, but the acquisition of it an almost necessarily damning activity. It was a dilemma for the ordinary person that James never solved satisfactorily.

At any rate, James himself was born free of the dilemma, and in other respects his situation seemed unusually fortunate. As to social and cultural position, the James home was a grateful rendezvous for almost every visitor of reputation, native or foreign, from Bronson Alcott to Thackeray. The father—friend of Emerson and Channing and Parker, of Carlyle and Sterling and Mill—was welcome in practically any circle he cared to enter on either side of the Atlantic.

Yet here is the picture of our small boy, the gifted second son of this favored household, pressing his small nose to the confectioner's glass of the world and staring with his large eyes at the withheld goodness! Why?

We are driven back, apparently, to the one element in his situation which, like a real enchantment, ruled all the rest: the element of place. The boy, with the spell of Europe cast upon him, was simply in the wrong place; changing the place would change everything. Every outline would fill in, every color brighten, every tone deepen by the flick of the magic wand. The drabbest prospect in murky Liverpool—"the damp and darksome light washed in from the steep, black bricky street"—would, and did, translate itself, according to the law of enchantment, into the finest mental glow; while the brightest and liveliest scene in New York harbor, by the same law, underwent an opposite transmutation. It was not a comparison of one reality with another, whatever their comparative qualities, but of two sorts of illusion.

You can find certain things in the boy's inheritance which may have helped weave his spell of Europe, and particularly, of England. For example, there is his Protestant-Irish heredity. If James's ancestry was to have been Irish, as it mostly was, it might signify that it was North-Ireland Protestant rather than southern and Catholic Irish. Everyone knows that the latter side of the Irish fence hardly feels itself close to England; while the former sometimes feels itself more English than the English.

Furthermore, Henry James could single out for particular attachment the one near ancestor who was not Irish, but of actual English descent. His father's mother, as the novelist fondly recalled, represented this "happy connection"; and even though the bond was attenuated by two generations in America, he fixed upon it, "for reasons and reasons," as most beneficent.

Even so, ranging all the ancestral forces one can on the side of Henry James, Junior's, feeling for England, there is left the large and important gap in their ranks represented by Henry James, Senior. This individualistic democrat showed little attachment to the old island home or the elegant *Via Media* of English culture.

Inveterate traveler and cosmopolite though he was, the more he experienced of European ways, the more he defended those of his native land. The most glittering of British intellectual circles left him of independent mind, and often of a caustically critical one. The talk of the Carlyle group, for instance, he once described as "depraving in the last degree" for what he felt was its mere literary interest in the state of society. Better talk, he boasted recklessly, could be had with the person sitting next to you in a New York horsecar. And near the end of his life he wrote patriotically: "No average American resides a year in England without getting a sense so acute and stifling of its hideous class distinctions, and of the consequent awkwardness and *brusquerie* of its upper classes, and the consequent abject snobbery or inbred and ineradicable servility of its lower classes, as makes the manners of Choctaws and Potawatamies sweet and christian, and gives to a log-cabin in Oregon the charm of comparative dignity and peace."

Such were the sentiments of the "paternal parent"; nor were they merely armchair ones. Unlike some gentlemanly equalitarians, the curious philosopher enjoyed the actual company of his fellow men. His remarks about the social advantages of the American horsecar were from first hand; he really took pleasure in riding in one. Nothing pleased him more, his son William wrote, "than fraternizing on the simplest and lowest plane with all the lowly persons he met," and the father's own language was characteristically more extravagant in declaring that a crowded Cambridge horsecar "was the nearest approach to Heaven on earth."

If the younger Henry James was in some respects his father's son—and I think he was—he was not in the above respect.

The novelist's own attitude toward his family endowment is curious for its mixture of appreciation and deprecation. There is no doubt of his pride in his family inheritance. In fact, the autobiographical books all but confess that our expatriate never really found in the world at large the counterpart of the little family circle for delicacy of the social relation and fineness of spiritual interest. Where else could be met that high, pure "transcendental" note just mellowed by Washington Square and Europe? In what other household was to be found so much brightness without hardness, geniality without softness, and play for personality on a plane that continually lifted to the more thrilling heights of the impersonal?*

"The great world," however much the novelist was prepared

* For evidence of the extraordinary quality of the family relationship, see the journal of the invalid sister, Alice: *Alice James: Her Brothers, Her Journal.* Edited by Anna Robeson Burr. New York.

to catch and celebrate its wonderful tones, never quite sounded such a note, and Henry James was to confront it with the lack from a hundred different approaches.

Nevertheless, the small family world seemed *outside* the great real world, or how can one explain Henry's wistful staring through the glass? This is the strange contradiction that we always have before us.

The author's gratitude toward the family life and American background was for a fortunate kind of *preparation* rather than a fortunate state of things in itself. James, in retrospect, saw the small boy starting from below zero, culturally speaking, and the happy fortune lay in the chance provided for rising upward, out of nowhere into somewhere. The momentum thus gained was what counted. One is prepared to "see so much" when one starts out with practically nothing to see! But the contrast remained one of negative against positive, with the great world the positive in its faults as well as virtues, and the small world the negative in its virtues as well as faults. This was the curious logic which the small boy acted upon and the novelist, looking back, found puzzling but still inescapable.

James's mingled admiration and bewilderment as he tried in his later years to evaluate the early family life in America turned on the question: How could it have shown a rather beautiful spirit when it so obviously lacked everything in the way of a beautiful form?

Form, of course, was the burden of the East Wind's message: order, tradition, style—form! Henry James would no doubt have stopped short of the rather rash statement once made by T. S. Eliot, that "the spirit killeth but the letter giveth life." James kept a high place for spirit, for a cherished brand of his own, as we shall see. But the letter, nevertheless, was enchantingly bright on the rich scroll of the elder cultures—the letter of tradition, the letter of accepted manners and customs and forms, the letter embellished and encrusted and complicated by the long slow centuries.

Unembellished to a pitiful degree he saw his own little family world when he looked back at it in the latter years. Yet again, he could not say it was lacking in spirit, in a very admirable spirit, in fact. And as for mere spiritedness, was there ever anywhere such a flow of it, in the household that included the elder Henry James and the older brother William, not to mention a host of vivacious, talented females—sister, cousins, aunts?

And how is spirit, intelligence, awareness, related to form? That was always where James, who saw no polarity, grew puzzled. "We came more or less to see," the novelist confessed, "that our young contemporaries of another world, the trained and admonished, the disciplined and governessed, or in a word formed, relatively speaking, had been made aware of many things of which those at home hadn't been; yet we were also to note . . . that, the awareness in question remaining at best imperfect, our little friends as distinguished from our companions of the cousinship, greater or lesser, advanced and presumed but to flounder and recede, elated at once and abashed and on the whole but feebly sophisticated. The cousinship, on the other hand, all unalarmed and unsuspecting and unembarrassed, lived by pure serenity, sociability and loquacity; the oddest fact about its members being withal that it didn't make them bores. . . ."

To translate the Jamesian "late manner" rather freely: the

outrageously free life of the little Jameses made for a great deal of fun and even for poise, while the correctly disciplined regimen of the other children was likely to produce (to be frank) little bores—and awkward ones at that.

Nor could James find that selfishness, thoughtlessness, or other unsocial tendencies were the result of the lively home atmosphere. On the contrary, he wrote, "there can surely never have been anything like their good faith and, generally speaking, their amiability. I should have but to let myself go a little to cite examples . . ." Which the novelist successfully avoided, returning instead to his main point, which is our point too, the same curious one we have been examining: "which is to recall again that whether we were all amiable or not (and frankly, I claim it in a high degree for most of us) the scene on which we so freely bloomed does strike me, when I reckon it up, as extraordinarily unfurnished. How came it then that for the most part so simple we yet weren't more inane?"

How came it indeed? Surely not because simplicity, after all, is not the same as emptiness, just as complexity is not the same as abundance!

The novelist, however, makes his own guess, which as a matter of fact quite abandons the thought that the one great need at home was more "form." "This was doubtless by reason of our inward life—ours of our father's house in especial I mean—which made an excellent, in some cases an incomparable, *fond* for a thicker civility to mix with when growing experience should begin to take that in." And he adds, concluding this section, "It was also quaint among us, I may be reminded, to have *begun* with the inward life; but we began, after the manner of all men, as we could, and I hold that if it comes to that we might have begun much worse."

Yes, one feels, Henry and William James might have begun much worse.

This chronic conflict in James's mind, never really cured, between the value of the inner life and the value of external forms for their own sake is illustrated concretely in a near-by passage of the memoirs. We might call the instance, using James's own term, The Case of the Dim Little Gentleman.

It seems that one of the mysteries of the James relationship was a marriage made by one of the female cousins. Herself of the type of able, spirited woman which anyone acquainted with James's heroines will at once recognize, Cousin Helen for some reason had picked for husband a small, feckless gentleman who seemed to the rest of the family a "most anomalous" choice. The novelist himself can hardly find words negative enough to describe him. Even to his wife, he remained an impersonal Mr. or an anonymous Dear, and James, "keeping it up" as he would put it, goes on to call him a "negative zero," "a consistent shade of nullity," "a blank from whatever view," "a natural platitude that had never risen to the level of sensibility." The only question was naturally "his early presumption in having approached, such as he was, so fine a young woman, and his remarkable luck in having approached her successfully."

This negligible individual never protested being trod upon, and apparently this was his common treatment by the rest of the family, including Cousin Helen. Not in a mean sense, of course, but only in the amiable one associated with a standing joke in an amiable family. But his place in James's family memories is obvious: it is as foil—negative contrast—to the positive character of the other members of the family.

Not too fast, however, for James the "restless analyst" is at work. Within a paragraph or so, a strange sea change has taken place in the whole visage and role of this dim little gentleman. Remember, James is recovering his early American world through the medium of some half-dozen decades of constant gathering of impressions in "the great world."

Details first emerge. The "blank from whatever view" begins to show features, blank enough in truth: "his long, slightly equine countenance, his eyebrows ever elevated as in the curiosity of alarm, and then the so limited play from side to side of his extremely protrusive head, as if somehow through tightness of the 'wash' neckcloths that he habitually wore and that, wound and rewound in their successive stages, made his neck very long without making it in the least thick and reached their climax in a proportionately very small knot tied with the neatest art." There was his characteristic posture: "his little rounded back, at the base of which his arms are locked behind him," and above which was "his bald head, yet with the hair bristling up almost in short-horn fashion from the sides . . . thrust inquiringly, not to say appealingly forward. . . ."

Clearly, these details are at first only insignificance made concrete, and James himself appears to us as a sort of literary predecessor of Mr. Peter Arno in having come across in New York an early variant of the latter's figure of fun: not the heavy "Major," but the little emotionally arrested, inconsequential clubman.

James, indeed, is promptly aware that the figure belongs in this class of comic types, his own "reference" naturally lighting upon Daumier. "I scarce can have known at the time," he ponders, "that this was as complete a little old-world figure as any that might then have been noted there, far or near; yet if I didn't somehow 'subtly' feel it, why am I now so convinced that I must have had familiarly before me a master-piece of the great Daumier, say, or Henri Mannier . . . the timorous Philistine in a world of dangers, with whom I was later to make acquaintance?"

The discovery is worth some paragraphs of development, in which wonder at this masterpiece's presence, in James's own back yard as it were, grows and grows. He scarce knows what the little man now does not suggest, "for the sharpness, of intensity, of type." This in turn leads to his asking "quite most of all" whether a person so marked, so brilliantly typed, "mustn't really have been a highly finished figure."

And if he was a highly finished figure, where did that leave the other members of the family? The revolution is almost complete; negative has become positive and positive negative. "That degree of finish was surely rare among us—rare at a time when the charm of the cousinship and the uncleship, the kinship generally, had to be found in their dispensing with any finish at all." In fact, the more our analyst reflects upon the dim little gentleman, "the more I make out in him a tone and a manner that deprecated crude ease . . ." (For this is what "pure serenity and sociability" have now become: "crude ease"!) "I remember his voice and his speech, which were not those of *that* New York at all, and with the echo, faint as it is, arrives the wonder of where he could possibly

[102]

have picked such things up." The little man's whole behavior suggested another world entirely, one "in which forms still counted." His own "forms" were certainly "adjusted and settled things; from what finer civilization had they come down?"

Whereupon the conclusion is inevitable. "Mayn't we accordingly have been, the rest of us, all wrong; and the dim little gentleman the only one among us who was right? May not his truth to type have been a matter that, as mostly typeless ourselves, we neither perceived or appreciated?"

Thus the poor dim little gentleman, after a half century of apparently merited oblivion, comes into his triumphant own! But his triumph was never complete; the conflict remained. James's heroes and heroines are not drawn from among dim ladies and dim gentlemen. Rather they are drawn, so to speak, from the "cousinship," from the lively and aspiring, who if they lack perfect external finish do not lack inner sensitivity and imagination.

Imagination and "the inward life" were of course rare in America to the degree they were present in the house of Henry James, Senior. But as we follow our expatriate in his uneasy wonder that simplicity could be accompanied by intelligence and that a cultural spirit could exist without a great deal of social ceremony, we cannot help wanting to remind him of the main idea of his own tradition. It should have made analysis easier, you would think, to remember that an effort at doing away with the extraneous in the realm of form and adhering to the intrinsic had been a definite aim on the part of James's spiritual forbears.

If the "inward life" of his father's household had any meaning, it had this meaning, for few individuals held it more firmly
than Henry James, Senior. The somewhat impatient philosopher
might be accused of carrying the idea too far, and slighting even
intrinsic form in his desire to dispense with every artificial aid
to inner grace. But if the idea itself—which might be traced
back as far as one pleased in the Old World, but which had
taken a characteristic turn in the New—if this idea were not
itself a tradition, and as a tradition a cultural fact of importance
to the analyst of the American scene, then it would be hard to
say what tradition or culture in essence might be.

Tradition or culture in essence, however—and hence possibly
in changed form—was not what Henry James was looking for.
Here we are back to our main point. James had connected culture with place—another place—and it was for that reason that he
disconnected spirit from form.

In this situation, America, though spirit, simply did not figure
as form, for it was Europe that figured as form. That was why
he was bound to see American forms as at once too sharp and
too flat—like the New England "meetinghouses" he derided in
The American Scene for not being English cathedrals. He was
bound to see the land itself as too wide, the railway trains too
big, the New York buildings too tall, and their towers too light
and too many-windowed. A respectable tower, in the other world,
was naturally in the way of a battlement. All these forms, by
the particular other standards and models, had gone astray. Not
that they had all come home to themselves in America; but James
showed little interest in what in their own way they might come

to. One can only shudder at what the "returned pilgrim" would have liked to make, ideally, of our native forms.

His own pilgrimage showed this divorce between spirit and form. In his character as an American he presents no "form" at all, as he comes as a young man to live in England. He is only sensibility, receptivity. "There were eminent gentlemen," he wrote of this time, "to 'meet' and, alas, awfully to interrogate me—for vivid has remained to me, as the best of my bewilderment, the strangeness of finding that I could be of interest to *them*. My identity for myself was all in my sensibility to their own exhibition, with not a scrap left over for personal show. (Yet) there were, it appeared, things of interest taking place in America, and I had had, in this absurd manner, to come to England to learn it; I had had over there on the ground itself no conception of any such matter."

What form, or external character, he takes on is thus certain to be European, and especially English. In personal manners, it led to that great external formality that struck so many visitors, and still strikes the viewer of the Sargent portrait in the National Gallery, which some Englishmen have been unkind enough to refer to as having the "perfect English butler" look.

But all these forms—the English and European ones—could be taken for granted; that is the happy fact for the young American who himself is all sensibility. He is unhappy, he feels "exposed," in America, where forms were still being made; but in the denser Old World, with its slow revolvings of ancient rites, its patina-covered monuments, its polished old surfaces—there the shy young man could almost lose his self-consciousness. True, there is something ominous in that same polish and finish of form. There is the flaw in the crystal, as we shall see. But so far as response to the forms and shapes themselves is concerned, the young novelist's "identity being all sensibility" was of course an advantage.

Even so, what were his resources, what was the deepest vision that served him, except that "inward life" which he described as so quaintly present in his father's household? What was his finest touchstone except that "good faith" of his family world, of which he wrote, "there can surely never have been anything like it?" It was by this light, unquestionably, that he saw the flaw in the crystal, even though he never took the light as worthy to be a new crystal in itself.

But let us see how this worked out in the novels, and in their famous "international situation."

In one of his prefaces (Volume XVIII of the New York Edition) James tells how much this "international situation" meant to him, and what its meaning was.

Europe, he wrote, was "constantly in requisition as the more salient American stage or more effective *repoussoir*, and yet with any particular *action* on this great lighted and decorated stage depending for more than half its sense on one of my outland characters."

This is very much, you see, like James himself arriving in England with his "identity for himself being all in his sensibility." A character from America has no significance in its own terms: not as an American who might expect to go on living in America. He is an "outlander," which is to say that America is but a province of, or poor relation to, the culture of

Europe. The significance of an American life begins only when it arrives at the center or capital of culture—Europe. Isabel Archer would never have had a life to live out—that is, a Jamesian life—if she had remained in Albany, New York.

But this is only half of it. Curiously, the center of culture by itself lacks life. It has no dramatic meaning until one of these sensitive provincials from America appears on it. For Europe by itself is but stage, lights, decoration—is, in other words, static.

Here I think are the basic elements of James's famous "international situation." Europe is being without becoming; America is becoming without being. Europe is status, America energy. Without America there would be no action, but without Europe no situation. To put it perhaps in its most general form, Europe is form without spirit, America spirit without form.

Other interesting things follow from this interesting proposition. America, as action, is necessarily the freer moral agent—and this is always true in a James novel. But Europe presents the only moral issue for America—and this too is almost always the case in Henry James's world. Europe, if we are to believe James, is America's fate.

So you might turn one light after another on James's central situation. Europe is beauty, America desire; America sincerity, Europe appearance. Europe manners, America morals; America innocence, Europe experience.

Most of the major works, from *Roderick Hudson* to *The Golden Bowl*, turn on this basic situation and trace the interaction of the two elements. The emphasis may shift a little from one side to the other, but the stories in which both forces are not present in some form or another are few and are definitely among the minor works. Some of these minor works, however, just because they avoid James's central theme and so escape its conflict, have a certain clear, firm quality quite different from the romantic tone of the larger works.

The two elements, as I have named them, are not to be taken too literally, that is, in their national aspects. Here for instance is *The Princess Casamassima*, which at first glance seems not to fit the international pattern, since the characters are all European (or like the Princess herself completely Europeanized) and the theme involves the special one of socialism. A little consideration, however, will show that the primary elements are present in only slight disguise. I should like to pause long enough to consider this novel as illustrating an early form of James's characteristic theme, and an early stage of his own artistic development.

It is unimportant that the little troubled hero of *The Princess Casamassima* is an underclass, underprivileged Englishman. Hyacinth Robinson might just as well have been one of James's inexperienced but sensitive Americans, so far as representing for James the sort of innocence coupled with aspiration which his heroes and heroines characteristically do represent. The important thing is that Hyacinth's dilemma, like that of the Americans, comes as he falls under the spell of the beautiful vision, the vision of the culture of "Europe." And the socialistic aim simply stands for the hero's original innocent spirit, that had been derived from his native condition and which gives him, to begin with, such moral impulse as he may have. It is like the "good faith" and "inward life" of James's own home. And, just as Roderick Hudson or some other American hero of James finds his original spirit put at hazard by the seduction of the beautiful vision of Europe, so Hyacinth's revolutionary morale fades under the spell, and the little protagonist goes down to destruction.

To take it from the other side, the factor of "Europe," as James felt and used it, is not necessarily represented by literal Europeans. Indeed, to illustrate this element in its most corrosive form James generally turned not to a native European but to a Europeanized American. He reserved for his Gilbert Osmonds and Madame Merles and Charlotte Stants and Christina Lights the role of representing "civilization" in its most seductive and destructive aspect. It was from this class of denaturalized individuals that James drew his greatest villains.

But the international opposition remains fundamental.

It is significant that *The Princess Casamassima* is among the author's early books, for the experiment of using a character not an American as protagonist in what is still the basic Jamesian drama is not one that James tried often. Moreover, Hyacinth Robinson is not convincing as an underclass Englishman. We believe in many of the other characters, but Hyacinth himself remains an abstraction. Intellectually, he is one of James's susceptible Americans in British dress; but he figures only for the intellect. He is a failure as an actual person.

The Princess Casamassima, however, remains especially interesting among James's novels for a number of reasons. It is the only important work of James that treats society as a dynamic rather than a static affair. History appears as a process and not merely a finished product and there is the problem of a changing order. The enchanted kingdom for once is not just a museum. It is a place in which people are trying to live, many of them against great odds.

Well, what is the drama of this situation, as our romantic young visitor sees it? It can be stated quite clearly, for this is one of the least ambiguous of James's books. The drama of young Hyacinth Robinson's situation as an underprivileged but rising idealist is that he must choose between justice and beauty—for James tended to see these two ideals as antithetical. Hyacinth's first ideal of changing the social structure so that its benefits might be better distributed runs into direct conflict with the other conviction that grows upon him: that it is precisely the system of privilege and injustice which has "created the monuments and treasures of art, the great palaces and properties, the conquests of learning and taste, the general fabric of civilization as we know it."

We may disagree with the logic of this opposition. It is in fact the logic of literalism and of romanticism—that "culture" is identical with some one form of it, and that two kinds of goods (beauty and justice) can be opposed absolutely, and still both be "good." But Hyacinth Robinson was so constituted, the novel implies, that he saw it that way and could see it no other. The reformer and the aesthete could not be reconciled—not when the reformer had sworn to change society, and the aesthete discovered that any change would destroy its highest glory. Hyacinth Robinson had been caught by a spell of beauty which transfixes life, and there is no escaping the fatality of it; Hyacinth if he chooses beauty must reject life. And *Casamassima* made the point in the most conclusive way its author was ever to make it. Hyacinth destroyed himself.

It does not necessarily follow that James feels with his weakling hero, that social justice and the conservation of culture are fatally opposed, though we strongly suspect this is about what James came to think. What we do observe, however, is that this particular question virtually disappears in James's work after *Casamassima*. Social inequality does not figure thereafter as a moral issue or a dramatic situation, nor society itself as a thing essentially in process.

This I think is not without its significance. Whatever James may have thought about social change, it is clear that he came to see it, for artistic purposes, as opposed to his "international situation." He could not go on dealing with English society as a process and at the same time find its greatest fascination to lie in its being finished. It is all to the credit of the young novelist that he should have been affected at this time by the sight of human suffering and wanted to dramatize it, but you soon see that this is not the main theme of the novel, or a main interest of Henry James.

James's conception of a better society appears in the end as naïve and hence not particularly relevant. It is mixed with such stereotypes as his hero expresses near the end of the book: that social reform "would cut up the ceilings of the Veronese into strips, so that everyone might have a little piece. I don't want everyone to have a little piece of anything and I've a great horror of that kind of invidious jealousy which is at the bottom of the idea of redistribution."

But after all, neither poverty as an evil nor socialism as a possible cure makes the real theme of the book. If it were so, we should have to find the author far on the side of fatalism with respect to the question of evil in the world. "What remedy but another deluge, what alchemy but annihilation?" Hyacinth asks himself as he walks through the streets of London almost overwhelmed by the vicious life he sees forced upon certain sections of society. These leprous spots in the social organism are horrible, intolerable. But there is no cure that is not worse than the disease; in fact, the disease is itself an ingrained part of the organism. For, "if it was the fault of the rich, as Paul Muniment held, the selfish and congested rich who allowed such abominations to flourish, that made no difference and only shifted the shame; since the terrestrial globe, a visible failure, produced the cause as well as the effect."

This is fatalism—the denial of man's essential moral freedom—and I think it fair to count *Casamassima*, to all appearances, the most fatalistic of James's books. None other presents a dilemma so hopeless or a denouement so completely disastrous. "Convert, convert!" is James's great word, but it is a word without virtue so far as the apparent theme of this book is concerned—evil in the social organism.

But James, in his own sphere, is not a fatalist, and that is why, I think, we must look for the true conflict of *Casamassima* somewhere else than in the social question: look for it nearer the author's real point of tension. For the question of social justice does not really cut deep into James's consciousness, or into the heart of the book.

No, the real drama of *Casamassima* is the familiar Jamesian one of innocence and experience. This is what Hyacinth's social dilemma comes down to, a conflict between one stage of cultural evolution and another, a lower degree of knowledge against a higher degree. Poverty, it is true, is a condition of Hyacinth's lower-class, underprivileged origins, but it is not the ruling condition. The ruling condition is ignorance, innocence, inexperience. Hyacinth might conceivably have been wealthy and yet innocent and "underprivileged" in the Jamesian sense of having missed the opportunity of culture, just as many of James's Americans are wealthy but underprivileged in this sense. Hyacinth's dilemma happens to involve social justice, but it might have involved any other moral question. Hyacinth would not have been saved by a deeper understanding of the problem of justice; he could only have been saved by greater knowledge, to begin with, of the world.

So Hyacinth is the brother of Roderick Hudson and of Isabel Archer, a victim of innocence, rather than of injustice. And James grants moral freedom in this conflict of innocence and experience as he seems to deny it in the realm of social justice. The "shame" of things is not ingrained and ineluctable when it figures as ignorance; it may be expiated. Hyacinth's expiation, it is true, is utter and tragic. But if we think of his dilemma not as a matter of having to submit to one or the other of two inescapable evils (social injustice, or the annihilation of "civilization as we know it"), but of having to choose between the old and the new light, we see that James has at least granted him choice.

This I think is the way to take *The Princess Casamassima* as a link in the chain of James's narrative dramas. It is not an odd link, so viewed, but a consistent one. In some ways it is the most rigorous, the least equivocal, exposition of James's characteristic problem.

To take this view, however, is not to dismiss what the novel seems to say concerning James's attitude toward society and justice. If the social organism is in fact dynamic—if in truth it *cannot* be stopped at some point of perfection and finish, like a motion picture at a lovely still—this truth is bound to bear on the work of an artist who paints society. I think it does bear quite seriously on the work of Henry James, who would have liked to deny that society cannot be stopped.

Let us return to "the international situation"—of the moral, aspiring but innocent American, as the active element, meeting his fate on Europe's "lighted and decorated stage."

We need to take a further step, and see that the affair is not quite as simple as this. The last thing to accuse James of is making things too simple. There would be no interaction of the two elements, no common ground between them, if the division were absolute. Drama requires that external force and internal character somehow correspond; an internal conflict provides the opening rift for fate.

So you will see that James's two elements are themselves each divided, divided within much as the two are divided without. "Europe" has its moral aspect, and "America" its aesthetic one; America has its moral weakness and Europe its spiritual strength.

The unpredictable quantity is of course American inexperience, naïveté. This is the "X" element in James's mystery whose presence precipitates drama and whose evolution solves it one way or another. James risks the intelligibility of his drama, it must be evident, on this "X" element of American innocence — of which more later.

But if "Europe" were all beauty and "America" all morality,

the two would never converge. No, Europe, to be as it were America's fate, must appeal on other grounds than the aesthetic. It must appeal, in fact, on moral grounds.

And so it does. To Lambert Strether and Isabel Archer and Maggie and Adam Verver, the "vision of Europe" is not only the vision of art and beauty. The vision of art and beauty is the vision of the "good life." James's chief heroes and heroines are not presented to us as mere wind-blown aesthetes. They are presented as persons of high ethical character. They would never lay their all, as it were, on Europe's altar of beauty and civilization were it not in the hope of the largest spiritual rewards.

This we might call the first phase of the Jamesian international drama. It is the romantic opening movement, in which a good American without form seeks European form in itself as a "good."

So here is Lambert Strether, in what is sometimes considered James's best novel, *The Ambassadors,* pondering "the Parisian scene" in a light that is finally ethical. The very nub of the matter is that the seeming disregard for moral considerations—as witness Chad Newsome's "unsanctified union"—is transformed, by its beautiful manners and intelligent sensitive spirit, into something essentially good. The narrowness and lack of culture in the life back home, to which Strether had been expected to return his protégé, this same Chad Newsome, more than cancel whatever pretense it may have had to superior virtue. The vision of what Paris means as liberation has come too late for Strether himself. But at least he can bless Chad's choice, even if it means blessing, on the grounds of culture, the fact of adultery.

Such, at least, is the claim of *The Ambassadors*: that manners can transfigure morals, beauty can save life; and the same thought appears in almost every novel. Adam Verver, in *The Golden Bowl*, catches the vision in the "boundless moment" that is the turning point of his career. Standing as it were on his "peak in Darien," the American financier sees before him the wonderful prospect. He will put the power of his wealth in the service of beauty; he will devote the remainder of his life in gathering the splendid objects of Europe's culture and bringing them to his fellow countrymen at home for their lasting inspiration.

But the other phase of the drama, the disillusioning phase, is equally important. This is what happens after the vision is actually followed. After all, there is a flaw in the crystal, a witch in the enchanted garden. Beauty alone may be emancipation, but it leads to bitter knowledge, complication, fatality. Now the two elements of "Europe" and "America" show their other sides. If romance pictured aesthetic Europe as spiritual liberation, experience proves it to be spiritual suffering—perhaps even bondage. And if romance had shown the American character in its susceptible and ignorant aspect, experience now brings out its moral and spiritual strength.

For tracing the Jamesian drama through its entire revolution, there are better examples than *The Ambassadors*, which is concerned mostly with the first phase of the drama. *The Portrait of a Lady, The Golden Bowl, The Wings of the Dove,* among others, carry the action through the second phase as well. Illusion is followed by disillusion, choice is made and paid for. Of these, let us follow through the novel which James himself felt to be his most accomplished, *The Golden Bowl*.

A glance at the actors of the drama shows the high plane on

which *The Golden Bowl* is conceived. On the side of "culture"
—that is, of European civilization, "finish," "form"—are two
resplendent figures: Charlotte Stant and Prince Amerigo. Charlotte
belongs to a class with which the reader of James has become
familiar, a class of international adventurers of greater or less
refinement that includes Madame Merle, Gilbert Osmond, Gabriel Nash, and others of both sexes. Their particular quality is
style—aesthetic sophistication. They make a great appearance,
and know how to carry off the most difficult situations. Morally
they are all more or less wanting, but in manners and general
social form they are "splendid." They are worth something, then,
simply as accomplished personalities, self-made objects of art,
so to speak. James does not hesitate to admit their value as
such. And among them Charlotte stands as one of the finest, for
she is pictured to us not only as displaying all the confident
external qualities of her kind—physical beauty, a fine free grace,
unshakable poise—but as possessing a good deal of inner strength
as well.

Charlotte's misfortune is of course her lack of wealth. Had
she possessed means to match her magnificence, presumably she
would have never been led into evil. And of course there would
have been no story, for the indigent Prince Amerigo would
have married Charlotte instead of Maggie. Lack of means, we
may note here, is a major factor in the duplicity of almost all of
James's villains, from Gilbert Osmond and Madame Merle to
Kate Croy and Merton Densher. With this fact should be noted
that fortune, for James, rarely means anything but already-
acquired wealth. As in an upper-class English novel, an indigent
character in James is not expected to improve his fortune by
earning it. Fortune is part of fate—hence the temptation on

the part of James's poor but ambitious persons to resort to dubious measures in influencing people of property.

In the case of Prince Amerigo, it is taken for granted that he deserves whatever success he may have in marrying wealth. He is like a splendid precious stone that has lost its setting; to provide him with a proper setting is no more than to do him justice.

And the Prince, to take up this second representative of worldly glory, is not at all a "hard" character, but a very fine one indeed. At the worst he only represents a different code of morality from that of his "puritan" American wife. He is continental Europe at its best, urbane, delicate, exquisitely cultured, if with too ancient a tradition behind him to be very much a free moral agent. But in a sense he is as innocent as Maggie. He is as innocent of wrongdoing, in his relations with Charlotte, as Maggie at first is ignorant of his own code. In the end, indeed, the Prince is the more innocent of the two, for Maggie is able to plumb the workings of her husband's mind, while the Prince remains mystified by the curious motives and intangible values that guide his wife.

Maggie and Adam Verver, meanwhile, are the highest examples of our "American" element—the innocent aspiring characters who are the free moral agents in the drama. They are a type James had been portraying and reportraying from the first, but never at so high a level. Adam and Maggie might almost be called "natural American aristocrats." You can be sure that Maggie's acquired title of Princess is not without its symbolic meaning, just as the kingly light in which her father again and again is revealed has its significance. Isabel Archer, though she had rejected her English Lord, deserved in all truth to be called the Lady of *The Portrait's* title. Maggie Verver is now granted the actual designation of Princess. But father and daughter are almost above the need to have their inherent aristocracy ratified. In the end, they can almost do without "the great world" itself: they are equally happy in redeeming or letting lapse their social position.

To such a calm, high "note" James here raises his lifelong fascination with high social form. And on such a plane, with characters of such inherent fineness on both sides, the drama of innocence and experience may now be worked out.

I have already suggested the main situation. Maggie Verver, our high-minded American, and Prince Amerigo, the brilliant Italian nobleman, have made a splendid marriage, but its success is threatened by a previous affair between the Prince and Maggie's friend Charlotte. The passion of this earlier connection has apparently not faded out for either of the two participants. Maggie, who had not known of it, at least in its seriousness, gradually comes to learn that it still persists after her own marriage. With this disturbing knowledge comes Maggie's dilemma: whether to expose the culprits and so destroy her own possibility of happiness (for to expose the Prince would probably be to lose him), or to make an attempt somehow to win back her Prince and save her marriage.

The situation meanwhile has been complicated in a very curious way by the marriage of the long-widowed Mr. Verver to none other than Charlotte. This strange venture was suggested oddly enough by Maggie herself, whose "innocence" on this count we are tempted to call by a harsher name—stupidity. But Maggie's idea is to provide the splendid and deserving Charlotte with *her* proper setting, just as the Prince had been provided his, and also to "protect" the rich Adam Verver from other designing females of a much less desirable sort than Charlotte. The thought also is that Adam, so protected, will remain all the more available as the beloved intimate of his daughter, the relations between the two having always been of the closest sort.

So what was a triangle becomes a quadrangle, and the liaison between the Prince and Charlotte, somewhat difficult to carry on before, now becomes, all "innocently" as far as Maggie's and Adam's designs are concerned, almost invitingly convenient.

Maggie's dilemma, which had not really become clear until this latter arrangement had been in force for some time, is thus much more complicated, since it involves her father as well as herself. To expose the offenders now would humiliate Adam both as a father and a husband, just as it would humiliate Maggie both as wife and daughter. And above all, it would mean to both of them that all their high faith in culture as liberation and in goodness as service to culture—and indeed their faith in good faith itself—must be discarded as a horrible delusion.

The weight of it all falls on Maggie; she is the key to the whole problem. Adam is too Olympian in his benignity even to be aware of the situation, or if aware, he cannot show it without destroying his Olympian quality. "Deep" man that he is, deep beyond anybody's calculation, he is perhaps quite aware of what is going on, but his hands are tied by his own ineffable role as the giver of all good and perfect things. Like God himself, he must rely on others to recognize and fight the battle of good and evil.

Maggie belongs among the mortals, the sufferers and victims and strugglers. She too is "deep"—perhaps the deepest and most "astonishing" of all, as Fanny Assingham (the Jamesian commentator) says—but she is vulnerable and responsible. Maggie is the moral agent in the drama; she represents the "X" quantity of original innocence and prospective experience which precipitated drama in the first place and must solve it in the last. She is the evolving factor, both acted upon and acting.

To conclude here the brief synopsis of events and anticipate the denouement: Maggie chooses the difficult course of saving the whole situation, saving the wonderful design, trying to put back together again the shattered fragments of the Golden Bowl. All without consultation with her father or any open admission between them that anything has gone wrong—though there is a good deal of silent exchange of intelligence—she accepts the moral responsibility and forces a fight which previously was brought to her. With a sense of mounting strength and even of cunning, she lets her antagonists know that she *knows*, and knowing she will fight back. But in fighting back, she makes it plain, she will use no vulgar weapons of publicity or even her "rights" as such. Her only weapon is the moral one of right itself, and the metaphysical one of knowledge. "I *know*," she seems to say to both the Prince and Charlotte, "and now *you* know; and if you want to continue in your wrong, you will continue not only against me, but against knowledge and truth itself."

Thus the dilemma is shifted to the other side; Charlotte and the Prince have knowledge and responsibility thrust back upon them. They are, indeed, convicted of the knowledge of their sins. And so comes the chance for these glittering and worldly ones to show *their* fineness, which both proceed to do.

The Prince, puzzled alike as he has been—with the reader!—by Maggie's earlier blindness and her later penetration, mystified both by her goodness and her cunning, at least sees enough to see that he has a remarkable wife. Maggie, he begins to realize, is worth cherishing in a more definite way than in the somewhat cotton-batting fashion he had cherished her before. And Charlotte, aware that she is beaten, responds in her splendid manner and with her splendid strength. Her head held high even though she is obviously shaken inside, Charlotte accepts her fate, which is to be "banished" to America, there to take up, with Adam, the work of carrying out his great dream of bringing culture to his native land. We have a sort of preview of her carrying off, with the greatest éclat, the role of hostess and guide in the great museum to be established in "American City"—a role for which her long acquaintance with European art has eminently fitted her—while successive hordes of hungry, benighted Americans hang upon her words with admiration and gratitude.

And Maggie, freed by her knowledge, is strong enough to go on without the close aid and comfort of her father. She looks forward now to reconstructing through her wealth and her fresh blood the Prince's ancient and honorable line, and taking her place in the noble tradition to which by nature she belongs.

All this is the story as we are told it. What such a summary leaves out is not only the excitement of James's method, the champagne bubbling of the Jamesian style, but also the under- and overtones of meaning. Some of these undertones fit with the above summary, but some do not.

Under- and overtones are gathered about the Golden Bowl itself—that ornate bit of the "loot of Empire" discovered (in the early pages of the book) by Charlotte in company with the Prince in an obscure London shop, and which she wants to secure as a wedding gift to Maggie. This "object of art" is somewhat overdone in its rich gilded ornamentation but exquisite all the same. But alas it doesn't ring true; it has a hidden flaw, a crack. The Prince, in his ancient canny wisdom, is wary of it, wants nothing to do with it.

"But it's exquisite," (says Charlotte).
"Of course it's exquisite," (the Prince replies). "That's the danger."

The danger of the exquisite, the flaw in the crystal, has been the constant dark note in James's picture of the beautiful life. It appeared in *The Portrait of a Lady* as the hidden evil in Gilbert Osmond's character. Osmond, the last word apparently in perfect taste—so perfect that he need not prove it by any vulgar activity, his own life being itself a work of art—turns out, unfortunately, to be an utterly selfish, in fact a cruel man at heart. And Isabel must expiate her choice of this finest blossom of civilized taste by suffering also its cold inner cruelty.

We may note here a certain progression from the earlier to the later James in his sense of what might be called the curability of the "flaw in the crystal." Hyacinth Robinson, as we have seen, could find no cure at all; he could expiate his own early ignorance only by killing himself. Even poor little Daisy Miller, hardly a responsible person herself, had to pay for her innocent reckless-ness by dying of a fever. Isabel Archer, while she possessed the strength of character to meet her fate—that is, to face the fact of evil—could do so only by doing a bitter penance the rest of her life. Milly Theale, the angelic heroine of *The Wings of the Dove*, while she succumbs to her long-standing illness in the sorrowing knowledge that her own good faith had been exploited, is at least vindicated after death through the influence of her uncorrupted spirit, the memory of which puts to shame her ex-ploiters. And finally Maggie Verver, though she suffers her term of anguish, comes out quite victorious. With evil conquered, she may enter the promised land of high civilization which had been denied or spoiled for her predecessors.

This is a most interesting development, showing James more and more confident as he grew older that somehow he could recon-cile his two opposed elements—have his cake of simple American "goodness" and eat his cake of high aristocratic European "cul-ture."

It is no accident that the symbolic Golden Bowl is called a bit of the "loot of empire." James seems to be recognizing here what his Hyacinth Robinson had recognized before; that "civilization as we know it" is like that, built on special privilege and in-justice. The Golden Bowl is just another small item in the total levy that high civilization makes upon humanity at large—just another chip as it were of the priceless Elgin Marbles, carried off to decorate and glorify the new center of imperialism. "Civili-zation as we know it" is greedy, selfish, heartless, and deceptive. But exquisite, precious, like the Golden Bowl.

Now, how does naïve goodness approach this precious but

deceptive thing? It approaches it, of course, according to its own spiritual law, what Emerson would call the "law of man" as contrasted with the law of things. It assumes reciprocity of moral feeling, expects value returned for value, faith for faith.

Much in this spirit Adam and Maggie Verver, like Isabel Archer and Milly Theale and the other romantic and high-minded Jamesians, come with their hopes and faith to the scene of beautiful civilization. They bring the best of motives, come holding out their largesse of fortune and good will, and expect a return, in the shape of "culture," equal to what they bring and extended in the same faithful spirit.

The Prince and Charlotte have these cultural values; they *are* civilization and culture. But alas there is the flaw, they are not quite faithful at heart. The simple-minded father and daughter gradually have forced on their consciousness that beautiful behavior may coexist with rather ugly intentions. Beneath the high form and gloss the other law is operating, of material self-interest. The hidden motive is simply greed—readiness to profit from a situation according to the rule of matter rather than of spirit.

In short, Maggie and Adam, like Isabel and Milly before them, come to see they have been "used." Charlotte and the Prince have taken advantage of their good nature just as Madame Merle and Osmond took advantage of Isabel's good nature, as Kate Croy and Merton Densher took advantage of Milly's.

It would be difficult to explain the credulity of James's heroes and heroines without calling in the "international situation," for James rests his case very largely, it is plain, on its being that of a young, rich, but untried race meeting up with an old, experienced one. Hence the result: the young illusioned one is "taken in," "used."

This is a little too simple—we will qualify it somewhat later. But to understand how it could have appeared as simple as this, one must go back to a more innocent world, James's world of the latter part of the nineteenth century and up to the World War of 1914-1918. That was the day, for James's Americans, of the "grand tour." The great energies released on the ending of the Civil War had brought about their unparalleled material expansion. The continent had poured its wealth upon many Americans, deserving and undeserving, and created a large new suddenly leisured class that wondered what came next. James's Americans were drawn from just this class. Many of them were discovering that man lives not by bread alone—at least when, after he has bought all the bread he can use, he has a good deal of money left over to buy something else. This other something was "culture," and culture, too, seemed a purchasable commodity. If purchasable, Europe was obviously the place to do it in—Europe with her beautiful old house at last in order, the bloody past more or less buried, and all its objects of art nicely arranged and put under glass. Millions of Americans did not share this view at all. Millions of Americans thought of Europe not as a museum, but as "the old country." But these were not James's Americans.

This was the background for James's international drama, a background that was to stay in place up to the World War of 1914-1918. The war itself was to break it, the war and the peace. Americans would go to Europe in larger numbers than ever after the war, but not in the simple innocent spirit of "the grand tour." The image of Europe as merely a beautiful museum was shattered with the bombs and shrapnel of the war, and would probably never be put together again in just the same way—as James tried to restore the Golden Bowl. Our postwar exiles were to have no images for restoration. They were the "lost generation." James's generation of exiles—Isabel Archer and Lambert Strether and Maggie Verver—was still the beglamored one.

The disillusioned part of our story of "going back" is to be told by T. S. Eliot, the spokesman of the "lost generation," for which we need another chapter. Here we have to conclude the illusioned part of the story, which is the one that James tells. The interesting thing about *The Golden Bowl* is that it has a triumphant conclusion. The drama goes from disenchantment back to enchantment again.

James's "international situation" does not ordinarily have this extra act. Usually—in *The Portrait of a Lady, Roderick Hudson, The Wings of the Dove*—the drama stops with disenchantment. The heroes or heroines, Isabel Archer or Milly Theale, have no power to restore the image to its original form. They can only have a "moral" triumph, Isabel in life, Milly Theale in death, but they cannot also have a romantic triumph.

Our wonderful little Maggie Verver can have both. She can have a moral and a material victory, a success of power and a success of virtue. She proceeds, with Isabel Archer, to the point of sad knowledge—the knowledge that her good faith has been abused—but then she leaves Isabel, and goes on alone to absolutely new regions of triumph. In fact, Maggie Verver is the female knight errant who wins the day, who redresses wrong, blows the trumpet, gives the word, restores the palace to its former life and beauty.

This is an ambitious project, to say the least, for it means a real act of redemption. Maggie, the innocent sufferer, is one thing; Maggie, the all-wise savior, is another. A savior cannot be mistaken. He must be sure of his understanding both of evil and good. He cannot have any illusions, nor can he have doubts. He really must be pure, and not merely innocent; and wise, and not merely good.

It is here we begin to have questions about our "American" element, when it appears as the free moral agent on Europe's stage, and comes all in good faith, ready to play the shining knight and rescue the damsel in distress.

For one thing, the American crusader is very rich, and the world has a right to wonder whether so much wealth can be so innocent. After all, wealth is one reward in itself; can it then buy itself another reward in the form of culture, or honor, or merit for service?

When excess wealth is out looking for good deeds to do, let it beware! It is fair game for schemers and false pleaders of all sorts, as philanthropists so often learn to their sorrow. So let rich America beware when it goes to "redeem" poor Europe.

The bargain between American wealth and European culture thus begins to look somewhat suspicious from both sides. If beautiful but needy Europe stretched out hands which were self-ish, the hands of the New World may be none too clean themselves, for all their gesture of sacrifice. They too may have been stained with a very material interest in "civilization as we know it." The knight with the shining armor, in brief, may have been fooled at home before he was taken in abroad. The right word for his moral confusion may be not innocence, but delusion.

Then there is the question of what the American emissaries to the Old World are really after. Do they want to redeem it from its ancient evils, or are they halfway drawn to share in its glamour and glories? We are troubled by questions of this sort, reading James's tales, as early as *The Portrait of a Lady*. What does Isabel Archer really want? A husband? Is she in love? Or does she want not love, but to achieve culture and refinement according to Europe's more aristocratic standards? These objects are not just the same. If Isabel confuses them, is that a form of innocence or a form of duplicity? We get little help on such questions from our author. Here we begin to enter the famous region of Jamesian ambiguity.

But Isabel is a clear-cut character compared to Maggie. Does Maggie want a husband, or a title? We will take up this question later. Here let us note that whatever Maggie wants, she has a tremendous lot of money to help her get it, much more than poor Isabel ever had.

The longer James wrote, the wealthier his Americans got, and the grander and higher plans James found for their money. It begins to look, finally, as if American wealth is going to redeem the world, both Old and New—so preoccupied is James with this theme. It was the theme he was working on in *The Ivory Tower*, the book that he had to drop at the beginning of the first World War. Great American fortunes, falling into the right hands of course, were to redeem the evil Old World (as in *The Golden Bowl*) by bolstering up tottering European civilization, and redeem the New World (as in both *The Golden Bowl* and *The Ivory Tower*) by bringing European civilization to it.

James is at some pains to make Adam Verver seem consistent as a man both of great acquisitive and great benevolent powers. "A wiser hand than he at first knew," we are told of him, "had kept him hard at work at acquisition of one sort as the perfect preliminary to acquisition of another, and the preliminary would have been weak and wanting if the good faith had been less." There are no details to substantiate this assertion, but this is the assertion given to make Adam Verver credible in his dual role.

Do we actually see the two men as one, the hard-driving, tremendously successful money-maker, and the quiet, scholarly collector of art of the novel (one of the most knowing in all Europe), a man immensely "deep," refined, and wise? Would the one occupation, when pursued with good faith, seem to be the perfect preparation for the other: good faith in high profits the perfect introduction to high faith in goodness and beauty? Perhaps so. But the reader does not put the two together. He does not believe in any such Adam Verver. He merely accepts a fiat character of this name and description, but one who never suggests a past, a profession, a personal history.

Then, as to Maggie, the daughter of wealth, and her marriage to the Prince. Did Maggie love the Prince? Had she at any rate given ordinary consideration to the claims of the marriage relation? We do not know. We do know that this was not the "great" motive in the Ververs' dealings, the real Jamesian sign and signet upon the affair. This is something presumably higher than the desires of Maggie's heart; it has to do more with the dreams of her imagination.

On a lower plane, the aims of the Ververs could be made to sound vulgar enough, for after all they are not different in kind from those of any newly rich family that wishes to rise culturally and socially. Money is the instrument in both cases; acquisition is precisely the word James uses to describe the Ververs' means of realizing the best both in culture and marriage. In fact, the two things come together: cultural aspiration is like a marriage; marriage is like cultural aspiration. The husband-Prince is simply the finest item in the collection of art that the Ververs are picking up in Europe. He *is* culture; he is, as we are told, "positively civilization condensed, concrete, consummate." And he can be bought, apparently, like a Florentine tapestry or an Etruscan vase.

But the Ververs' ideals are *not* on a vulgar plane. That is always the puzzling thing in a Jamesian marriage contract! That is what has Prince Amerigo so absolutely bewildered. What was the bargain, anyway? Did not Maggie get her title; did not the Prince get his money? Does not that satisfy the essential conditions?

No, it does not! The Prince and his paramour, Charlotte, are quite mistaken if they think the Ververs are satisfied with any such crude interpretation of the bargain. That is the very point— the transcendental meaning of the marriage to the Ververs, as against the worldly meaning understood by the Prince. The Ververs' ideals, far from being vulgar or worldly, are so other-worldly that a mere Italian nobleman simply cannot make them out!

Well, what *does* really move Maggie? Why is it that she is to be treated neither as a rich heiress who has bought a title, nor a true-hearted girl who loves and wants to hold a husband? How are we to take this creature at once so otherworldly and so ambitious, so innocent and so "deep," so mild and so formidable? We may well ask, for here we find ourselves in the deepest thickets of James's ambiguity.

It is a region which perhaps only a transcendental American puritan, bedazzled at the same time by the spectacle of "the great world," could have imagined—and left us to wander bewilderedly in.

Fanny Assingham, the stage-manager of the drama, and a person a good deal responsible for the marriage, is almost as puzzled as the rest of us at Maggie's mysterious ideas of love and marriage. When the clouds have gathered around the marriage, and the storm seems about to break, Fanny is questioning Maggie to try to discover how it is she can remain so calm. Maggie explains:

"Because—don't you see?—I *am* mild, I can bear anything."
"Oh, 'bear!' " Mrs. Assingham fluted.
"For love," said the Princess.
Fanny hesitated. "Of your father?"
"For love," Maggie repeated.
It kept her friend watching. "Of your husband?"
"For love," Maggie said again.

Maggie's "love" is indeed something to wonder about. If it is love of her husband, what can you say of a love which does not sense a rival until the rival has been invited into the very household of the wife, almost thrown into the husband's arms?

THE ENCHANTED KINGDOM OF HENRY JAMES

If it is love of her father (and the bond between them is apparently so strong that each comes first in the other's regard, even after the double wedding), what can you say of this form of attachment, persisted in at such length and at such a pitch? So dominant a love between father and daughter is generally viewed as something not only odd but wrong.

Well, Maggie says "for love"—love itself, the pure universal emotion, which might be all very well if this actually were Maggie's meaning. But would even Plato suppose Maggie could have reached this peak of clear vision by such clouded and vague steps as are represented by the concrete loves of husband and father? I think not.

The mystery remains, and very mysterious it is, because we get no help from the author in solving it. Indeed, for dramatic excitement, the unexamined and unexploited area of *The Golden Bowl* attracts one with a great fascination. If James had only shifted the interest from what he tells to what he does not tell, the reader halfway envisions—he hardly knows what—but something very astonishing indeed. Let us look at it.

In this unexploited drama, we should certainly be interested in the possible retribution upon a father and daughter with such a bond between them for taking on a supernumerary wife and husband more or less known to be lovers themselves. We should like especially to have Maggie's character read and revealed in the light of her actions in bringing this about. In such a light you begin to have the feeling that Maggie, the lovely Princess of the fairy tale, might turn out instead to be the bad witch.

For to have done what Maggie has done: to have bought a Prince for a sort of household pet or charm, to think so little of him as a husband that one spends three fourths of one's time with one's father, then to make a further purchase of a female charm or pet for the same ménage and deliberately throw the two into each other's company, remaining the while serenely and almost calculatingly unaware of what they may be doing to pass the time away: is this not a piece of contriving that opens up—as James himself might say—the more lurid reaches of the fiendish?

The least one can observe concerning such a situation is that the Prince and Charlotte have excellent grounds for astonishment and resentment on their own side. If any persons might think themselves badly "used" in this extraordinary business, they would seem to be the two casually acquired and casually neglected spouses.

But in the James drama, the Prince and Charlotte may only furtively try to puzzle out their odd status in relation to the other half of the quartet. Furtively, like naughty children, they may indulge their own unhallowed passion, not knowing whether it is blessed, ignored, or condemned by their benefactors. They have no right even to question the high motives at all times of Adam and Maggie.

Here we come to another portion of James's ambiguous kingdom. It is true that James presents the physical relationship of Charlotte and the Prince with more candor and definition than he usually gives to human passion—only perhaps the affair of Kate and Merton in *The Wings of the Dove* being drawn with as much intensity. Presumably it is a real passion, and in fact we are so convinced. But a real passion, in the less ambiguous kingdoms of the world, is a fact of importance in itself. It is not to be easily dismissed.

THE ENCHANTED KINGDOM OF HENRY JAMES

It is not exactly dismissed in *The Golden Bowl*, but it is most readily and conveniently cured. Surely two lovers never so docilely resigned their love as did Charlotte and the Prince. If the Prince entertained a true passion for Charlotte, we must at least think him a cad for having abandoned his love with so little show of fight. And if Charlotte was deeply in love with the Prince, her loss or sacrifice entitles her at least to our sympathy. But if the Prince and Charlotte were after all only having a light meaningless affair, are they worth the Ververs' trouble at all? There is no real story, if there is no real passion.

Yet Charlotte is no more granted a pathetic or tragic sympathy than the Prince is viewed with a certain critical irony. Charlotte is simply spanked and sent home like a naughty and misguided but after all penitent and brave little girl; while the Prince—more or less a passive figure throughout—simply resumes his accepted role as the lustrous "catch" that he was, with perhaps added luster drawn from the creditable showing he has made as he becomes initiated in the higher laws of the Ververs.

The Prince's behavior might perhaps be accepted on the grounds that he had never put too high an estimate on his own moral worth. He had understood from the first his limited role in the Verver household. He was to have his fortunes rehabilitated in return for the title and other values of high civilization which he could offer. Though a little puzzled as to what else might be expected of him, he is perfectly ready, through experience, to learn what that else might be. We can perhaps see him shrugging off, as an unfortunate miscalculation on his part, the incident of Charlotte. But then we must wonder a little whether, in the prospective splendid life of Maggie and the Prince, there shall not come over both of them occasionally a rather dry sense of the merely convenient nature of their whole relationship.

We are much more dubious as to the future life of the Adam Ververs. If Charlotte, after her defeat, is not a tragic figure she must remain a highly suspect one. Erring and spanked once, will she not err and want spanking again? We cannot quite see this high-spirited adventurous young woman, married to her elderly philanthropist husband, settling down tamely to the routine of public service in "American City"—for all the careful playing out or playing in of Adam's "silken cord."

Incidentally, this "silken cord" of Adam's, which he has about Charlotte's neck and by which he holds her to him, deserves a chapter by itself in our revised *Golden Bowl*. It belongs with Maggie's mysterious "love." Why does Adam need a cord to hold Charlotte, silken or otherwise? Is she not attached to him voluntarily, by respect and gratitude at least if not by love? Why and what is the cord? Is it the power of his money? But that would be something like bribery. Is it the threat of exposing Charlotte and the Prince? But that would be a kind of blackmail. Adam's "silken cord" is only another of those unexplained items in the inventory of James's ambiguity.

But as to Charlotte's role in our revised drama, there must come upon her often, we feel, black moods of bitterness at her purchased ornamental status and dark impulses to compensate somehow for her galling, virtually unrecognized defeat.

In fact, the reader's imagination on which James always counted heavily has been much too stimulated to be quieted by the dropping, however grandly, of James's own last curtain. It is still fixed on those undealt-with matters that lie off stage. If light were to be thrown there we are almost sure it would reveal further, and rather horrible, happenings in this extraordinary drama.

The key to this unfinished business would certainly be Charlotte—the squelched and humanly aggrieved factor in James's story. I think she would need a part to herself, called "Charlotte," which James never allowed her in the book. It would deal with Charlotte's revenge. We know the real target of her revenge; it would be that crafty-innocent, smugly virtuous, coolly victorious little Princess. How she might get at Maggie would be the question; Adam's silken cord would probably snub her back from any move to follow the victorious couple to Rome and once more seduce the Prince away from Maggie and so triumph. But there is Adam himself, the all-benign and beloved father of the Princess and Charlotte's own jailor-benefactor-husband. The logic of motive and situation point to him as the proper medium of Charlotte's revenge.

We can even see where the scene would take place; it would be in some off room of Adam's great museum in "American City," among the priceless purchased and transported treasures that represent "civilization positively condensed and consummate." Here would come the second crash of the Golden Bowl, the really devastating irreparable one. We falter a little as to what actually happens. We cannot believe that Charlotte has a chance really to triumph; she is herself too much in the toils; she is flawed with the same flaw of the Golden Bowl.

Our imagination, however, makes a last flight. As the gilded captive struggles with her jailor, amid the toppling of treasures, will not Adam be forced to use his power; will he not slowly tighten now his silken cord? And would not the final horror of this act lie perhaps in some Hawthornesque transformation, one quite in keeping likewise with the James of *The Turn of the Screw*, which we see taking place in the visage of Adam himself?

It is a wild flight, but if the daughter-princess is a witch in disguise, the father-king may well be a wizard. Power like Adam's, at any rate, that stands on a golden throne and holds a silken cord, cannot be granted for good without its being granted for evil. And in enchanted strange kingdoms, the surest thing is that things are not what they seem.

On such a merry chase James's ambiguity leads the reader. The guessing game, widely participated in these many years, promises to go on indefinitely.

I am aware of one suggested theory which credits James, at least in the case of his most deliberately mysterious story *The Turn of the Screw*, with a hidden but illuminating "key" of his own. The key is that of morbid psychology. The story is a Freudian fantasy arising in the mind of a sex-starved spinster.

Sexual pathology of greater or lesser degree and of considerable variety may certainly be read with little trouble into many of James's stories. I have already hinted that the bond between Maggie and her father seems in effect much too strong to be accounted for as an ordinary father-daughter affection. But that James himself recognized, to say nothing of intended, anything unusual in the relationship is scarcely to be believed. In fact one feels James would have been the person most horrified at the idea.

Yet there are scores of places in James's works where only a reference to abnormal psychology could explain the intensity of certain emotions. Consider for example the short story called *The Pupil*, which is a tale of the friendship between a moneyless young tutor and a precocious youngster belonging to a family of shabby cosmopolitan adventurers. The tutor is ill-paid at first and later not paid at all. In order to keep his job he must submit to sordid indignities on the part of the family and make devious shifts of his own, the climax of which is his securing money from other sources in order to support himself and his pupil, in part, as well. That the situation is inglorious to say the least is evident from the tutor's repeated resolutions to break it off—resolutions, however, which he finds impossible to carry out. Aware that the attachment is ruining his own career, he nevertheless is somehow helplessly caught in it, only the death of the boy at last releasing him.

Such a story begs at once for Freud, or one of his colleagues. People do not ruin their lives for other people unless deep emotional centers are involved, and when the case is that of an adult young man and a precocious small boy, we may be excused for sensing something off the normal pattern. Did James want to suggest an abnormal passion between the two? It is much to be doubted. He makes no effort to hide the fact of great affection between the man and the boy, displayed once or twice by an embrace, but this very circumstance makes us question any further implication.

This is not to say that the reader may not deduce, as something of which James himself may have been unaware, the presence of an unusual emotional substratum in the very nature of the story. The deduction seems inevitable. But it does not follow that this is the point of the story—James's point.

The point of *The Pupil*—James's point—has to do with the intangible compulsions of the spirit rather than with those of instinct, normal or not. The plight of the precocious youngster is a spiritual plight and calls for a spiritual response. Whatever reward there may be to offset the sacrifice of the tutor comes from the knowledge that a fine little spirit, found struggling in sordid surroundings, has not been left in the lurch. If there is fatality here, it is the fatality of imagination. The young man, once aware of the pitiful call for understanding, and aware that he alone has heard and can meet it, simply cannot fail his knowledge.

Something of this sort, you gather from the story and from James's preface, is James's own "point." It may or may not be adequate to explain the actual events of the story—I think it is not—but that is another question.

With regard to *The Turn of the Screw,* I can see no reason for refusing to believe James's own plain words in the preface as to what his intentions were. His problem, he says, was to make evil "portentous," and to do so he felt that giving it some particular form would be ill-advised. Rejecting the "comparative vulgarity" of such a "limitation," he decided on just the opposite, that is, to give it no form. "Only make the reader's general vision of evil intense enough," he writes, and "his own imagination" will supply sufficient particulars. James in fact was chagrined when certain readers charged him with a "monstrous emphasis" of evil in the story, and he is at pains to insist again that "my values are positively all blanks save as an excited horror, a promoted pity, a created expertness . . . proceed to read into them more or less fantastic figures."

THE ENCHANTED KINGDOM OF HENRY JAMES

James was often enough indirect, but deliberate misstatement for the purpose of throwing his readers off the track is, I believe, out of character. There is every reason for thinking that James would find Freudian "figures" read into his blanks as fantastic as any other kind, and equally the result of a "created expertness."

But again, what James may have revealed unintentionally and unconsciously in *The Turn of the Screw* is something else. A good case might be made, in fact, for the morbidity or even immorality of the very method of presenting evil as a pure blank. This charge, to which the generality of "good clean murder" and other horror stories is open, is much more one to which James seems liable. To excite horror without at the same time throwing as full a light as possible upon its concrete causes and the human values at stake is surely a form of artistic indulgence, and one of which James is sometimes guilty. The whole group of stories which includes *What Maisie Knew*, *The Pupil*, and *The Turn of the Screw*, show a certain fascination, not free from the morbid, for the situation of childish innocence surrounded by shadowy viciousness, only partly named and illuminated. The morbid note lies of course not in the situations themselves nor in the presence of evil, all of which is the proper concern of art, but in the partiality of treatment. We feel a certain abuse of the childish consciousness, at once so innocent and so precociously aware.

Here we come much closer, I think, to the nature of James's ambiguity. For are not even his adult heroines too childishly innocent and too precociously aware? James had come to see, sadly enough, that the enchanted garden in the fairy tale contained a witch. He left the witch, however, as mysterious as the enchantment. James appeared loath to reduce either form of wizardry to terms of human experience and daylight knowledge.

It may appear an anticlimax to suggest that the secret of James's ambiguity, and of the "glamour" of James as well (for the two go together), is simply innocence, or virginity, itself, which yet is coupled with great intellectual powers and an intense curiosity concerning "the world." In terms of psychological origin, I think the word for this particular quality is "precocity"—an advance of ideation over experience. And do we not recall Henry James the infant in long clothes, "taking in for all time" the look of a square in Paris? Such a key, I believe, opens up on the one hand the extraordinary range and minuteness of James's imagination, peering at and circling about the motives and acts, the conspiracies and plights and compulsions, of people in the "great world," and even hesitating in fascination about the simple "fact" of what these things are; and on the other hand leads back to the extraordinary inward glow and spring of power in the novelist himself— the glow and power of the pristine consciousness, the unbroken web of illusion.

Other features fit in with this view, either helping to explain or being in turn explained by it. There was the fact that James, though he chose to live most of his life in England, chose to keep almost to the last year his American citizenship. Here again is the separation of idea and experience. James's life did not need to mean citizenship, nor did citizenship need to mean a life. He had neither helped construct his wonderful "Europe," nor did he have to keep it going. In so far as he felt moral involvement, it was perhaps with the more rudimentary young world on the other side of the water. The underprivileged young people of the small world back home remained on his mind, and their prospective introduction to "life" lay on his conscience. But this "life" was to be in the already-finished enchanted place. James, too, had his independent means. If he was not exactly a visiting prince to his enchanted realm, he was at least a well-provided-for baronet. Thus, what he owed economically and personally was mostly to the other land, the one in which he did not reside. What he owed romantically was to the enchanted realm, but the one in which he had little physical stake. He himself was happily free of the compulsion to put both in the same place, and answer the question posed for his Hyacinth Robinson concerning the problems of a going society. He could cherish the charm without running up against the problems.

All this may help explain why most of James's heroes and heroines react wholly, in the first instance, to the purely "ideal" aspect of their situations, and have the strangest disregard for the most ordinary physical considerations. James allowed his villains and villainesses a certain grasp of the material features of their circumstances, including the sexual life, but his heroes and heroines are surely among the vaguest of the children of light.

Even Isabel Archer, one of the most clearheaded of James's heroines, shows this strange vagueness as to the physical aspects of her marriage to Gilbert Osmond. It is as if a film came before Isabel's eyes, so that the common instincts and intuitions of womankind, instincts which we feel Isabel should possess in a healthy state, are suddenly rendered impotent. She apparently has caught no real sense of Gilbert as a person, a man and prospective husband with whom one is intimately to live.

Were Isabel deliberately drawn as a vague type we could understand this blindness; but she is not drawn so at all. Or if there were some queer quality in her, some rather perverted taste, hitherto dormant, for the gamy flavors of high civilization, we could understand her attraction to Gilbert Osmond and his cold perfection. But Isabel is no more queer than she is vague; she is decidedly the opposite on both counts.

So we have the same mystery presented, the same half-caught vision of something off-shade and perhaps spicily ambiguous. Yet once more I think we will be disappointed in looking for a "secret," whether titillating or offensive. Or rather, we shall find the secret to lie just in a virginal overlooking of the entire sexual aspect of Isabel's marriage.

The truth is that, while James's heroes and heroines (especially heroines) face and meet mature human situations, their characteristic decisions turn upon the fancies of childhood. It is possible to understand Isabel's choice of Osmond only if we think of her, for the moment, as an unripe girl for whom the physical aspect of marriage hasn't been comprehended or counted in. She is not falling in love with a man, but only an idea. Only the bad people in James fall in love with other people.

That is one law, then, of James's ambiguous country. Mature people, when they enter the enchanted palace, will behave like children acting out their personal fairy tales. True, after they have acted according to the law of make-believe, they suffer more or less according to the law of reality. Isabel finds herself the responsible wife of a bad man, and she responsibly, if somewhat quixotically, stays by her deceiver. Maggie finds herself married to a continental European, with a different moral code from her own—and she prepares to deal with this situation.

THE ENCHANTED KINGDOM OF HENRY JAMES

If we will grant James's make-believe law, we can believe, for the time being at least, in the situation that follows. The Jamesian drama then tightens up in its highly intricate form.

This is the artistic achievement of James in which his devotees—and he is a writer with devotees—are most interested and in which they find their chief satisfaction. And this artistic, or technical achievement is of course the subject of most of the comment and criticism of James. James perhaps is too consciously "the artist," but there is no question of his accomplishment on this side. He is "tough-minded" as an artist. He hated amateurishness extremely, and the stories he wrote specifically about artists and their problems are among the best of their kind. Jamesian irony is strong but his ambiguity entirely absent from such stories as *The Lesson of the Master* and *The Real Thing*, stories I think that have not received their due among James's work. As the bride of art, James had torn the veil.

As the bride of life, however, he tended to leave the mystery all the more mysterious. The word for James's emotional effect is glamour—the glamour of the spell woven, the light played, the illusion fostered. And does not this explain why, though everyone has found this magic of glamour in James's prose, no one has found the magic of poetry? For poetry's magic brings us closer to inner reality, while glamour's magic takes us farther away. There is something misleading about the glamorous effect. Its rainbow colors, like the sheen of oil on water, break down into other elements altogether—and not very pleasant ones.

So James's rainbow colors tend to break down into other elements, and often quite dubious ones—queer attachments, conspiracies, falsehoods. Beauty is not what it seems, and even good-ness is not what it seems.

There is our good Maggie, for instance, so "mild," as she says, and yet the cunningest person around. Maggie is James's magic personified. She is the one that is going to work the miracle. She is to put the Golden Bowl of beauty and high civilization together again—cracked though it is—and save both the glamour of her dreams and the substance of her worldly position.

How is this to be brought about? I do not want to make light of the means Maggie supposedly uses. It is "inward grace," the power of good faith over bad faith. It is not hard to see where this comes from in James's experience. This is the "good faith," the "inward life," of the remarkable James household back home. James's father had said "convert, convert"—convert lower to higher by the use of the spiritual law. Here is the place where we are to see "the dim little gentleman," as it were, converted from a mere object of art to a spiritual being.

The only question is how it is to be done. Other heroines of James—Isabel Archer and Milly Theale, for example—have been sustained in their own lives by "inward grace," but only with the sacrifice of their illusions. They have all lost the dream of their "dim little gentlemen." Maggie is the only one who saves both her soul and her illusions.

Maggie's time of testing provides James with one of his scenes of high theater. There is the grand setting, the great house at "Fawns," the card party proceeding within one of the splendid rooms, and Maggie outside on the terrace, outside the long lighted windows, suffering her agony, hovering like a soul in purgatory.

At the card table are the three other souls whose fate are in her hands (plus Fanny Assingham, the inevitable fourth, shall we say, at Jamesian bridge).

"Spacious and splendid, like a stage awaiting drama, it was a scene she might people, by the press of her spring, either with serenities and dignities and decencies, or with terrors and shames and ruins, things as ugly as those formless fragments of her golden bowl she was trying so hard to pick up."

The players proceed with their game, abiding by the rules, resting on the forms of civilization, while Maggie struggles alone with the shapes of terror and temptation in the outer void. Her temptation is to give way to her sense of righteous injury, "the horror of finding evil seated, all at its ease, where she had dreamed only of good; the horror of the thing hideously *behind*, behind so much trusted, so much pretended, nobleness, cleverness, tenderness. It was the first sharp falsity she had known in her life. . . ."

To give way, to retaliate according to the law of the world; or to suffer and forgive according to the spiritual law; these are Maggie's choices. Maggie has taken in the glances, the unspoken appeals of the other three. She pictures herself momentarily as "the scapegoat of old . . . charged with the sins of the people" that must go forth into the desert to sink under his burden and die.

But do they want her to die? If she is to take up the burden of the others' sins, must the result be to make a martyr of herself?

No, the insight comes to her, that is precisely what they don't want. The other three want her to live, "live on somehow for their benefit, and even as much as possible in their company, to keep proving to them that they had truly escaped and that she was still there to simplify."

The terrible temptation to give way to her sense of wrong gradually passes. Maggie understands that "the rights of resentment, the rages of jealousy, the protests of passion" are not for her. No, "for *her* husband's wife, for *her* father's daughter," these crude expressions of injury appear now, in a fine figure, "nothing nearer to experience than a wild eastern caravan, looming into view with crude colors in the sun, fierce pipes in the air, high spears against the sky, all a thrill, a natural joy to mingle with, but turning off short before it reached her and plunging into other defiles."

So the crisis passes, and Maggie's "better nature" has won. Maggie returns safe from her midnight Gethsemane into the lighted drawing room, the magnificent house of civilization. She has accepted her burden, but not to sink under it. The next scene is not Calvary, but somehow has become the triumphant entry into Jerusalem. The others understand, with little or nothing spoken, the triumph for all of them. Maggie has performed the inward magic which keeps the outer magic whole and perfect. There has been no vulgar "scene," no ugly hurling of charges and recriminations. All has been saved by the tacit inner act.

And afterward Maggie notes, as a clue to both the past and the future, that "if the beauty of appearances had been so consistently preserved, it was only the golden bowl as Maggie herself knew it that had been broken. The breakage stood not for any wrought discomposure among the triumphant three [the Prince, Charlotte and Adam]—it stood merely for the dire deformity of her attitude toward them."

With "the dire deformity" of her attitude corrected, evil has been exorcized and good will reign.

I have not tried to disguise my impression that we have here a species of spiritual legerdemain. Surely it is much too good to be true, that lower can be converted to higher simply by preserving the beauty of appearances.

For if this is a study in spiritual law, it has strange features. Charlotte and the Prince, presumably, are the only wrongdoers— but it is Maggie whose attitude alone is one of "dire deformity." Maggie, presumably, is the sacrificial agent—yet Charlotte and the Prince are the ones who must renounce a real passion. Maggie's time of testing finds the real battle already won, just as the Prince and Charlotte's sacrifice is not considered a test at all. *The Golden Bowl* gives us a Gethsemane without a Calvary and a resurrection without a death. Mary Magdalene has regained her virtue without stooping to wash anybody's feet; and Pilate, no longer a skeptic, has found a beautiful answer to his question. Truth is appearance and appearance is truth.

As I have already suggested, most of James's other books find no such easy victory for the side of righteousness.

What we can make out, however, is that "the beauty of appearance" has remained a cardinal value to James, and here at last takes the highest place. *The Golden Bowl* is the triumph of the romantic James. If James wished at the same time to put forward the value of inner faith and simple goodness—the heart's truth—it is only as a servant, not the master of appearances. From the time that Hyacinth Robinson had chosen death rather than risk destroying "civilization as we know it," all of James's troubled protagonists have called upon their spiritual resources to support the "beauty of appearances" rather than to give up the deceptive value itself.

Almost any sacrifice for beauty's sake—for glamour's sake, rather—is preferable to renouncing or revising this fascinating appearance. The little story called *Flickerbridge* shows to what absurd lengths James could carry this rule. It tells of a young American artist in London who is engaged to a young woman, also American, who "writes up" European subjects for American papers. As a preliminary to the marriage, the young man makes a visit to the home of a distant English cousin of his fiancée, a lady whom the girl herself has never seen. He expects his girl to join him there shortly, but, arriving first at the cousin's country home, the romantic American finds "Flickerbridge" such a quaint vestige of an older England, and the spinster cousin so unconsciously perfect in her setting, that he cannot bear the idea of his excitable young lady "discovering" the whole charming place inevitably to exploit and spoil it. Rather than risk being a party to such a sacrilege, the young man prefers to give up his marriage. So he calls off his engagement, calls off the girl's visit, and quietly leaves Flickerbridge to its sleeping enchantment.

This little fairy tale approaches somewhere near the limits of fantastic abnegation. Yet it differs only in degree from the characteristic pattern of the James drama.

Renunciation of life, strangely enough considering our bedazzled pilgrim's sense of expansion under the magic of his "great lighted and decorated" European scene, is the real moral again and again of James's stories. In so far as James's world yields a universal meaning, this is it: that life must be sacrificed for glamour.

This meaning is more explicitly told than usual in the scene of Isabel Archer's disillusion, when she has become aware of what she has lost in having chosen life with Osmond. She has lost the right to impulsive and generous action. "Action had been suddenly changed to slow renunciation, transformed by the blight of Osmond's touch." Isabel must substitute now for the happiness of expression the sad virtue of constriction.

This moral is of course the moral that truly befits the tale of the little girl who dreamed of a fairy prince in a fairy palace— the moral, too, of the story of turning back in search of the lost heritage. There is no real happiness for flesh and blood in the dream palace. And the clock cannot be turned back. Not life, but death, awaits the human heart bewitched by the enchanted past.

As for *The Golden Bowl* and its miracle of redemption and fulfillment, it is rather surprising that this fascinating fable has not been seen for what it is: Henry James's great dream story. It is the one version of the fairy drama in which all the magics really work, all the dreams come true, and prince and princess, in their shining palace, live happily ever afterward.

The striking fact about James's world with *The Golden Bowl* left out is its lack of continuity. For all the passionate vibrations of James's people to it, life simply is not prepared to go on for them in the wonderful place. Strether with his brave dim smile, giving up his Maria Gostrey; the spinster Maria herself in her perfect Paris setting sterilely surrounded with the *objets d'art* of a foreign culture; Chad Newsome and his love for beauty's sake;

Isabel going back to her loveless bed; Milly Theale dead a virgin; Roderick Hudson's small talent turned to futility: these are the characteristic pictures left with us, and over them all is the bright, cold glitter of sterility.

It is not a question of the tragic or happy ending. It is a question of what has come to pass. "Ripeness is all," says Shakespeare. But there *is* ripeness, and with ripeness there may be reproduction; there may be an eternal ripeness, even. But what James tells of his enchanted realm is that there is no ripening there and no generation. There is the adolescent dream, and the disenchantment, and a certain brave pathos. But the frost comes with the flower; the fruit itself never develops. Such is the devastating reality which James allows us to see beneath the glamorous illusion.

This unripeness differs from ordinary immaturity. We sense instead the uneven development of precocity, with its lack somehow of the principle of growth. James's innocents do not make the crude errors of the immature, but rather the overimaginative errors of the precocious.

We know the immature American, and he does not act like a Chad Newsome or even an Isabel Archer. If he is "innocent," and he is in his own way, he is innocent in the manner of those "innocents" of the *Quaker City*, Mark Twain's exuberant fellow travelers, whose crude deportment abroad must certainly have humiliated our passionate pilgrim.

We must narrow James's international drama to its actual meaning—the drama of a certain type of American who has always sought to reconnect himself with the mother culture. We know that James's Americans exist, and in some quantity; they remain one of the elements in the mixed New World pattern of nationality. They are the element which naturally considers culture and authority to lie in the Old World. Their story of re-encounter with ancestral scenes and ancestral culture is the one James tells, and it is a true tale, thus delimited and reinterpreted. It is not a story of the native American, whether at home or abroad.

With a turn for Freudian analysis, one might find the note of sterility in James's world to be the result of a sort of cultural mother complex. James's susceptible children of the New World have not severed the silver cord, and the unnatural liaison prevents them from forming more equal and fertile connections.

We should be on our guard, then, when we come to the one marriage in James that is not only beautiful but fertile. Our "astonishing little Maggie," as Fanny Assingham has every right to call her, is the heroine of this episode too. She has done what no other Jamesian heroine has managed to do, she has had a baby. Not only has she captured her dream Prince; not only has she kept the marriage from breaking to pieces; but she has insured that the dream and the house of dreams will go on after her own death. Maggie's little Principino carries the burden of a Jamesian posterity. So far as I know, he is the only second generation in the whole of James's fictional world.

The bambino serves as sufficient warning that in *The Golden Bowl* we are likely to find all the more intractable elements in James's beautiful but deceptive world falling nicely into place. We are not mistaken. The merger of dream and fulfillment takes place all along the line. At last James's conflict, unresolved since the problem of choosing between the "cousinship," with their excellent human qualities, and the "dim little gentleman," with his empty perfection of type, has been settled. One does not have to choose—at a sufficiently high level of beautiful form.

It is the dream quality of *The Golden Bowl*, I am convinced, which gives it its peculiar fascination among James's works. We soon begin to feel that the theater of this drama, while nominally James's England, has somehow been translated to a kingdom all its own. Even the European "lighted stage" has removed itself to a distance, and comes to us in faint tones. The two worldlings, Charlotte and the Prince, are permitted their excursion to the magnificent house party at Matcham (where they meet incidentally the First Royal Personage himself), but Maggie and Adam have really established a court and sovereignty of their own. During the few occasions in which they receive the outer world they are preoccupied and almost indifferent. Maggie's mild vague smile, Adam's quiet inner "hum," need no support from the outside and recognize no allegiance. These two ineffables weave their own spell and commune with their own gods.

Nor is it an accident that the great scene on which the final curtain falls, the one in which Maggie and the Prince receive and bid a last farewell to Adam and his lady Charlotte, takes place in a London of the off season, with all the "notes" of the great world in abeyance. "The time was stale, it was to be admitted, for incidents of magnitude; the September hush was in full possession at the end of a dull day. . . ."

Stale the time, dull the day, all that is irrelevant. Rather, the drab background only throws into relief the brilliance of the occasion. James at last has created and peopled a "great world" of his own, with its own rank and decorations and ceremony. It is this world and its figures which now shine against the faded-out real one. No red carpet is laid down on the pavement of Eaton Square, no outward props are needed to signalize the occasion. But make no mistake about it: an incident of magnitude is exactly what is taking place.

Maggie and the Prince are rather impatiently waiting. Maggie is pretending to read a book, but meanwhile dealing, in her astonishing mild-tyrannical way, with her last delicate problem of appearances. It is one raised by the Prince. The Prince has a crude idea that he ought to indicate in some way his own reformation. Should he not somehow demonstrate, in the presence of his erstwhile paramour, his complete renouncement of their old passion and complete allegiance to his wife, and so correct any false impression that may remain? He suggests as much to Maggie.

Maggie: "What business is it of yours?"

The puzzled Prince: "Isn't it my right to correct her—?"

"Maggie let the question ring—ring long enough for him to hear it himself; only then she took it up. ' "Correct" her?'—and it was her own now that really rang. 'Aren't you rather forgetting who she is?' After which, while he quite stared for it, as it was the first clear majesty he had known her to use, she flung down her book and raised a warning hand. 'The carriage. Come!' "

Charlotte happens to be the wife of Mr. Adam Verver! That is "who" she is. If there is still any question of what that means it is soon settled. The Prince had jumped at Maggie's "Come!" and, "when they were below in the hall there was a 'Go!' for him, through the open doors and between the ranged servants . . ." and he goes. "He received Royalty, bareheaded, therefore, in the persons of Mr. and Mrs. Adam Verver, as it alighted on the pavement, and Maggie was at the threshold to welcome it to her house."

There is no doubt what sort of an occasion is transpiring. It is an occasion of Royal State. And upon such an occasion, how can any question of common ethics be raised? The poor Prince, in his blundering proposal to tell Charlotte just how things stood, was in danger of the crime of lese-majesty against the Queen.

And as for the queenliness of Charlotte herself: "The shade of the official, in her beauty and security, never for a moment dropped; it was a high cool refuge, the deep arched recess of some colored and gilded image, in which she sat and smiled and waited, drank her tea, referred to her husband. . . ."

Once, true, there is a delicate moment, when the Prince in his capacity as host is about to present to his erstwhile lover "a plate of *petits fours.*" Would the unofficial, the underneath, the "inward life," betray itself by any slight flicker in this official act?

Ah no, Queen and Prince are both equal to the situation. Amerigo carries it off perfectly, and as for Charlotte, Maggie can only be grateful again for the consummate way in which she "cleared her acceptance, cleared her impersonal smile, of any betrayal, any slightest value, of consciousness."

In fact Maggie is now so assured of the triumph of appearances that she can safely leave the two former lovers together while she joins her father at the other end of the room.

"It's all right, eh?" says Adam, referring to a picture on the wall, one of the perfectly selected masterpieces from his collection which he had recently presented to his daughter.

"Oh my dear—rather!" is Maggie's answer, and both of them know that it applies not only to the picture on the wall but to the other picture, the living tableau of Charlotte and the Prince at the tea table, with all that it signifies. King and Princess allow themselves mutual felicitations on the final success of their new alliances. The house of the Ververs has been strengthened, culturally, by the two marriages. "The two noble persons seated in conversation and at tea fell thus into the splendid effect and general harmony: Mrs. Verver and the Prince fairly 'placed' themselves, however unwittingly, as high expressions of the kind of human furniture required aesthetically by such a scene."

Nor is the gratifying assurance of a succession forgotten. The Principino has been "ordered" for half-past five, of this afternoon of state, and the Princess assures the grandparent, "Trust him, my dear, not to fail you!"

We know he will not fail, for how can there be failure in this kingdom where dreams come true?

So the state occasion is carried off to the last perfect letter, with King and Queen, Prince and Princess, and little Prince-of-line, all taking their proper cues and keeping to their proper roles. "It's success, father," cries Maggie, gratified that she can meet his eyes with every evidence of joy in hers, just as she had been gratified a moment earlier by the sincere ring she had heard in her own voice when she had cried "Father, father—Charlotte's great!" And just as Adam had joined her in saying "Charlotte's great," so now he joins in and echoes her "It's success."

When people have to listen to themselves for the note of sincerity, we may be pardoned for wondering if all is really well. When success means the successful covering up of something, we can only wonder if the something itself does not mean failure.

But what is the impression which has been hovering in our

minds as we watch this little party? Where have we seen its ritual before and heard its particular accents?

Maggie's imperious "Aren't you forgetting who she is?"

And: "The carriage. Come!" The majestic "Go!"

Royalty received bareheaded—the grand entrance—the ceremony of the tea table—the *petits fours* passed—the visitor's perfect impersonal smile. There is needed only the slightest turn to bring out the exact effect of a children's make-believe tea party. "Ah, *do* have another, Mrs. Verver"—"And your little son, the Prince?"—"I have ordered him for half past the hour; Miss Bogle is perfectly trained"—"A charming child, Princess!"—"Well, we must be leaving, our carriage awaits ——"

The final scene of *The Golden Bowl* suggests nothing so much as a splendid make-believe tea party acted out by some unusually imaginative children. We marvel at the perfect play-acting, the forms so beautifully mastered, the really convincing show the children put on. But the marvel is at the make-believe. And if the children reveal, or rather hide, strange knowledges of the schemes and shames of grownups, we marvel further at their precocious, ambiguous awareness.

We are not likely soon to see anything like another Henry James. It took the combination of a certain phase of New World youth with a certain period of Old World glamour to produce him. As I have already noted, this could not survive the World War of 1914-1918, and is even less likely to survive the war that began in 1939.

How much James himself, at the end of his life, was aware of the breaking up of his imaginative world—even as the grounds for enchantment—is hard to tell. There is the well-known letter I referred to earlier which expressed his terrible shock at the outbreak of the war. "The plunge of civilization into this abyss of blood and darkness . . ." he wrote, "is a thing that so gives away the whole long age during which we have supposed the world to be, with whatever abatement, gradually bettering, that to have to take it all now for what the treacherous years were all the while making for and *meaning* is too tragic for words. But one's reflections don't really bear being uttered. . . ."

There is no call to arraign James for not being a prophet. Nevertheless, he had deliberately used his "Europe" during this whole long age that now proved treacherous as a mere "lighted and decorated stage," a static background for his supersubtle international dramas. No actual going society could stand being used that way. Certainly European high society, resting on what it rested on—empire and balance of power and the rest—could not stand any such pure aesthetic use.

James had not always ignored what was behind and beneath his beautiful Europe of country houses and leisure-class culture. *The Princess Casamassima* showed how much he had once been impressed at the inequalities on which "civilization as we know it" rested. When he turned his back on such knowledge, he had himself dug the pit from which came this agonized cry in 1914.

James did not live to see the end of the war, and the role played by his own young America in coming to rescue "European civilization," much as one of his own rich romantic American characters might arrive on the European stage to act out a drama of innocence and experience. There was the same misunderstanding about aims and ideals on the part of the rescuer and the rescued. There was the same feeling by the Americans, after the rescue, of having been "used." But there was the same ambiguity, too, about the role of the wealthy savior, America. Were his own motives so pure? Had not this romantic rich rescuer perhaps fooled himself at home before he was fooled abroad?

If there was a "Maggie" in this actual, historical drama, it was Woodrow Wilson. For Wilson, like Maggie, was cast in the role of the wonder-worker. He was the free moral agent in the situation, able to convert lower to higher by true idealism, and so redeem the beautiful old culture of Europe from its ancient burden of evil. He was to cure the flaw in the crystal.

The parallel extends further, in a rather remarkable way. For Wilson at Paris, like Maggie at "Fawns," had his "time of testing," when the question was whether to expose the players in the game—the great international card game of the treaties after the war—or merely to correct his own "deformity" with respect to what the other players wanted of him.

Wilson decided as Maggie decided, not to expose the players, but instead give way on the more embarrassing points of his own high program. In this way the form could be saved; and no sacrifice would be required by anyone—except the actual losers, the Central Powers. Theirs was to be the role of Charlotte. Thus the Golden Bowl of Europe was put together again, much as Maggie put the broken pieces together, and the official forms were gone through at Paris and Geneva in much the manner of the tea party at Eaton Square.

In real life, the story of course went on to the sequel. The proud vanquished power was not bound by a "moral act" which had cost the victors nothing, but instead actually gained them more. It was soon struggling against the ambiguous "silken cord" which for a moment held. The cord broke in real life, as it must have in the aftermath of James's story. The Golden Bowl crashed once more.

Was James himself saved from the crash of the Golden Bowl, the "treachery" of the long period before the war in which his work was essentially done? I think in a certain sense he was— saved by that same personal nonparticipation in "the great world" which allowed him to see it with glamour. He is not to be praised for cultivating the glamour and leaving the falsity ambiguous. Yet as to his own personal fate, I think it fair to say that renunciation saved him. He did not eat of the fruit. He was virtually a monk of art, a dedicated, withdrawn soul.

This almost religious dedication is illustrated in a remarkable personal memorandum found by Percy Lubbock and published by him in his introduction to James's letters. It is a notation made apparently during the troubled early months of the war itself, and, as you see, is a sort of conversation of the artist with himself, or communion with his muse:

"I take this up again after an interruption," the note begins; "—I in fact throw myself upon it under the *secousse* of its being brought home to me even more than I expected that my urgent material reasons for getting settled at productive work again are of the most imperative . . . I needn't expatiate on this—on the sharp consciousness of this hour of the dimly-dawning New Year, I mean; I simply make an appeal to all the powers and forces and divinities to whom I've ever been loyal and who haven't failed me yet—after all: never, never yet! . . . Momentary side-winds break in every now and then but I come back, I come back, I all throbbingly and yearningly and passionately, oh *mon bon*, come back to this way that is clearly the only one in which I can do anything now, and that will open out to me more and more, and that has overwhelming reasons pleading all beautifully in its breast. . . .

"Oh celestial, soothing, sanctifying process, with all the high sane forces of the sacred time fighting through it, on my side! Let me fumble it gently and patiently out—with fever and fidget laid to rest—as in the old enchanted months! It only looms, it only shines and shimmers, *too* beautiful and too interesting; it only hangs there too rich and too full and with too much to give and to pay; it only presents itself too admirably and too vividly, too straight and square and vivid, as a little organic and effective Action. . . .

"I seem to emerge from the recent bad days—the fruit of blind accident—and the prospect clears and flushes, and my poor blest old Genius pats me so admirably and lovingly on the back that I turn, I screw round, and bend my lips to passionately, in my gratitude, kiss its hands."

One would have to go to the literature of religious mysticism to find the parallel of this expression. The muse that appears here, however, is not the great universal muse, with her deep golden note that rings upon necessity. This angel, as you see, is still the one who waves the wand of enchantment. She is a romantic. And the time itself (the war time) which only a few months ago was too tragic and black for words has now become, under the wand, high and sacred.

When you remember, however, that this is the expression of

a man over seventy years of age, you can see how young in heart James's dedication to his genius had kept him. One might say of Henry James and his whole long enchanted pilgrimage what Conrad says of the romantic young African explorer in *Heart of Darkness*. Obscure evils lay about him; one could not tell what lay behind the ambiguous appearance of things; the event was to prove the illusory nature of much of the quest. But as for the pilgrim, the artist himself, "glamour urged him on, glamour kept him unscathed."

CHAPTER VII

Henry Adams and the Hand of the Fathers

~~~~~~

A FEW months before the outbreak of the war in 1914, Henry James in England received a letter from his friend Henry Adams in America. James wrote in reply:

"I have your melancholy outpouring of the 7th, and I know not how better to acknowledge it than by the full recognition of its unmitigated blackness. *Of course* we are lone survivors, of course the past is at the bottom of an abyss—if the abyss *has* any bottom; of course, too, there's no use talking unless one particularly *wants* to. But the purpose, almost, of my printed divagations [*Notes of a Son and Brother*] was to show you that one *can*, strange to say, still want to—or at least behave as if one did . . . I still find my consciousness interesting—under *cultivation* of the interest. Cultivate it *with* me, dear Henry—that's what I hoped to make you do—to cultivate yours for all that it has in common with mine . . . You see I still, in presence of life (or what you deny to be such) have reactions—as many as possible . . . It's, I suppose, because I am that queer monster, the artist, an obstinate finality, an inexhaustible sensibility. . . ."

Henry Adams, in March of 1914, was already referring, it seems, to that "abyss" which Henry James was to see open a few months later. The two men had much in common. Almost of the same years, they were both products of "the whole long age" before the War that James wrote of. They were world tourists, spiritually, each having left his simpler, more puritan home background to look for an education in "the great world." They were fastidious, self-conscious men, instinctively exclusive in taste, shrinking from everything "common" with about an equal aversion. Both had as little as possible to do with the general public, and the general public had in both cases reciprocated.

But there were important differences, as James's letter indicated. James was that "queer monster, the artist." Adams was not. He was not quite the artist, as he was not quite the scientist, the historian, the politician, or anything else specific. Adams had halfheartedly tried everything, but given himself to nothing. James had given himself absolutely to his mistress, Art.

That told the difference, and why James still "had reactions," and was "an obstinate finality." True, James had given himself aesthetically to what was partly an illusion—the glamour of the Golden Bowl of high European civilization. But this glamour, this enchantment, had led him on all these years, had kept him, in a sense, unscathed. It could do so as long as the "long age" held, and the enchantment was not broken either by James's personal participation in it, or by rude outside events.

Adams was no innocent, no glamourist, and no pure dedicated spirit. Unlike James, he was drawn himself to participate in the glittering life of power. We suspect that if a place in the sun had been offered him at the right time, on his own terms, he would quickly enough have taken it.

What were his terms? They were the terms of hereditary aristocracy, very much the same sort of terms of "high civilization" that James so admired in Europe. The trouble was that Adams's opportunity, like his heredity, lay in America. But America was a democracy, and alas would not meet Adams's aristocratic terms. They presupposed a privileged elite, an established social class, a political hereditary system, that simply did not exist in the United States. Adams could succeed in the hereditary political pattern only by joining in the democratic political melée. But this is what a fourth-generation Adams would not care to do.

Henry Adams is our outstanding case of the hereditary aristocrat in a democratic world. That was his dilemma, and that is his interest as a figure. Unlike James, Adams signifies more as a character than as an author. He may not be remembered much for anything original in the way of art or thought; he will be remembered for something distinctive in the way of a fate. Adams, who always felt that energy was hopelessly dissipating, never had a better idea for gathering his own than when he sat down to write his *Education.*

He is no simple figure, and *The Education* complicates as much as it explains. Adams showed various instincts, but the instinct he showed most strongly was the instinct for protection. He will not expose himself. Adams was always wrong, but no one else was right! Adams knew nothing, but no one else knew even that much! When he was a young man in the embassy at London, he had already got hold of this formula that was to become a lifetime defense. Writing his brother Charles who was fighting with the Army of the Potomac, Henry was sure that "while my time *may* be wasted, I don't see but that your time *must* prove so."

Charles Francis, Junior, the most downright of the fourth-generation Adamses, made the only possible answer to such a dictum. "Now, my dear fellow," he wrote back from his field camp, where presumably he was well occupied saving the American Union, "speak for yourself."

It is what the reader would like to tell the author of *The Education* many times. Dear Henry, speak for yourself!

Henry would not speak for himself without also claiming to speak for everybody else. If energy seemed to him to be running downhill, then it was necessary to show that the universe was running downhill. At last he found a generation to listen to him, the disillusioned generation after the War. Henry Adams was dead, he could not hear himself being heard, but finally a weary world was ready to listen to Adams's story of futility.

Henry Adams was in a good position for disillusionment, this position of a hereditary aristocrat in a world that had outlived that pattern. He fits very well Thomas Mann's description of the Biblical Joseph, that he was "late . . . in time and in his soul, a very good specimen of a descendant, volatile, witty, difficult and interesting."

Such was Adams, and not only was he a "difficult descendant," but a descendant of a difficult tradition. His fathers were all a little like that. They had all fought in their way for American democracy, and all distrusted democracy except when run by an Adams. They had all found themselves opponents of European empire and class rule, and yet as Henry wrote, they all owed much to Europe and the aristocratic idea. The truth is the Adamses were in a class by themselves—aristocrats in America, democrats in Europe. The home estate was just on the edge of the New

World, and faced back toward the Old. The Adamses had never looked into the interior. Henry as a boy could watch the ships leaving Boston harbor for Europe, and they seemed to be asking him to go along. But he also expected to be sent to Washington.

The Adams world was an in-between world, in between the Old and the New, in between the eighteenth century and the twentieth, in between *Vox Dei* and *Vox Populi*, in between religion and science, in between science and politics, in between politics and art. Only one thing seemed a certainty: the place and integrity of the Family itself, under God's will and instruction. But suppose even this certainty, during the nineteenth century, should begin to look doubtful? If the Adams line should feel this rock of faith in the family shake—or even worse, the rock of Faith itself—it would be truly tragic. And something of this sort seems to have happened about the fourth generation if not, as Brooks Adams insisted it already had happened, in the second.

The result in the fourth generation was the books on social decay written by Brooks and the books on the degradation of energy written by Henry.

This was why Henry, who had seen his own tradition fading away, was in an excellent position to speak for the traditional world that broke up in Europe in 1914. His disillusion had sharpened his eyes for disintegration anywhere. Long before 1914 he had foreseen the threat to Henry James's Golden Age of British Empire of the expansive force that lay in imperial Germany. He had no answer or remedy himself. Like T. S. Eliot, his eyes were open only to disaster. But after the War, he looked like the very spirit of postwar disillusion.

Young men who had seen meaningless sacrifice in Flanders

hailed him as brother. He would have understood Dadaism in Paris, and Noel Coward in London. Henry Adams's *Education*, that had got nowhere in an age of belief, got everywhere in an age of unbelief. It took its place with Proust and Hemingway and Joyce and Eliot as postwar literature, the literature of the Lost Generation of exiles and international wanderers, which had followed on Henry James's beglamoured generation of pilgrims and aesthetes.

Here was a postwar mind that had somehow developed in the prewar period. If Henry James expected to comfort such a mind with his own rapturous aesthetic creed, he was doomed to disappointment. An Adams, unable to comfort himself, would not be comforted by anyone else.

No woman, Henry Adams wrote in his *Education*, had ever driven him wrong; no man had ever driven him right. This I think is the clue to Adams's life and to the meaning of his books, especially the later works which often seem to disguise more than they reveal. His life was a struggle between the line of the Fathers in him, the Presidents and the public men who set the pattern for a career for which he was not fitted, and his own nature, which was sensitive, intuitive, artistic. Adams's writings break down into the books he wrote for men, and the books he wrote for women, and they are miles apart. Women urged him to follow his own nature, and Adams wrote *Esther* and *Mont St. Michel and Chartres* for them, and charming letters such as those from the South Seas. Men tried to draw him into public life, or told him to write history, and Adams broke himself in two again and again trying to live up to the dictates of the Fathers.

[169]

The conflict went on and on, to the last, a public man versus a private man, as Mabel La Farge, one of his favorite nieces, has written in her sensitive memoir. The public man still wrote for the world of men, wrote *The Rule of Phase*, for example, to satisfy the Fathers. It was all power and force and intellect, and described a universe without a spark of feeling in it. And it was a universe doomed, doomed to prove that a world that had allowed the Adams line of public men to run out must itself have run down. The rejected Fathers and their hard Law must be vindicated though the heavens fall.

Then there was *Chartres*, which turned against Law and the Fathers completely. It turned the universe over to the pity and caprice of lovely woman, who had always led Adams aright, and would forgive him where he had gone astray. It was as far on one side as *The Rule of Phase* was on the other, but at least it expressed the private man, the man of feeling, instead of the public manikin of irony and erudition. "No, sir, you can't do it, you can't impress God that way," William James had bluntly written Adams concerning *The Rule of Phase*—not by "wit and learning" in treating a tragic subject. Adams knew it at heart. *Chartres* admitted that God couldn't be mocked. It threw Adams's case upon the mercy of the Virgin.

As for *The Education* itself, it was on both sides at once; it answered everything double. One sentence confessed what the next denied. The inner and humbled Henry Adams begged to be understood for the tyranny worked upon his nature by the outer Henry Adams and the pattern of the Fathers. At the same time, the outer Henry Adams, with mockery and irony, defended himself against the world.

HENRY ADAMS AND THE HAND OF THE FATHERS

The preface to *The Education* came as close as Adams could publicly to asking for understanding. The preface said that it was only the manikin the book presented. Yet—and who can miss the whispered plea?—it just hinted that there was a suffering man behind the mask. "It must have the air of reality," he wrote of his puppet figure, "must be taken for real; must be treated as though it had life. Who knows? Possibly it had."

Naturally it had, and I think you can find the place in *The Education* that tells of the first serious break in Adams's life, which drove part of him inside a mask. It was when he was a young man in the years just after the Civil War and had put himself in a fair way to achieve a career that for once did not depend on the family position and the family inheritance—all that "nest of associations" signified by "the First Church, the Boston State House, Beacon Hill, John Hancock and John Adams, Mount Vernon Street and Quincy."

Young Henry had been his father's secretary in the embassy at London during the war years. After the War, Henry had perhaps hoped for an appointment in the incoming administration of General Grant, which he and his friends had somehow believed would be a "reform administration." The appointment, or whatever, did not come, and neither did "reform." Instead America's gaudiest period of high finance set in, and Henry with his brothers Brooks and Charles decided to take to their pens, and set up as critics of those public affairs which they had not been invited to help run themselves.

The result was the "Session" articles which appeared in magazines both in England and America. They were something new in American journalism: closely reasoned, factual articles exposing the inner workings of finance and railroads and government policy. They anticipated by many years the "muckraking" journalism of the twentieth century, and were in fact to be rediscovered as almost the first serious efforts at analyzing finance capitalism in the United States.

The important thing for our story is that they had a great success. Even Henry Adams, who could make anything look like failure, from Harvard College to God, had to admit that this venture looked like "a sufficient success." The articles were reprinted, pirated, and made political capital of by the thousands or hundreds of thousands of copies, all over the United States.

This venture was probably the nearest Henry Adams could come to reconciling his particular ambitions and divided genius. It was close to the world of action, which fascinated him, but away from contact with the public, which distressed him. If it was not actually literature, for which he had real feeling and talent, it was in that direction. Above all, it promised to give him a name of his own, an independent position, and a sense of confidence in his own powers, from which point a talented young man might go nearly anywhere.

It even showed that a fourth-generation Adams, with all his hereditary handicaps upon his head, might make a place for himself in a democracy.

But then what happened?

"No sooner had Adams" (wrote Adams in his *Education*) "made at Washington what he modestly hoped was a sufficient success, than his whole family set upon him to drag him away. For the first time since 1861 his father interposed; his mother entreated; and his brother Charles argued and urged him to go to Harvard-College."

It was Henry Adams's little theory in *The Education* that his "failures" were all due either to lack of power in himself, or opportunity in the world. Either he lived in the wrong century, or else he lacked the right equipment; in any case, fate always stepped in to snatch victory from him.

Here is the instance that does not fit this theory. Neither Adams's powers nor his opportunity had failed; nor did fate step in, unless you call family opinion fate—which, in a deeper sense, it was. But this "failure" lay simply in Adams's own willingness to follow the family opinion instead of his own.

We happen to have evidence that Adams himself did have a different opinion from the family's in this case, and had already chosen differently on the question of Harvard. For it so happens that the offer from Harvard College first came to Henry when he was alone in England, about to return to America, and Henry without the family had decided against it. Henry with the family, however, was too much for Henry. When he arrived in America and was met by the solid family front, he decided against his decision. It is quite right as *The Education* puts it: to Harvard College went Henry, aged thirty-three, because, as Henry aged seventy wrote, his brother argued, his mother entreated, his father interposed.

It is not hard I think to find the family's reasons for the pressure put on Henry, and the point is that they were precisely reasons of family. Henry's "Session" articles, while they might be true, gave comfort to the wrong party, the non-Adams party. It is true, the Adams party was for the moment quite non-Adams,

and full of improper people. But an Adams would do his reform-
ing inside his party and not outside of it, in public. Henry's articles might be Henry's success—they might be Henry's salvation—
but they were an Adams scandal, and they had to be stopped.

"So, at twenty-four hours' notice," says the autobiography in
summary, "he broke his life in halves again in order to begin a
new education on lines he had not chosen, in subjects for which
he cared less than nothing; in a place he did not love, and before
a future which repelled." You must allow here for Adams's usual
exaggeration for the sake of neatness and symmetry. But I think
the general sense is true. The incident seems crucial in Henry's
life. This is where the sense of defeat begins. This is where the
chapter heads in the autobiography become names of despair. Nor
can you explain it on external grounds, for apparently this is
just where Henry went on from success to success. He now became a brilliant teacher, a successful editor, a celebrated historian
—elected president of the American Historical Association. The
defeat was an inner one, just as those chapter headings in *The
Education* tell an inner and not an outer story. Only to the inner
sense could these most successful years of Adams's life, after his
removal to Harvard and before his wife's death, be called *"Chaos"*
and *"Failure."*

The next chapter heading must tell an inner story too—*Twenty
Years After*—since it fails to tell an outer story at all. Twenty
years after what? Twenty years after the death of Mrs. Adams,
of whose existence there is no hint in *The Education.* Yet in this
same *Education* she was certainly the most important single character besides the author, as her death by her own hand was cer-

[174]

tainly, tragically, the most important single event. This was the greatest "breaking in halves" of Adams's life. No wonder we must read *The Education* by opposites! Disguising as it reveals, this is the place where it reveals most by telling nothing at all.

Nor can any outsider pretend to fill in this gap which Adams and his intimates have seen fit to leave blank. Adams had married Marian Hooper in 1872. He resigned from Harvard in 1878 and moved to Washington, where the Adamses became the center of a select and brilliant circle of Washington society. They were building a large house, designed by Richardson, just across the park from the White House itself—the hereditary focus of an Adams's ambition. Mrs. Adams's death occurred just as they were to move into the new home.

But Henry had long ago given up any real purpose to take part in national politics. The removal to Washington, the select dinner parties, the private intimacy with public men, the new house on Lafayette Square—all these were at best the simulacrum, not the substance, of a public career according to the way of the Fathers. No woman, Adams wrote, had ever led him astray, and we cannot believe he excepted his wife. Did Marian Adams instinctively distrust this life in the capital, to which they were now all the more committed by the house they had just built? She seemed discontented with her own lack of life direction. Did she perhaps feel that Adams's private indulgence of a passion for politics which he could no longer hope to exercise openly only increased the indirection of both their lives? Did this enter into her dilemma?

I do not know. Other reasons are suggested for her act: that she had brooded over the death a year before of her father, of whom she had been very fond. There is the fact of childlessness, a matter of special importance, one might suppose, to Henry Adams himself, bound up as it would be with continuity of the hereditary line.

We do know that it was some years before Adams could face returning to the Washington home, and that the experience marked the turning of the private man toward a different element in his nature—the feminine element—and away from the pattern of the Fathers. It was at this time that Adams wanted to renounce his historical writings, and professed his regard for only one thing he had ever written, the novel *Esther*.

Esther is not a great novel, but it is about a woman's predicament; it involves among other things the death of her father, and the question of the heroine's faith in life; and it is written with sympathy for the woman's point of view. By all reports, the character of Esther was based specifically on Mrs. Adams, but the important thing is that it is a woman's book, and that Henry Adams in his bereavement liked to recall it. Adams had finally chosen, at least privately, between the Fathers and the Mothers. He had chosen the Mothers, and dethroned the Fathers from their rule over his soul.

Not that this happened all at once. Both Henry and Brooks Adams had long been interested in "feminism," and especially their theory (like the medieval one) of woman as the "fixed" element in society and man the roving one. As early as 1876 Henry had lectured on "The Primitive Rights of Women." Certain women among Adams's relatives and friends had been favorites, all the way from a grandmother down to a half-dozen real or nominal "nieces." These women saw and felt in him, apparently, what no man had seen or felt. In the South Seas, where Adams traveled during his years of exile, he had a chance to study matriarchy itself, as an actual surviving institution, and he left as a record the privately printed *Memoirs of Marau Taaroa, Last Queen of Tahiti.*

The death of Mrs. Adams touched this line of feeling with religious intensity. From this point (as Mr. Robert Spiller has also noted in his study of the book *Esther*), the road runs plainly to *Chartres* and the twelfth-century Virgin. This was the step from secular to sacred, from matriarchy to mariolatry, but it was a logical step granting Adams's early and fundamental sense of conflict between the feminine elements in his nature and an over-masculine world that he was supposed to master. It was perhaps too late to straighten out what stood for law and what for love in the real world of men and women, and so put together the broken halves of his life. But it was possible to go back in fancy to a bygone world in which he might reclaim the lost heritage of his nature—beauty and feeling and woman's intuition.

The "Prayer to the Virgin of Chartres," as Mabel La Farge has intimated, told the spiritual history that *The Education* disguised or was silent upon. This was the enigmatic poem in manuscript, found among Adams's papers at his death, and not published until Mrs. La Farge printed it in her memoir. It cannot be called a success as a work of art—*Mont St. Michel and Chartres* was much more that—but more than any other writing it traced the intellectual route by which Adams arrived at the altar he set up in private. It is well worth examination, especially by those who have tended to take Adams at his own public evaluation. It began:

[177]

THE WIND BLEW FROM THE EAST

GRACIOUS LADY:—
Simple as when I asked your aid before;
 Humble as when I prayed for grace in vain
Seven hundred years ago; weak, weary, sore
 In heart and hope, I ask your help again.

You, who remember all, remember me;
 An English scholar of a Norman name.
I was a thousand who then crossed the sea
 To wrangle in the Paris school for fame.

When your Byzantine portal was still young
 I prayed there with my master Abailard;
When Ave Maris Stella was first sung,
 I helped to sing it there with St. Bernard.

And so the verses go on to sketch briefly what *Chartres* builds out more fully—the time and place that Adams had now fled to in fancy and where he conceived that the inner Adams might have had a chance for expression. That was northern France in the day of the building of the cathedrals, when the Virgin Mary ruled the Church and the Church ruled much of the world, and both together in this particular place inspired some of man's greatest and loveliest works.

To understand the salutation "Gracious Lady," however, we must think not only of the twelfth-century Virgin, but of the medieval Lady of Spiritual Love, whom we know most familiarly now in Dante's Beatrice of the *Paradiso*. Lady Beatrice, we recall, had been a real woman adored afar by Dante when she was alive. But after her death her role was even more important; she became the poet's spiritual mentor in divine philosophy and guide

[178]

to the throne of the Virgin in heaven. Following once more a clue of Mrs. La Farge, we understand that the memory of Mrs. Adams figures in this invocation of "Gracious Lady." She has assumed a place somewhat like that of Dante's Beatrice, as an ideal mentor in spiritual matters. While it is the twelfth-century Virgin to whom the prayer is actually addressed, we know that this personal significance often lies just beneath the surface.

But it is the historical recapitulation of Adams's spiritual conflict that most interests us, and whose meaning we are trying to decipher. Significant in this connection is the character of the twelfth-century Henry Adams. He is an "English scholar of a Norman name," and do we not already foresee, for the imaginary Adams, the fate of the real one? Is not this the hand of the Fathers all over again? For what could be more socially correct for an Adams to have been in the twelfth century—out of all the million possible ancestors—than an Englishman of a Norman name; and if this were but the instinct for family correctness, would it not again be the death of the real man? Would it not mean that, even in the twelfth century, a Henry Adams could not be among the indistinguishable, even if to be so were to be one of the unknown architects of Chartres itself?

This choice may be a witting and sorry one, rather than for pure preference. Possibly Adams is telling himself that he *would* have been just that in the twelfth century, an English scholar of a Norman name. Even then, he may be saying, he would have had to turn back across the channel to reach the scene of the great flowering. Even then he would have been outside the common cause of faith. He would have come only "to wrangle in the Paris schools for fame."

Now, whether Adams saw that the wrangling for *fame* rather than for truth was also part of his twelfth-century doom, we cannot tell. From what follows, I rather think that he did not see this distinction even in his prayer to the Virgin—that this was part of the unconfessed rather than the confessed error. It is the "wit and learning" all over again, which William James said would never impress God. But in any case, it was to wrangle and not to believe that Adams saw himself as part of the great period of Catholic belief. And we see already that, though he had also prayed for grace to the Virgin, he had prayed in vain; and this thought is developed as we go on:

> For centuries I brought you all my cares,
>   And vexed you with the murmurs of a child;
> You heard the tedious burdens of my prayers;
>   You could not grant them, but at least you smiled.

Whatever this verse may mean in terms of Adams's problem, it must mean something different from the earlier verse about the "wrangling scholar." The petitioning child and the wrangling scholar must be different aspects of Adams's personality at least from his own view; though to the observer they might be closely related. The scholar is looking for truth and, if he merely wrangles, failing to find it; the petitioner is asking for mercy, for a boon, perhaps for an indulgence which not even the Virgin could grant. But the one character does not admit personal need while the other does—a most important distinction in the case of one hoping for help.

Just what these boons and murmurs might be, in terms of Adams's inner life, remains obscure, but we must believe they are

closely related to the central conflict. Was it the boon of greater
energy that Adams asked? He seemed always preoccupied by the
question of energy. We know that his general energy was such
that he could do the necessary research and writing to produce
the eight or ten volumes of his *History* in a relatively short time
for such a task, meanwhile carrying on other work such as teaching and editing. Yet his physical inheritance, or illness, as he half
suggests in *The Education*, may have left him limited in some
particular energy, perhaps emotional, which was the subject of
these murmurs against fate. On the other hand, psychological
factors may have been the more important even with respect to
such a matter; and the petition here may have been for the grace
to overcome these difficulties in himself. There is the further
possibility that the murmurs and tedious burden represented simply Adams's desire for success and fame according to the hereditary pattern, and were indulgences which heaven must deny because they could be got only by the genuine efforts of the man
himself. In this last case we would find the scholar wrangling for
fame and the child begging a boon identical.

But in any case, whether Adams asked for what fate absolutely had denied, or whether he asked insincerely for things
which only his sincere faith and effort could have brought him,
it is evident that the boons asked *were*, in a real sense, indulgences
which could not be granted. What signifies is Adams's own description of them as the murmurs and tedious burdens of a child,
who, unlike a mature man, asks for purely wishful things.

The prayer so far, in any case, gives us a Henry Adams with
his conflict unsettled. Whatever kept the genuine nature from
freeing itself is still present, and it is interesting to ask whether

some way of emancipation had ever been possible. Surely we must allow within the range of possibility an actual triumph of the genuine man over the necessities that confronted him. Was the celebrated Adams name and heredity, in itself, such a handicap as to amount to "fate" for Henry Adams?

Charles Francis Adams, Junior, a fourth-generation Adams himself, made perhaps as true a comment on the subject of celebrated ancestors as can be made when, in the biography of his father, he described the latter's experience of five years of activity in the Massachusetts legislature. Charles Francis, Senior, too, was a marked man, "ticketed for life," as Henry wrote of himself, and he ventured only with misgivings upon his first attempt at public life. His son wrote, however, that the experience was happy and encouraging rather than not. "Gradually and insensibly he came to realize that no prejudice, either personal or because of family, really existed toward him; but, on the contrary, the great mass of the community actually felt an interest in him and a kindliness to him because of his name and descent—an interest and a kindliness which, had he himself possessed only a little of the sympathetic quality, had he been only a degree less reserved in nature and repellent in manners, would have found expression, then and afterwards, in ways which could not have been otherwise than grateful to him."

I think the same comment might stand for Henry Adams's case. The "fate" of having celebrated ancestors was a matter of attitude inside Henry, rather than of circumstances outside him.

Nor can we take at face value the theory of Henry in his *Education* that he would have been "made" in John Adams's time by the same heredity which unmade him in his own time. John

Adams was not a fourth-generation celebrated Adams. Henry Adams was not an unknown poor schoolteacher. Henry could start from where he started, with three generations of famous names behind him, or he could imagine himself in the situation of his great grandfather, starting with no name and from nowhere, like Abraham Lincoln or Ulysses Grant, but he could not argue they were the same situation.

No, I fear the fatal element was much closer to simple pride than to anything irreducible in Henry's situation. In this sense, the family pattern became a handicap; in this sense it was "fate." The triumph of the personal Henry Adams would have meant the humility of the family Henry Adams, and that was not the sort of humility that Henry was prepared to cultivate.

There remains the further possibility, even in later life, of his recognizing fate for the insuperable fact that it appeared to have become. In other words, there would seem to have been possible a whole view of life providing it were now truly a tragic view.

Most of Adams's writings, as a matter of fact, had called logically for a tragic view—certainly *The Rule of Phase*, as William James insisted; just as certainly, in its different way, *Democracy*, as Mr. Commager has implied in his essay on Adams. If the fate of humanity is what Adams said it must be, in *The Rule of Phase*; if the fate of America is such as Adams claimed its institutions inevitably determine it to be, in *Democracy*; then erudition and irony toward the one prospect and flippancy and derision toward the other were pitifully weak responses for any human being to make.

If one were to ask further why the tragic view of life was denied Adams, we can only return to our central point. We are dealing with the nemesis of a sense of born superiority. And if Adams felt himself above the common human lot to begin with, the same assumption insisted he was above the common lot even after his nemesis had treated him with uncommon severity.

This becomes a tragic fact to the observer, who realizes that fate had abused Adams's merit to about the extent that Adams had thought his merit above fate. It explains too why Adams is more important than his work. For we can see Adams as a tragic figure, while Adams in his writings could never see himself as other than an ironic or a pathetic, in a word, a futile one.

The case of Mr. T. S. Eliot, another son, or grandson, of New England troubled by the hand of the Fathers, shows how far the nemesis of a sense of superiority may drive a distinguished artist without making him a tragic poet. A truly tragic view of life brings unity; despair, like that expressed by "The Waste Land," remains a matter of division. In Adams's case it should be plain that his irony, derision, self-mockery, parade of erudition, and occasional pathos (as in *Chartres*) showed in their various ways the divided man. Even the "Prayer to the Virgin" went on in alternations between Adams the wrangling scholar and Adams the erring child:

> If then I left you, it was not my crime,
>   Or if a crime, it was not mine alone.
> All children wander with the truant Time.
>   Pardon me too! You pardoned once your Son!
>
> For He said to you:—"Wist not that I
>   Must be about my Father's business?" So,
> Seeking his Father he pursued his way
>   Straight to the Cross towards which we all must go.

HENRY ADAMS AND THE HAND OF THE FATHERS

So I too wandered off among the host
  That racked the earth to find the father's clue.
I did not find the Father, but I lost
  What now I value more, the Mother,—You!

I thought the fault was yours that foiled my search;
  I turned and broke your image on its throne,
Cast down my idol, and resumed my march
  To claim the father's empire for my own.

Crossing the hostile sea, our greedy band
  Saw rising hills and forests in the blue;
Our father's kingdom in the promised land!
  —We seized it, and dethroned the father too.

And now we are the Father, with our brood,
  Ruling the Infinite, not Three but One;
We made our world and saw that it was good;
  Ourselves we worship, and we have no Son. . . .

Perhaps no further comment is needed on the more personal elements suggested in these lines. What concerns us is the historical analogy which the scholar Adams has built up to explain the erring child—and which we cannot help but feel is in part a defense even against his own impulse to confession.

Yet something may be said for the victim of a historic process. Descendant of a long line of Protestant patriarchs who tended to put the Law above the Prophets and the Old Testament above the New, Henry Adams had felt the harsher breath of his tradition, while a certain exclusiveness had kept him from knowing its more grateful side. (The Adamses never could stand an Emerson or a Channing.) It is not hard to make out the meanings in the verses.

The Father stands for Law and Rule—the hereditary Adams pattern. The Mother stands for Love, and Henry Adams had got an overdose of law, while far too little scope had been allowed the principle of love.

The effort to trace this conflict back to the founder of Christianity himself is surely a dubious expedient. It is the witty scholar we are sure who here makes a play on words in order to try to make us believe that Jesus was seeking Rule more than Love—or some other kind of rule *than* love.

Nevertheless, we know that the Church, unfortunately, after the manner of institutions, tended to lean toward the Law, and perhaps because of the personality of its first great instituter, Paul, leaned away from love even when it stood for Love. And one half of the condition for any sort of human love, whether she stood in the relation of Wife, Mother, or Daughter, was allowed no such standing in the Church as had Father, Husband, Son. Yet the womanly, the motherly, the daughterly had to come into the Church somehow, and come in they did by way of the Virgin Mother (even, too, as the Daughter of St. Anne), who slowly and surely worked her way up to the very top, above the Trinity, as Adams delightedly insisted in *Chartres*.

Then came the break in the historic process which produced the actual Henry Adams—the Reformation—and there was a certain misfortune in the fact that the chief reason for the break, the need of the human mind to be sure it looks at the thing instead of merely the image of it, struck most hard at what had become most an image, the Virgin Mary. For with the removal of the image, much of what she had stood for was removed also, so that in this respect the Church was back to something like the barrenness as well as the purity of the primitive communion, except so far as it tried the even more doubtful expedient of bringing in the missing element by way of curling the hair and beard and softening the lips and eyes of its founder, the truly long-suffering Jesus.

What might be valid, then, in Adams's analogy is the dominance, especially in Calvinism, of the Father as all-powerful judge over the Mother as the agent of love and forgiveness. I need not dwell on the judicial-ecclesiastical-patriarchal type which actually did dominate so much of the life of early New England. Brooks Adams, in fact, wrote a book, *The Founding of Massachusetts,* to show the terror of a regime built on the identification of God's will with the edicts of a small group of self-righteous men. And even the ancestral mother, Abigail Adams, could collaborate in the harsher sort of Puritan rule with a firmness that would have pleased a Winthrop or Mather, as witness this admonition from a letter written to her eleven-year-old son, John Quincy Adams: ". . . for dear as you are to me, I would much rather you should have found your grave in the ocean you have crossed, or that an untimely death should crop you in your infant years, than see an immoral, profligate, or graceless child." In view of this background for the notion of "God, the judge," we can sympathize with the fourth-generation Henry Adams, the exception to the family rule for its men, not judicial and stern, but sensitive, shy, aesthetic, intuitive, in a sense, feminine, who yet found himself thrust perforce into a ready-made masculine mold which broke him rather than he it.

So much the historic analogy explains; yet we cannot press it to the length that the arguing scholar Adams here presses it without its once more becoming false. With regard to the question of woman's place, for instance, there is the other side to the medal of Puritan Protestantism. After all, the simple fact was—and it was a fact of simplicity—that wife and mother probably never before in the world had found truer places of respect than they did in Puritan New England. Respect was the key word, not chivalry or idealization, and before we are sure that women prefer chivalry to respect, we ought to hear the testimony of the two other principals in Dante Alighieri's triangle of sacred and profane love: that is, of the honored but unused Lady, Beatrice herself, and of the used but unhonored woman, the nameless wife who bore Dante seven children in ten years and afterwards passed from his life we know not how.

The very meaning of the Puritan movement had to do with the integration of truth—closing the gap between sacred and profane—and even when it looked as if the integer had been made needlessly narrow, it was in a real sense an effort to make a whole. Nothing became more characteristic of Puritan New England than that a worthy place was to be found for a thing or no place made for it at all. If it were in fact sin, it was to be cast out rather than accommodated, and this done withal in the world and not out of it.

True, this made for a strain, especially upon consciences sharpened to an exaggerated sense of sin, so that they saw it in areas of human life which Nature herself knew were good, for example in the natural rest and pleasure periods of living. It was just this unhappy tension, somehow prolonged into a more liberal day, which in fact produced such neo-New England Puritans as Henry Adams and T. S. Eliot, the conscience-stricken but not the conscience-cleared.

Yet we cannot take the testimony of the conscience-stricken that a new day of grace had not come to pass, that the same discrimination that had sought to leave out bad could not leave in good. There is no question what Henry Adams wanted to bring back: it was natural emotion, intuition, freedom, forgiveness, mutual pleasure—all that makes for the livability and flow of life as distinguished from (even when prospered by) its mere ordering. These he began to see, somewhat romantically, all centered in the nature of woman. It was she who refused to abide by masculine law, whether human or divine; it was she who worked according to another principle, inspiration, favor, desire, creative instinct—love. And so it was that the stricken widower returned to the past age that he felt had put woman at her highest: which had celebrated, adored, worshiped her. Yet we cannot take his word that the spirit he wanted, and which his inherited and legalistic conscience had frowned upon, could not have been found in his own world and time by anyone who cared to look for it where it actually was.

The rediscovery of most of what Adams meant by the Mother—Nature—had been the great intellectual movement of his family's time. Speaking broadly, it had transformed almost every sphere of life, from government to poetry, and affected almost every part of the Western world, except here and there an insulated spot like the Adams family estate itself. New England itself was in large part the child of this general movement, whose beginnings Adams had called a "wandering" But if it was a wandering away from the Virgin Mother of the Church (as it

was only in a sense), surely it was a return to the mother of
life, and on a plane, say in Emerson or Wordsworth, that did
credit to the imagination of man. The sense of the wholeness of
truth remained; and if something had temporarily been left out
that was needed, now it was brought back as a good to be loved
and not an evil to be feared.

All this the scholar Adams, in these verses, chose to ignore
even while the penitent begged for the knowledge that would
fill his ignorance. The knowledge, as I have suggested, could
have been found by Adams almost any day a few miles from
the Adams's Braintree, at Emerson's Concord; or if Concord
were too rustic, it could have been got a little later at Camden,
where Whitman lived, not far from Washington. Adams in his
old age did in fact recall that Whitman had provided a place
for Nature in a manner unmistakable, and unmistakably different from the way in which any New Englander would allow
her a place, even when, like Emerson, he seemed to allow her
every place. So far as the education of Henry Adams was concerned, the *Essays* of Emerson would have done just as well as
Whitman's *Leaves of Grass*. Nothing could have been more in-
structive to a young Adams, in fact, than that Emerson as a
young man had left the narrower way of the Law both on a point
of conscience and a point of legalism. For Adams had been fated
to do just the opposite: to stick by the legalism and deny his
conscience. And in a hundred different forms Adams might have
read the lesson that he was looking for: that reason and nature,
love and law, meet at the point of man's conscience, to the greater
and not the lesser freedom of both. Call it grace or virtue, freedom or control, it comes to the same thing. Man's conscience

and his nature work best together, not at cross-purposes; they do so according to man's nature.

Concord, in short, might have saved Adams a trip back to the twelfth century. But Adams no more than T. S. Eliot after him could see truth so close to home. Emerson and Concord looked "naïf" to young Adams. He had to grow much older and sadder before he learned that "naïf" meant native, and became a charming adjunct to truth in medieval France.

Much of the difficulty no doubt—and it was a difficulty—lay in the fact that a great deal of truth, like Emerson, had left off its ecclesiastical vestments. Its face did not shine with the same glory, or frown with the same authority, when reflected in the light of the open sky rather than an altar candle. Transition meant change; change meant death and life; and the process always found some caught in between, with an old world dead and a new powerless to be born.

But the truth is that truth had long been making its way, much of it, into the world, and doing well on the whole. A good case might be made for this having been an object of most religious prophets: to drive truth back into the world. But if truth cannot be divided, one thing is certain: it is a most partial view which holds that ecclesiastical truth by itself is whole in a world that has secularized a good deal of it. The opposite view is equally partial: that truth itself is now profane and need not be abided by.

Henry Adams, one of the victims of the transitional process of his time, shifted characteristically between the two partial views. Sacred truth, to him, was alone respectable, but it was no longer true; secular truth was true enough, but it was not respectable. Poor Esther, in Adams's novel, fell into this predicament, and in fact practically all of Adams's books somehow dealt with it. As if to illustrate it once more, his "Prayer to the Virgin of Chartres" went on to include an absurd "Prayer to the Dynamo," which he asked the Virgin to listen to for a moment as "the last of the strange prayers humanity has wailed."

According to the theory that Adams was pleased to occupy himself with in his later years, the Dynamo in the twentieth century promised to take the place of the Virgin in the twelfth. That was where science was leading the world, he insisted, toward the worship of pure force. Science may well be left to speak for itself, in countries where it is allowed to speak for itself, but it is fairly clear that Adams was not speaking intelligibly for it. The Dynamo may symbolize anything one cares to make it symbolize: pure energy, or progress, or man's ingenuity, or power, or what, but it does not stand for a thing to be worshiped except to those who want to worship such things. In the twentieth century as in the twelfth there might be many who worshiped power or force. True scientists and philosophers, however, continued to be devoted to knowledge and truth, and not to power.

The twentieth century promised confusions enough, as Henry Adams clearly foresaw. Adams's own efforts at clarifying them, however, remain but one confusion the more. Concerning this "Prayer to the Dynamo" there is really no comment that improves upon the one Henry's brother Charles had made long before in a similar connection: let Henry, dear fellow, speak (or pray) for himself.

And so he went on to do, pray to the twelfth-century Virgin, in words not a little moving:

> Help me to see! not with my mimic sight—
>   With yours! which carried radiance, like the sun,
> Giving the rays you saw with—light in light—
>   Tying all sun and stars and worlds in one.
>
> Help me to know! not with my mocking art—
>   With you, who knew yourself unbound by laws;
> Gave God your strength, your life, your sight, your heart,
>   And took from him the Thought that Is—the Cause.
>
> Help me to feel! not with my insect sense,—
>   With yours that felt all life alive in you;
> Infinite heart beating at your expense;
>   Infinite passion breathing the breath you drew!

And finally the prayer concludes upon a note that curiously mingles piety and mockery. The mockery is all for the Father, the piety all for the Mother. It sounds worse blasphemy than it really is, since Adams had simply turned over the attributes of divinity from a Father-God to a Mother-God, as the preceding three verses indicate. But there is little question what the verses tell. They tell the final drastic revolt of the son from the law of the Fathers, his partisan devotion now to the rule of the Mothers. I say partisan and drastic, for it is plain that the new faith is not an integration, but a displacement: of knowledge for instinct, reason for love. The Woman-God now reigns alone and supreme; the Man-God, a total failure, is banished to outer darkness:

> Help me to bear! not my baby load,
>   But yours; who bore the failure of the light,

THE WIND BLEW FROM THE EAST

The strength, the knowledge and the thought of God,—
  The futile folly of the Infinite!

Yes, it is as one-sided and perverse as *The Rule of Phase*, this final private creed of Henry Adams. Where the public man had made the intellect a tyrant, the private man now set up the heart as a simpleton. *Chartres,* the book written for women, pays a dubious compliment to the sex by celebrating irrationality as woman's peculiar virtue. She is not only compassionate, this Virgin Mother according to Adams, she is indulgent, and she is not only indulgent, she is stupid. Whole chapters in *Chartres* are written to show that the Queen of the Court of Heaven can be fooled. Adams had to have it all one way or all another. If the Fathers were reason without love, the Mothers had to be love without reason.

But we can understand the drastic reversal, for it is Henry Adams turning on Henry Adams, turning on the part of himself that had followed a false pattern, confessing the wrong that had been worked not only upon his own life but also, perhaps, upon his wife's. It was drastic, for it was a form of atonement.

This is an overturn and not a cure, and it is not to be recommended for general usage. The ills of the twentieth century would be helped as little by Adams's indulgent Virgin as they would by his tyrannous Dynamo. Yet as to the personal and private case, judgment is not for the outsider. Attitude is everything in such matters as Adams hinted at in his "Prayer to the Virgin"—for I question whether even here he exposed the really private man. We cannot know for certain the private attitude, and whether or not Adams had resolved in some part at least his conflict between Law and Love, and saw that Love, after all, is only a higher form of Law.

CHAPTER VIII

Orpheus in Hell: T. S. Eliot

THIS book deals with the question of turning back and especially the fate of the New World spirit when it returns to old forms. Finally we come to the most deliberate return, or at least articulate and systematic. Where youth and glamour led Henry James, and protected him in a manner to the last; where Henry Adams fled in private and fancy from a broken life to a thirteenth-century image; T. S. Eliot with open eyes and publicly proclaimed for moderns the ancient order. This self-consciousness added a new element, in fact made a new mode. The experiment was incomplete as this was written, and whatever could be said about it could be said only provisionally.

But no one could doubt the seriousness of the venture. This was real and this was earnest, as every line of the poet said, even when it spoke most frivolously. There was something of the ultimate about the effort, as if a man should wall himself around, stone on stone, so as not to escape the position he insisted was inescapable. Here, one said, is farthest north in something or other. God according to Spinoza does infinite things in infinite ways, and no doubt this too had to be done. The man's choice and ordeal exempts his fellows'; this thing, thank God, need not be repeated.

The role of this last pilgrim-exile to the elder world was not to be envied—but one appreciated his report. It was a bitter document. Just the worst time for a journey, as the poet wrote of another pilgrimage, the ways deep and the weather sharp, the very dead of winter. The omens had been bad from the first. Somewhat as the Greek warriors in their disastrous expedition against Syracuse had the misfortune to sail just at the time of the mourning for Adonis, and had to pass between rows of ritual coffins piled on the wharves, so our American sailor had the misfortune to choose the period of the first World War for emigrating to Europe. What wharves were not soon crowded with the coffins of young men dead before their time? The American expedition, if it did not meet physical defeat like the Greek, found its action only led to the most serious moral confusion in our history. What more unhappy day for the voyage of a New World Adonis?

And so his bitter truth. The glamour was gone that had held Henry James. The Golden Bowl was broken, the silver cord loosed. The nymphs had departed. Buried beneath some snow-deep Alps the eagles and the trumpets. The New World knight had come to the Castle Perilous, but there was a great question whether any word could be found to end the bad enchantment. Our pilgrim attempted a few incantations, in a number of dead or strange tongues, but they delivered no one, least of all the knight himself. They were not his truth. He could speak in plain enough English when he wanted to. He said he thought they were in rats' alley. He would show them fear in a handful of dust.

It was not tragedy in the grand manner, nor was it free from some shadow of personal distress. If anything, the whole mode was too much of the time, place, and person, and most of all where it built on other modes, men, and times. Mortality sounded through it all too plainly. Yet it suited what it suited. If the setting called for this sort of muffled tragedy, or grisly comedy, the visiting author would oblige. Like Hieronymo at the Spanish court, or Hamlet at the Danish one, he would play mad and "fit" them—with the play they asked for, and every courtier a part to his order.

This is the poet's truth, bitterly, even jeeringly uttered, conceding good faith to no one in the modern world, but harshest toward his own coterie and himself. "The Hollow Men" marks perhaps the high point of this utterance, in that it is least mixed with the attitudes of piety and impiety that complicate so much of the poet's work. But if his truth is one thing, his teaching is another. The work divides itself between them, between a truth—the poetry—and a way—the essays—and never the twain do meet. You cannot find the Life in either, any more than Madame Sosostris in the horoscope of "The Waste Land" can find the Hanged God. Which is perhaps why the way is so barren and the truth so bitter.

Yet there are hints and glimpses of a good life, haunting suggestions of what might have been or might be. It is not to be found "on the sea or on the islands, not on the mainland, in the desert or the rain land." There is no need to make a mystery of where this "life" had been glimpsed. The poet was a New Englander in his deepest feeling and inheritance, and New England had been the scene that most quickened his spirit. There for a time at least the bird had sung down, the fountain sprung up, and wherever there is a thought of the flow and flowering of life, it is a thought of New England.

There is, for example, the haunting "hermit thrush" passage in the last section of "The Waste Land," which seems to recall a place where the poet had found just a little water and life, "the sound of water over a rock, where the hermit thrush sings in the pine trees." Set off as this is against the painful picture of the dead lands that has just preceded, it is a note of grace—not much grace, but a little—and the note is of New England. If there were any question of this, we have the author's own note on the habitat of the hermit thrush, to make the point clear. Here is the note:

Turdus aonalaschkae pallasii, the hermit-thrush which I have heard in Quebec County [Maine?]. Chapman says (*Handbook of Birds of Eastern North America*) "it is most at home in secluded woodland and thickety retreats. . . . Its notes are not remarkable for variety and volume, but in purity and sweetness of tone and exquisite modulation they are unequaled." Its "water-dripping song" is justly celebrated.

Later on we are going to see how much of the meaning of "The Waste Land" rides, like an iceberg, down in these authors' notes. Here you will have to take my word that these remarks on *Turdus aonalaschkae pallasii* are all to the point. This is the spirit of New England poetry, if I am not mistaken, a shy creature, most at home like Thoreau or Emily Dickinson in secluded woodland and thickety retreats. Its song is not remarkable for variety and volume, but the strain is pure and sweet when it comes. Perhaps also we are to connect this hermit thrush with the one that sings from a bleeding throat in Whitman's "When Lilacs Last in the Dooryard Bloomed"—lilacs being the flower of New England. As for "exquisite modulation of tone," this we must reserve especially for T. S. Eliot's own poetry. In fact the whole passage, with the note, might tell of the original habitat and gift of our poet. That it is meant also to describe the spirit of beauty in Northeastern America is the point I am making.

New England was not T. S. Eliot's birthplace, however. Our poet was born in St. Louis, Missouri, as you would not gather from anything written by our poet. The absence of reference on this point—as Henry James might put it—is somewhat too pronounced. Fourteen or fifteen years do not fall out of a life without a sound, or rather, when they do, the silence becomes a fact in itself. I think this is the case with T. S. Eliot and his blanked-out boyhood in Missouri.

Still, if I am not mistaken, there may be found with a little trouble one or two references to the poet's uncelebrated birthplace. Here is a passage from "The Waste Land":

> But at my back in a cold blast I hear
> The rattle of the bones, and chuckle spread from ear to ear.
> A rat crept softly through the vegetation
> Dragging its slimy belly on the bank
> While I was fishing in the dull canal
> On a winter evening round behind the gashouse
> Musing upon the king my brother's wreck
> And on the king my father's death before him.

[199]

This is what the poet left behind in his journey eastward, this is what is at one's back in a "cold blast" so to speak, and I think it is St. Louis. The "dull canal" might be the Mississippi River, with the St. Louis gashouse landmark above it, and the Negroes on the wharves grinning and shooting craps. But the "rattle of the bones" is death, too; and presumably the pursuit of gain has corrupted this scene. If the boy was fishing for truth in these waters, preparatory to his mission in the world, he had chosen an unlucky spot—or so I understand.

There is another line later in "The Waste Land" that perhaps recalls the Middle West. It interrupts the "hermit thrush" passage I referred to earlier with a memory of "the cicada and dry grass singing"—typical prairie sounds. Since in its context this is also a dreary and rejected note, we are advised to believe that nothing good could have come out of Missouri.

The same might be said for life in the United States as a whole, to judge from another reference to the sounds that the exiled poet heard behind him:

> But at my back from time to time I hear
> The sound of horns and motors, which shall bring
> Sweeney to Mrs. Porter in the spring.
> O the moon shone bright on Mrs. Porter
> And on her daughter
> They wash their feet in soda water. . . .

The horns and motors of the United States are telling only of vulgar love affairs; and whereas people with better customs and traditions have consecrated their lives with the holy water of religious ceremony, in the United States the national refreshment is soda water—or something of this sort I understand from the passage.

Then there is the short poem "Animula," which reads like a miniature spiritual biography, and in it are these lines descriptive of a boy's world:

> The pain of living and the drug of dreams
> Curl up the small soul in the window seat
> Behind the *Encyclopaedia Britannica.*

Here I think we come a little closer to the actual lad in St. Louis. It is the case again of Henry Adams and the ships that were offering to take him to Europe, when most boys are simply living from dawn to dark in the center of the universe. It is like Henry James and the smell of London books in the New York bookshop. Life does not begin in St. Louis; St. Louis is outside the confectioner's glass of the world. Real life would begin only somewhere else, and meanwhile there is the *Encyclopaedia Britannica* for a somewhat heavy dream to drug the pain of living— in St. Louis.

As with Henry James, the comparison is not of one reality against another reality, whatever their comparable qualities, but of one dream against another dream.

Thomas Stearns Eliot was born in 1888, the youngest son of a family of early New England stock. The father was a manufacturer. The mother, a Boston girl, was literary, and the general background was strongly scholastic and ecclesiastical, in the New England manner. The grandfather, the Reverend William Greenleaf Eliot, had been the pioneer who emigrated from

Massachusetts to Missouri before the Civil War. He came from
Harvard Divinity School directly to the Western settlement in
the spirit of this letter written to a friend at the time:

"What matters it if the few years of life be spent in cities or in a
wilderness? I am doubtful but very decided. The self-sacrifice, though
it sometimes comes over one like a cold hand on the heart, in general
means nothing at all. Let them know in some way that a youngster is
ready to come there to live, to spend his life among them if they will
provide food and lodging—for if I come, I come to remain, and to
lay my ashes in the valley of the Mississippi. . . ."

If you can read a certain missionary condescension in the young
man's decision, as if he might be leaving for the Amazon instead
of the Mississippi, its resolute spirit is just as evident. He was
as good as his word. The Reverend Mr. Eliot came to St. Louis
and stayed: to found the First Unitarian Church, to found, build,
and act for many years as chancellor of George Washington
University, and in many other ways to make himself one of the
chief public figures of the region. His decision to live in the
wilderness seems to have been less of a sacrifice in a worldly
way than he had anticipated, to judge from the gifts of money
which he was increasingly able to make to various institutions.
His benefactions to the university alone mounted from fifty
dollars at its founding to ten thousand dollars in 1860 and fifty
thousand dollars in 1885. He had opportunities to test his vow
of leaving his ashes by the Western waters, but remained firm.
He seems never to have hesitated in turning down, for example,
such attractive offers as that of the ministry of Kings Chapel
in Boston.

In the crisis of the Civil War, Reverend Eliot assumed a leadership in his region remarkable for its energy and enlightenment.

ORPHEUS IN HELL: T. S. ELIOT

He was a factor in the decision of Missouri to remain in the Union, and during the war years he became head of the Western Sanitary Commission—the Red Cross of the time and place. His moderation of view during this time enhanced his ability to serve his community, partly southern as it was, though it lost him the regard of some of his fiercer abolitionist New England colleagues, one of whom voiced his doubts that a man could be pastor of a church in St. Louis and a man of God at the same time.

Such, in brief, was the conspicuous close ancestor of our poet, and his achievement in the Western wilderness, as you may learn from an able biography written by the poet's mother. I think it makes up a near tradition as you might say—a New England-Middle Western inheritance—not lightly to be overlooked. That it was dropped out completely by our poet, too completely for nature or truth, is what we have to consider.

Henry James had kept a place for an "American element" in his international situation. It represented for him a "value," a certain gift of innocence and good will, that met its testing on the "decorated and lighted stage" of Europe. T. S. Eliot, publicly at least, kept no place for such an element or value. In fact, James's "American element" of innocence and good will, as well as the "inner light" of the Puritan—James's "inward life"—were precisely the qualities Eliot found most repugnant in his official criticism. Our exile sought to make, apparently, a complete break with his American background, and pick up as it were the very threads of the tradition that his ancestors had dropped three centuries ago, when they left old England for New England. It is an interesting fact that Eliot's corrected line of tradition takes up at just about this point, in seventeenth-century England, at the time of the Puritan disaffection. His various volumes of criticism, while they include many minor English figures, do not include any American figure, major or minor, with the exception of Irving Babbitt.

So we will look for no drama in Eliot's work on the order of James's international drama of innocence and experience. Eliot had suppressed whatever original "innocent" value might have been carried with him from his own world and inheritance. The conflict is there, I think, but it has been driven underground. Publicly, the poet arrived on "the lighted and decorated stage" of Europe already garbed in its own costume, proclaiming for truth its own traditional word. Childe Roland to the dark tower came—prepared to excel in all departments of the tower life.

Too much tension remained, however, to suggest that the account of the inheritance had been settled. The important thing is not whether the poet had found his own tradition sufficient or not—only a provincial finds his own tradition sufficient. The question is whether he had measured it at all—and only a provincial of another sort finds his own tradition not worth measuring. This second kind of provincial, who exaggerates the local by supposing it beneath consideration, is the type this book treats of.

But there was too much "wavering between the profit and the loss" ("Ash Wednesday") to suggest that a satisfactory estimate had ever been made of the whole American background. The loss could never be written off so long as the value had never been appraised. Instead, there is alternation between the two opposing attitudes of remorse and detraction. On the side of detraction is the impulse to pull the beard of the fathers, so to speak, in order to write down the value of the loss. To this I think we may refer the two curious uses made in Eliot's poems of the image of Ralph Waldo Emerson, who for general purposes would stand for the American ancestral image. ("This Savonarola is a disciple of Schleiermacher, Emerson, Channing, and Herbert Spencer"—T. S. Eliot in an introduction to "Savonarola," dramatic poem written by his mother, Charlotte Stearns Eliot.) In one of these, Emerson becomes a mere "frowning father"—strange role for the nonauthoritarian Emerson—"guardian of the faith, the army of unalterable law" ("Cousin Nancy"). In the other ("Sweeney Erect") our unoffending sage is invited, all unsuspecting, to witness the spectacle of Sweeney engaged in lustful love. But it was impossible by such means to expunge the face of the fathers, and so on the other side there is the impulse to confession which runs through the poems, reaching its height in the fifth section of "Ash Wednesday" with its refrain: "O my people, what have I done to thee."

After all, there is a great deal in common between one cultural tradition and another, New England and Old England, Catholic and Protestant, Emerson and St. Augustine. There is much in common between places—London and St. Louis, Oxford and Boston. They are at the least all actual. But if actuality were unimportant because it existed also in Missouri, would it be substantial in England? If the "inner light" were suspect because it was Unitarian and Emersonian, would any faith be satisfactory in the absence of "inner light"? Such questions as these we have to consider in trying to explain the bitter turn taken by Eliot's feeling and thought.

The teaching of the essays is in keeping with the way taken

by the man. The essays, too, mistrust everything local or "home-made." They fear the good judgment of the individual. They continually look for some external authority that has nothing to do with the accidental nature of the individual person, who might, as it were, have been born in St. Louis.

First the essays taught that this external authority might be found in literary tradition. Yet it was soon obvious that the necessity of personal choice or "inner light" is not removed by literary tradition, which has never been codified into a complete external system. The attention of the essays moved, then, from the aesthetic toward the religious, and within the religious, toward authoritarianism. The characteristic words of the essays changed from tradition to dogma and classicism to orthodoxy.

Here lies the real question of the essays, not the question of God or truth or reality, but of dogma, institution, and authority. The critic is fond of quoting Dante's famous line:

la sua voluntade è nostra pace

—thy will is our peace—and nothing could be better Calvinism or better Emerson. But this is not the question raised by the essays. Nor is it the question of the usefulness of institutions in themselves—no one, or few, will deny the place of institutions. The question is whether, at the level of genius where the point is relevant, a man can trust his own vision of truth, or must still trust someone else's—for dogma is other men's visions codified into a system.

The argument of Dante versus Shakespeare, which runs through the essays, turns on this point of primary and secondary authority. Can writers of this stature be trusted to trust their own insight into truth? Eliot's criticism answers double. Dante, it seems, could be trusted to trust his own insight, but Shakespeare could not. But again, the reason Dante could be trusted and Shakespeare not was that Dante lived at a time when everyone, including Dante, had a trustworthy method, rule, and belief already given him. "Dante's advantages" [over Shakespeare, the essay on Dante says] "are not due to greater genius, but to the fact that he wrote when Europe was still more or less one," that is, under the Church at Rome. Consequently, "He not only thought in a way in which every man of his culture thought, but he employed a method which was common and commonly understood throughout Europe."

But again the same essay says that Dante at his best could dispense with all institutional authority. Eliot quotes Dante's Virgil to that effect, in the lines from *The Divine Comedy* in which Virgil, who was not good enough to go with Dante into Paradise, was still good enough to anoint Dante for the heavenly journey:

No more expect my word or sign, [Virgil to Dante]. Your Will is free, straight and whole, and not to follow it would be sin: wherefore I crown and mitre you (king and bishop) over yourself.

Dante's will is free; Dante is now king and bishop over himself; Dante may now follow his own "inner light," quite as if he were a good Quaker or Unitarian. Or as Eliot puts it: "Dante has now arrived at a condition, for the purpose of the rest of the journey, which is that of the blessed: for political and ecclesiastical organizations are only required because of imperfections of the human will."

So there is something higher than institutional dogma and authority—if you have disciplined yourself to reach this state. Dogma and authority, it seems, are only means to an end. The next question is whether Dante's means are the only possible means.

To come back to Shakespeare, as Eliot always does, the question is whether Shakespeare had not also mastered his own will; whether he was not, perhaps, as reliable as Dante in moral judgment on others; and had not found his way, so to speak, through his own purgatory (of *Hamlet*) to the calm of Prospero's island (*The Tempest*); and if poor Shakespeare did not deserve, quite as much as Dante, to have some Virgil or Ben Jonson crown and mitre him king and bishop over himself.

> Though with their high wrongs I am struck to the quick,
> Yet, with my nobler reason, 'gainst my fury
> Do I take part: the rarer action is
> In virtue than vengeance: they being penitent,
> The sole drift of my purpose doth extend
> Not a frown further. Go, release them, Ariel. . . .

Shakespeare may have been unacquainted with certain modes of religious feeling known to Dante. I think he was. Still anyone may judge whether these lines suggest lack of insight on Shakespeare's part into moral or even Christian truth. Eliot's argument did not come to a conclusion, even on the moral question. But no conclusion is possible upon the secondary grounds (of institutions, authorities, and different modes of thought of different times) taken by Eliot's essays.

Shakespeare haunts the essays, just as Jesus haunts the poems. Again and again the essays find it necessary to assure the reader that Shakespeare is "great," in quotation marks, or "universal," in quotation marks, lest the reader be misled by the essays which again and again tell the reader that Shakespeare could not have been universal or great. Shakespeare had a debased philosophy, which could only lead to something bad. But did it lead to something bad in Shakespeare's case? No, it cannot be said that it did. Shakespeare had an inferior audience, while the little group of aristocrats around the Countess of Pembroke, for instance, had all the advantage over Shakespeare and Marlowe of not having to cater to the general public. But was the Shakespearean drama inferior for that reason? No, it cannot be said that it was.

Then there is the "Dialogue on Dramatic Poetry," which is haunted from beginning to end by the greatest writer of dramatic poetry, William Shakespeare, and yet which twice puts forward the strange proposition, Why does Shakespeare fail us?

No answer. There is never any answer, and Shakespeare's ghost walks through the essays, unlaid, unscathed, and unappeased.

There is no appeasing any great ghost I fear, Dante's any more than Shakespeare's, by the burnt offerings of the essays. They are like a pyramid with the top cut off. They do not allow for the highest, but are addressed rather to the superior, and when not to the superior, then to the exclusive. Their highest value is not greatness or genius, but distinction; and indeed this is the quality of the poet's own work. This is the land divided by lot, as the poet wrote.

Actually, the teaching of the essays leads to the bitter truth of the poems. The poems understand and demonstrate high distinction, technical brilliance hardly surpassed; and the essays too understand technical and poetic distinction, and never praise bad poetry. Poet and critic are both alive to "exquisite modulation of tone" and all that has to do with the sense of the ear. In the realm of the human spirit, the poems understand despair and human bondage; and the essays too understand human bondage and the divided will. Neither the poems nor the essays understand, or at least demonstrate themselves, release and freedom, and it is too bad that they pretend to.

The greatest insight of the essays is into those literary works which do show spiritual division, failure to reach a conclusion, and either conscious or unconscious doubt. This is the literature of suffering, suffering without catharsis, prayer or penitence without purgation. A great example of this is Baudelaire, and Eliot wrote with insight, "He was one of those who have great strength, but the strength merely to suffer. He could not escape suffering and could not transcend it, so he attracted pain to himself. But what he could do, with that immense passive strength and sensibilities which no pain could impair, was to study his suffering."

Donne, in a way, "is such another," and so, strangely enough is the Tennyson of "Maud," of whose curious underground conflict Eliot made an astute analysis. And it is at this point that the essayist, a little gloatingly I think, catches up for once with Shakespeare's ghost. Hamlet, the equivocal and ghost-ridden, provides the chance, and Eliot's study of the Hamlet problem makes its point, just as it is made with the infinitely lesser affair of "Maud." But the point is the same: Hamlet, the seething soliloquist, like the seething monologuist of "Maud," was "dominated by an emotion which is inexpressible, because it was in excess of the facts as they appear." Disgust with his mother does not cover the whole situation. There is something else, something which even Shakespeare, apparently, has not isolated.

The truth is, Hamlet is disgusted with himself, and this self-disgust is prior to everything else. If this is not true (and if I may here add a note) how explain the speech of Hamlet to Ophelia: "I am myself indifferent honest, but yet I could accuse me of such things that it were better my mother had not borne me." What are these things Hamlet might accuse himself of, in terms of actual deeds done—in terms of drama? We do not know. If they are evil deeds, they are probably not of a crudely vicious sort. Nevertheless, they are "offenses," in Hamlet's own eyes, such as lead him to say of himself ". . . with more offenses at my beck than I have thoughts to put them in, imagination to give them shape, or time to act them in." Now, does this not mean that what really weighs on Hamlet is not his mother's offenses, but his own? If so, should they not be "thought, shaped, and acted" in the play, if we are to know Hamlet's tragedy instead of merely his confusion?

Hamlet, in any case, is the play of Shakespeare that you might most nearly describe in the terms Eliot uses for Baudelaire: suffering that could not be escaped or transcended, but attracted more pain to itself. They are also the terms that you can use very well to describe "The Waste Land," "The Hollow Men," "Ash Wednesday."

From the humorless and anxious essays it is a relief to turn to the poems, much as one might leave an unseaworthy ship

[211]

that is continually taking on more water than it can handle, and take to the lifeboats. The water is cold and the going difficult, but at least this medium will support you.

Somewhere Eliot has written that the difference between criticism and poetry is that criticism must point to ideals, while poetry need only express actuality. Nothing could be further from the truth so far as his own work is concerned. The poems point to all the values which the criticism refuses to acknowledge, and the more actual the poems are, the more they leave a place for the higher values. They know the second best from the best, and if "Ash Wednesday" says:

> I no longer strive to strive toward such things

it is not because the poet does not recognize that "such things" are worth striving for.

And whereas the criticism argues for orthodoxy that may be got from outside the individual head and tamped in, like sawdust, the poetry jeers:

> We are the hollow men
> We are the stuffed men
> Leaning together
> Headpiece filled with straw. Alas!

If the essays overemphasize measure, control, self-denial, and all the negative virtues, concerning which the greatest philosopher of measure, Aristotle, wrote a book to say that too much denial is exactly as bad as too much indulgence (but poor Aristotle, he was unacquainted with the "genteel tradition" of later New England, and so could not imagine anyone, as he said, with "a *defect* in respect of pleasure")—if the essays exaggerate denial, there is the truth about Prufrock in the poem, who mourns:

> I have measured out my life in coffee spoons.

If the essays outline a way that puts the letter above the spirit and suspects love and all outward movements of the heart, there is the confession of the unhappy soul in "Animula":

> Unable to fare forward or retreat,
> Fearing the warm reality, the offered good,
> Denying the importunity of the blood,
> Shadow of its own shadows, spectre in its own gloom,
> Leaving disordered papers in a dusty room. . . .

And so on. What the essays leave out the poems put in, and what the essays argue for the poems rebel against, according to the best laws of compensation known to Emerson and Plato. Or as the ancients put it, Nature expelled with a pitchfork returns just the same.

Truth and nature, as well as beauty and art, lie with the poems —no man can sing without somehow singing truly. The poems may sing the song of the minstrel, like Arnold in Dante's *Purgatory*, who weeps and goes singing. Again, they may recite the ditties of the court fool. Hieronymo's mad againe. But in any case, there are qualities and quality in the poems. There is no pleasure, no fun, not even wit or eloquence in the essays, with their stiff official tone and magisterial stare. No laughter in the courtroom. The poems are full of fun. No one could be as solemn as the official figure of the criticism, so there is the unofficial figure of the poetry who continually exposes solemnity.

Even Prufrock, in the author's first important poem, is aware of this side of the character:

> At times, indeed, almost ridiculous
> Almost, at times, the Fool.

For a complete picture of the Fool, in all his motley, there is the portrait drawn of him "in demotic French," in the verse called *"Mélange Adultère de Tout"*—Mixture Adulterous of Everything. He is all quick-change disguises: *"En Amerique, professeur; en Angleterre, journaliste,"* and so on through a dozen other masquerades. With long strides and in a sweat you'd scarcely keep up with this terrific fellow. In Yorkshire, a lecturer; in London a small-time banker; really, you'd give your head! In Paris you'll find him wearing the black cap of *jemenfoutiste*, or, I suppose, Dadaism. In Germany he's a transcendental philosopher, transported to the seventh heaven. Hither and yon he flits on his various brilliant triumphs, all the way from Damascus to Omaha. He celebrated his last birthday at a water hole in Africa, disguised in a giraffeskin. They'll be pointing out his monument some day on the burning slopes of Mozambique.

This is not only good fun, it is strength, the power to turn over the other side of the medal of Jove. That is the power the poems continually show, as the essays never really do.

The fun can be much less pleasant than in *"Mélange Adultère de Tout."* The turnabout exposure can be grisly, as in "The Hollow Man," or "Lines for an Old Man." Still, humor is its redeeming grace, even when mordant. The poems provide their own antidote. There is no protection against the magisterial stare of the essays. Your innocent reader, your unformed young person looking for the correct thing, your dull scholar, is outstared and coerced by the essays, quite without conscience. But anyone should know how to take this Old Man of the poems, dreadful as he is. Let the young, the innocent, the dull beware:

> When I lay bare the tooth of wit
> The hissing over the archèd tongue
> Is more affectionate than hate,
> More bitter than the love of youth,
> And inaccessible to the young.
> Reflected from my golden eye
> The dullard knows that he is mad.
> Tell me if I am not glad!

We know where we are, here. It is our own fault if we think we must be mad just because this malicious old fellow's eye looks so sane. Even more, we know that malice self-exposed becomes something a little different from malice.

So we know where we are, on the whole, all through the poems, if we understand them at all, which I admit is another question.

The difficulty of Eliot's poetry follows partly I think from the position outlined by the critic, which in turn followed on the way taken by the man. The way was away from everything native or "home-made." The theory, too, is not to trust the individual nature, integrity, or power of expression, but to look for some external model—that is, somebody else's way of trusting and expressing himself. Hence, everything in Eliot's poetry tends to be at a remove. Hence the myriad disguises and ventriloquisms of the poems, which the young poet of "The Portrait

of a Lady" had already said he had to use in order to say anything at all:

> And I must borrow every changing shape
> To find expression . . . dance, dance
> Like a dancing bear,
> Cry like a parrot, chatter like an ape.

Somewhere I believe Eliot has mentioned how many lines in his
poetry up to the time were both satisfactory to him and his own—
fifty or sixty if I'm not mistaken. At any rate, the phenomenon
was extraordinary, extraordinary because the poetry is at once
so borrowed and so personal. There is no mistaking an Eliot line;
there is hardly an Eliot line that is Eliot.

How can this be? How explain the genuineness so to speak
of the forgery? (If forgery sounds like too harsh a word, and
it is, I refer you to the backhanded dedication of "The Waste
Land": "to Ezra Pound, *il miglior fabbro*"—the better forger—
a clearly false accusation however you want to take it!) I think
the explanation lies in the one faculty of the poet which keeps
its authority so to speak through all the various transformations,
the listening faculty. "The eyes are not here, There are no eyes
here," so the poet writes in "The Hollow Men." But the ear,
the still and unexpressive organ in man, is always there, and
is one of the finest in poetry. Wherever the ear's cadence is
heard, in other poetry, or in the music hall, or on the street, the
poet picks it out. When it reappears in Eliot's verse it is unmistakable; it has the stamp on it and has been subject in turn to a
hundred imitations that do not have the stamp.

This is the faculty of the hidden hermit thrush. For the rest, on the side of personal feeling, the answer to Eliot's style is the same one we have been giving. The style is the man; this method of taking at second hand was the choice and life of the person. The man had turned spirit and letter around. Spirit followed on the letter—waited for some other letter to answer its need. What we know (the man and critic had said) is not the same great reality that all the poets and philosophers know, dead or alive, and that God himself is, but the picture of reality other philosophers and poets have made. This means in effect that the poet could recognize his own reality only through other recognitions.

Nevertheless, it is a personal reality the poet waits to recognize, very personal in fact. The touch, through the gloves of other poets, is extremely sensitive. Whatever words of someone else tell the exact position and feeling known to the poet become alive, like a second skin or a third ear drum. The spirit lives as it were in the skin, ear, tongue, heart of other poets.

There is something ghostly about this, and it is no wonder the poet was fascinated with the bodiless voice of Philomel, voices singing out of empty cisterns and exhausted wells, the hidden thrush, and so on. One has to be a ghost to enter into other bodies; likewise one's own body, losing its ghost, loses everything that is breathing, living, and less tangible than dried guts and bones.

Lady, three white leopards sat under a juniper tree
In the cool of the day, having fed to satiety
On my legs my heart my liver and that which had been contained
In the hollow round of my skull.

Such, too, was the lot of Webster and Donne, as the poet supposed:

> Who found no substitute for sense,
> To seize and clutch and penetrate;

and who consequently could find no comfort in thought:

> But our lot crawls between dry ribs
> To keep our metaphysics warm.

But this would be the worst kind of metaphysics, in fact it is not metaphysics at all. It is a form of superstition, or confusion of matter and spirit—the unfortunate feeling that ideas ought to be tangible to be true, while matter ought to be immaterial if it is to be good. It is like saying that one gets the virtue of the doctor's prescription by swallowing the piece of paper he gives it to you on. No wonder the poet was to see only fear, and not life, in a handful of dust. Emerson, with his distinction between the law for things and the law for man, would easily answer the point. But if Emerson were too much a home-made product, one could not do better than hear Thomas Aquinas on the subject, who presumably belonged to the right line of the Fathers. No body can receive the substantial form of another body, said this philosopher, unless it lose its own form by corruption. But an intellect is not corrupted, but rather is perfected by receiving the forms of all bodies; since it is perfected by understanding, and understands by having in itself the forms of things understood.

Let us eat real bread or meat—matter going through changes of form—for the sake of the body, but for the sake of the mind, let us imagine all things in their own forms everywhere, wherever we happen to be. In this way one might put the local and the general in their proper places, and grow wise in Omaha. But our poet, who had supposed the ideal life depended on being in the right physical locality, was to find that all appeared local and physical in the ideal one, as we gather from the sorry conclusion in "Ash Wednesday" that:

> . . . time is always time
> And place is always and only place
> And what is actual is actual only for one time
> And only one place. . . .

But the method of the poems, again, is the method of literalism, as if one *could* find the right time and right place, verbally speaking, on the dead dusty rolls of papyrus and ink which have come down from the first cave scribbler. The poet does find the places that corresponded to his own feeling with astonishing, if laborious, aptness. The labor is the reader's too. He must read through Eliot's reading in order to find what the poet found for his writing. Strangely enough, the more one reads of this erudite author's reading, the more personal the poetry becomes. In spite of the quotations in six or seven languages, the poems are quite the opposite of academic exercises of a library-filled head, for example, Mr. Pound's literary revivals. They are personal, even private, in extreme.

The method makes for its own peculiar quality and tone, the tone that echoes twice in the reader's ear—the echo of an echo, the glass that reflects again. There is always an extra note, a shadow, between reality and understanding. Listen:

> Because I do not hope to turn again
> Because I do not hope
> Because I do not hope to turn

or

> Here is no water but only rock
> Rock and no water and the sandy road
> The road winding above the mountains
> Which are mountains of rock without water
> If there were water we should stop and drink
> Amongst the rock one cannot stop or think. . . .

or the brilliant single line:

> Stone, bronze, stone, steel, stone, oakleaves horses' heels

or almost in parody of itself:

> If the lost word is lost, if the spent word is spent
> If the unheard, unspoken
> Word is unspoken, unheard;
> Still is the unspoken word, the Word unheard,
> The Word without a word, the Word within
> The world and for the world;
> And the light shone in darkness and
> Against the Word the unstilled world still whirled
> About the centre of the silent Word.

Beautiful and haunted, listening for the word that is already an echo, chiming again, gong answering gong across an empty space: such is the lovely unmistakable quality of Eliot's verse. "The Waste Land" itself is like a great hollow gong, echoing from beginning to end, echoing in large units and small, and chiming both with itself and a hundred smaller and larger units of other works; so that at two removes, and muffled, reality sounds.

This makes the difficulty, the twice-reflected image, and further, the associational image that depends not on the general associational character of language, but upon some particular association that happened to have been fixed in the poet's mind by his reading. "The Waste Land" is the height of all this complicated cross-reference. There is first an impression, and that may be a good deal in itself, lovely and haunting, but impressionistic: a blur of images of decay and drought and fear. More precise meaning waits on uncovering at least one layer of images, and sometimes three or four. This uncovering process is certainly not an aesthetic act, or aesthetic satisfaction. It is a detective act, if you like mystery stories. The poet has determined his readers to be one part reader and three parts sleuth, if they are to get any general satisfaction out of "The Waste Land."

Finally there is the question of what "The Waste Land" is and means when at last it is uncovered. What kind of a poem is it—epic, lyric, drama, or monologue? If drama, is it tragedy or comedy? Does it deal with grief, or only a grievance? All such questions wait on finding first what it is really about.

There is no space here to go through a detailed unraveling of "The Waste Land," even so far as the present writer thinks he might. Someday no doubt the proper exhaustive scholar will exhaust the subject. It is a cryptogram, as I have suggested, with meanings for the initiated and meanings for the uninitiated, and three or four levels of meaning at that. I can perhaps give here a few clues, which our exhaustive scholar will doubtless multiply to a hundred.

A great deal of help would come from knowing *The Divine Comedy*, for Eliot has taken over much of Dante's method, as to symbolism, levels of meaning, and so on. Our scholar will need a thorough acquaintance with medieval imagery and its multiple usage—literal, historical, personal, mystical, if that is correct. He will want to understand many of Dante's own symbolic values for the words he uses, such as fire, light, water, earth, river, lady, dog, and so forth, and remember that Dante sees a "good" and a "bad" aspect to almost all phenomena. It appears that Eliot often uses the same or similar meanings, and in fact leans heavily on Dante's whole view of the universe and its symbols. Eliot, however, has not followed Dante in the form of his poem, but has used a quite different and modern form, one related apparently to a work of music, with recurring themes.

Then one is to remember that back of Dante and the *Inferno* is Virgil and *The Aeneid*, for Eliot has drawn greatly on both. Indeed, it may be useful to look upon "The Waste Land" as one of a series of poetic "descents into hell": Virgil's being into the classical infernal regions, Dante's into the medieval hell, Eliot's into a modern hell; for we strongly suspect that the author has seen his work in very much this light. Milton's *Paradise Lost* may figure in the series too. In the case of "The Waste Land," the descent of the poet is not followed, as in *The Aeneid*, *Divine Comedy*, and Milton, by a visit to the happier realms of Elysium and Heaven. The point is important, as we shall see later. Yet for purposes of elucidation, the works of the author's great predecessors, and especially the first two, are always to be kept in mind.

The allusions to great works and cultures of the past do not stop here, by any means. The alert reader will catch echoes and hints of meaning that seem to come from Plato's myths, from Homer, from Old and New Testament literature, from the Hindu wisdom literature. And the sad loves and fates of all the exquisite youths of song and story—"Lycidas," "Adonais," "The Prince's Progress"—such things as these are in the poem. Some of these allusions are pointed out in the poet's notes, many not. But our reader, or scholar, will want to go directly to these notes—fifty or so of them—for leads as to what the poem is really about. These notes, which fortunately the author published with the poem itself, are I suppose unique in literary method. They are not simply comments and elucidations of meaning, they actually contain much of the meaning.

One example, a very simple one. Here is a line from the poem that stands by itself near the end of Part III:

To Carthage then I came

Now, in a reasonably self-contained poem we should gather from this that someone—the "I character" of the poem—had come to a city that was somehow like ancient Carthage, and the context would tell us in what way. The context gives no such information, hence the need for the author's note, which tells us where the line comes from, and what its context *there* is. The line is from Saint Augustine's *Confessions*, and the rest of the sentence reads "where a cauldron of unholy loves sang all about mine ears."

[223]

Now, this is the real meaning of the line. This is the context we need to have—not merely the context of the poem, but of the reference. Our "I character" had come to a city where a cauldron of unholy loves sang all about his ears. But this is only the beginning of our scholar's work. He may need to know a great deal more about Saint Augustine: for example, that he is the author of *The City of God*, a study of a city or society "built without hands," a truly holy city, and one in strong contrast to the pagan city of Rome, of his day. Are we to understand some similar point made with respect to the London of Eliot's day? Perhaps. Anyway, the investigator has the job of fitting this clue, "I character here equals Saint Augustine in Carthage," into the context of the poem—which means into the context represented by the other fifty notes, as well, not to mention the hundred and fifty or so more that might also have been appended.

The over-all equation and clue, we must suppose, is the one pointed to in Eliot's first note, the equation between ritual and romance as made by Miss Weston in her book on the subject. This equation is not out of keeping with Dante and medieval thinking, but very much in line with it. For it was much this synthesis, between courtly and heavenly love, between sensuous and religious imagery, between the quest of the Christian Grail and the ritual of the ancient vegetation and solar myths, that was gradually being made during the Middle Ages and which culminated in Dante. It ties in also with *The Aeneid*, and the quest of its hero for his "ancient mother"—symbolically, the land where he shall establish his race. Our scholar will want to have a sharp sense for this equation and its possible variations. The ancient vegetation story—the death of the god, his going under-

[224]

ground in the fall and resurrection in the spring—is like the search for the Holy Grail in the medieval romances. Both heroes are tested and suffer, must die to themselves before they are born again. This is also like human love. It is also like the Eucharist, or Communion sacrament, which memorializes sacrifice, death, and resurrection.

The reader may see some of the darker possibilities in such an equation, especially if its values get turned around, and I think he will need to have such possibilities in mind in reading "The Waste Land." "The Waste Land" is the underground part of the cycle, the sun-god in Hades, love in hell. The sacred meal here is possibly profaned, and eating of the god may be like eating of the mate—or even eating of the children, the fruits of love. The land must suffer so long as the god is thus detained underground. The god, too, may turn and devour the land and the people. Everything is upside down. In any case, our exhaustive scholar will want to ponder a good deal on this key equation: sacred meal equals fertility rite, and vice versa.

Another note on the symbolic meanings of words. While Eliot seems to have followed Dante often in such meanings, still many of Eliot's words have extremely limited and special meanings, which apparently can be referred only to the author's own private feeling or experience. These private values represent one of the levels of meaning, at any rate, and our scholar will have to become an adept at divining for example what hyacinth garden, boat, rat, dog, bone, hair, rock, shadow, eyes, sea, and other words may mean in this highly personal idiom. One thing is fairly clear, these values are quite specific and fixed, when they can be deciphered at all. It is like a code. Certain of these code

[225]

words run all through the poem, and not only through "The Waste Land," but other poems of Eliot's as well. Wherever our scholar finds them in "The Waste Land," he can write in the code values, and thus help piece together the meaning of the poem.

Perhaps I have suggested enough to suggest what sort of a task our redoubtable scholar has before him—almost as difficult as the hero's quest in "The Waste Land" itself. He must be prepared for a labyrinthine journey, for even an amateur could see how corridor opened on corridor, and catacomb under catacomb. You could not avoid the question, why such indirection? Presumably the purpose must have been revelation even though the method is disguise. Well, we must take what we can get; the poet must keep what we cannot receive. Meanwhile, since my own interest is in meaning and not in explanation, the reader will have to take my word for what I proceed to make out of "The Waste Land," and pardon me where I have made of it something wrong.

Let us keep in mind our questions: is it an epic or not; is there a hero and if so who? There certainly seems to be a hero, a quest, a test of some sort; and it seems to be a fable, or form of epic, at least on one level.

There is the mythical setting, a strange kingdom and land-scape, a mythical cosmology. There are semimythical characters, king, prophets, gods and goddesses, hero, ladies, and so on. The hero has come to the enchanted kingdom, where a spell has been cast, and all is decay and drought. The king is old, sick, or maimed. The people perhaps have sinned and followed false gods. Desire fails, the crops die. What needs to be done? Perhaps the old king needs to be sacrificed; perhaps the people need to repent; perhaps the hero needs to accomplish his task, say the word, release the spell. Or perhaps the hero himself needs to be sacrificed, die, and go underground, like the vegetation god. Perhaps the hero has failed altogether, and there is no hope anywhere. All these things are possible, but this seems to be the basic fable, and the question is how it is used and meant.

Here, anyway, is the first part of the poem, "The Burial of the Dead." Who is dead and where are they buried? Well, I think it is a whole generation—our famous "Lost Generation," let us say—and they have gone underground, to that part of Dante's inferno reserved for the ambiguous, the neither this nor that. Heaven chased them forth, Hell receives them not. They are the dead-alive, who have lost the good of the intellect without getting the bad of their passions; or, as in Eastern mysticism, they are "the living dead" who are without knowledge of the spiritual meaning of life. They were only "for themselves," and now they are like dogs, living a purely animal life. In fact the Dog Star is in the ascendancy throughout the poem, and by that, I take it, our author means that "naturalism" or animalism or democracy is the reigning philosophy, there is no sacredness to anything, and people live like the Cynics of the Grecian school, performing their functions publicly and mechanically—like Diogenes in the public square.

Anyway, here we are, underground in the Unreal City, which is also London, where the masses mill in a circle and the shades walk in daylight, while the bell sounds the ninth hour when Jesus himself cried, "My God, my God, why hast thou forsaken me?"

What is the trouble? Well, in their youth they felt free, this generation—too free. I think Rousseau may be the villain here and Shelley and Swinburne and democracy and liberty and perhaps German freethinking and the Reformation itself. Summer surprised with a shower of rain—there was a quick short flowering. But the soil was too shallow, the seed shot up only to fall back and die.

Down, down they went, this unfortunate Lost Generation, into the earth and the life of dogs and materialism, some of them perhaps crying like the French symbolists to the Virgin Mary as they slid down. Free love led, as with Tristan and Isolde, only to the funeral pyre. Now they are in this indeterminate nether region, neither dead nor alive. This region is like the one in Swinburne's poem "Tiresias," where "the holy hand of law can set no tune on time":

> Yea, surely they are now transformed or dead,
> And sleep below this world, where no sun warms,
> Or move about it now in formless forms
> Incognizable, and all their lordship fled;
> And where they stood up singing crawl and hiss
> With fangs that kill behind their lips that kiss.

That is perhaps the trouble. Like the drowned sailor, Palinurus, in the *Aeneid*, they are dead but not buried. If somebody would only bury them properly it might be better; there might then be the hope of a resurrection. Call for robin redbreast and the wren to cover with leaves and flowers the friendless bodies of these unburied men!

Among those present in this unhappy place are a number of characters as told about by "Madame Sososstris" (Blavatsky?): the

Fisher King, with his trident, and I think he would be Father England, and an old man much in need of relief; Belladonna, or Circe, the Lady of Situations, the designing female, who tries to stir desire with charms and sorceries; the drowned Phoenician sailor—our author's own card—suggesting perhaps the case of Adonis or Osiris, young gods of the ancient world borne out to sea—Osiris in a coffin—after being wounded in their first meeting with love; and also Ferdinand, the wrecked prince of *The Tempest*, who sings of his drowned father; but most especially the young pilot Palinurus in *The Aeneid*, who was required as a sacrifice by Neptune, and being put to sleep by Lethe dews fell out of the boat on a calm night, carrying the rudder with him. There is the one-eyed merchant, who has only a half-vision of the truth, and who sells all the latest currents and carries a burden on his back: who might in some aspect, on a long guess, be James Joyce, and in another aspect our author again. There is the Wheel of Fate or Fortune, with probably some reference to the Buddhist theories of great cycles. There is also a friend named Stetson, who made the Great Refusal (of love), and who on a chance might be Ezra Pound. There is the Hyacinth Girl, or true love, whose memory, like the hyacinth flower itself, which sprang from the blood of a slain youth, returns with every spring. But she perhaps is not present here in Hades, but remains above.

What of the quest of the Grail, and the burial of the vegetation god? Well, this is it. This is the burial of the young god, stricken in his early flowering. This is the testing of the young knight, Gawain or Parsifal, brought up by women, too sheltered, in the woods far from the world, and starting on his quest not knowing what the quest is. He failed to ask the question in the

Hyacinth Garden, just as Adonis failed in the first test of love, ran from Aphrodite, and was wounded by the boar. The god or knight has flourished in his short spring and is withered by the first rays of the sun, or blighted by an unseasonable frost. The women mourn his untimely death; woe for Adonis, for Attis, for Osiris, the blighted young god, broken and buried. Woe for the drowned Phoenician sailor, his eyes now clouded like pearls, cloudy with sleep, blinded in the dark, cloudy with death. Woe for the Hyacinth Girl, left burning like Dido.

Woe then, too, for the land that is blighted because the god is dead, for the corn that grows not, for the tree that does not stand, for the field that does not bloom. Who is at fault, the god or the people, the hero because he failed or the land he came to because it was decadent? We do not know—there may be some discrepancy here. But anyway, this is the Burial of the Dead, the burial perhaps of the very organ of fertility itself, like a corpse. Nothing grows out of this rubbish; which is only a heap of broken images, and our "I character" will at least show us fear in the shadow of death, under the red rock of suffering.

In the second part, "A Game of Chess," we have the effort to revive the dead god, and what life and love is in this kind of a dead-alive world. Here is the goddess Belladonna, or Circe, with her synthetic rites, and I think our questing hero is going to be initiated. His initiation might be along the lines of the rites of Demeter, according to Frazer: "the preliminary fast of the candidates, the torchlight procession, the sitting of the candidates, veiled and in silence, on stools covered with sheepskin, the use of scurrilous language, the breaking of ribald jests, and the solemn communion with the divinity in a draught of barley-water from a holy chalice."

Belladonna, anyway, appears to be the latest of a long line of goddesses and queens of dubious virtue, from the Biblical whore who sat on the waters to Venus and Cleopatra down to Modern Love. She may well be modern London, or the Goddess Britannia, who rules the waves and keeps her home fires burning with huge seawood fed with copper, as becoming the daughter of the old sea-god Poseidon—Britain with his three-pronged fork of power. She is, anyway, the bad, or underworld, aspect of the Lady of Love, and here she is trying to work her charms of incense and soft lights, trying to revive the vanished powers of our hero. She is trying, perhaps, to revive Endymion, the sleeping hero of Keats's poem and sleeping youth of English poetry.*

No success. What has happened to the goddess's powers? The oracle does not speak, the mystery does not work. Her nimbus spreads out in fiery points (perhaps like our own goddess of liberty in New York harbor), almost glows into words, but then is savagely still.

Well, I think the poet gives us a little English history to explain what has happened, by way of the antique mantel above the fireplace. It looks back like a window on the past, from which a fresh air blows—only the past being alive to our poet—and tells of the change of Philomel, by the barbarous king so rudely forced, and this king I take it is Henry the Eighth. Like Tereus he put away his true wife and in taking another mistress cut off his wife's tongue so she could not tell on him. Her tongue

* The aesthetical loves of the Pre-Raphaelites are no doubt also alluded to in this section, notably the tragic affair of Rossetti and the copper-haired Elizabeth Siddal, who became his *"Beata Beatrix"*—the all night vigils, the use of drugs, etc.

became the nightingale, a bodiless voice. This was what happened with Henry's putting away of Mother Church and the forced embracing of the English Church—it cut the great tradition, and left the English muse a bodiless tongue, while the body became dumb.

True, this nightingale, the bird of English poetry, appears to have burst into a very rich song just at this juncture, during the reign of Elizabeth, and not so very bodiless a song either, we would think! But this is our poet's story—this is the genesis of Elizabethan literature—a cut-off voice singing in a wilderness, with Puritanism and pagan naturalism on the way. Still she sings and still the world pursues this pagan muse in a day of "dirty-ear" democracy. Other "withered stumps of time"—cut-off tongues of tradition—were told on the wall; staring forms—dumb bodies —lean out; but the life stream was already cut off, even in Shakespeare's day, or so the poet suggests. That is why the priestess is in such a bad state tonight.

Meanwhile our hero waits for initiation; presumably has fasted; been welcomed by a torchlight procession, like the ominous triumph of Jesus' entry into Jerusalem; and now comes the all-night vigil, sitting in silence, veiled, on a stool covered with sheepskin. Still nothing happens, and the goddess waits on him, just as he has been waiting on her. Why doesn't he speak, what does he think, speak, think, what? He thinks he is in rat's alley, where the dead men lost their bones. He hears nothing but the wind of time, or death, knows nothing, sees nothing, remembers his false spring, but feels no present creative urge. He does hear Shakespeare reduced to jazz; and people go through the motions. But it is only an all-night vigil, a game of chess, like the game in Middleton's *Women Beware Women*; and the players are preoccupied while those in high places, who ought to provide an example of virtue, seduce the innocent, and everybody waits for the end, the knock of doom.

Let us follow out the rest of the initiation, the use of scurrilous language, the breaking of ribald jests, and the solemn communion with the divinity in a draught of barley water from a holy chalice. Now we have come to our Sacred Meal, I think, and it takes place in a public house. The divinity, we suspect, is the taproom host, and he is just about to close up shop. Hurry up it's time. The boys are back from the trenches, there may be a new king pretty soon, and all of them want a good time. Still further changes seem threatened in the way of "liberalizing" the Church, the State, the marriage code. The jazz age is here, birth control, divorce. HURRY UP, PLEASE, IT'S TIME.

It was a bad moment for the arrival of our would-be initiate, questing knight, and partaker of the Sacred Meal. The communion drink is beer or perhaps gin, the chalice a can, and the bread of life is a pork joint, or a "hot gammon." It is like King Tereus's meal, you will remember, who had his son served up to him in a meat pie. They are sacrificing their children. No wonder God is about to close shop. Good night, Bill Shakespeare, good night, sweet ladies of old England, as Ophelia cried, good night, ta-ta, goo'night.

The next part is "The Fire Sermon," and somehow in it we have a full-fledged prophet. He is an ascetic, something like Buddha and Saint Augustine, but more like the old Greek mythological character Tiresias, "old man with wrinkled female breasts" whose initiation into prophecy was curious. Tiresias, it seems, was walking in the woods one day and saw serpents coupling, whereupon he beat them apart with a stick. For this act, the gods struck him blind and changed him to a woman; but again, years later, he saw, or sensed, serpents coupling and beat them apart with a stick. After this he reached his final state, both man and woman and neither, "throbbing between two lives," yet gifted with second sight. This second sight is not happy; everywhere he sees the folly of life; everywhere he sees death, and most of all in the act of fertility. Tiresias, in short, is a Puritan of the more unpleasant sort; he dislikes the conjugation of the sexes. Quite likely he hints at perverse forms of sex, such as homosexuality, or at sadism, which may be a sort of perverse asceticism.

But for the modern story, Tiresias the prophet preaches a message of asceticism to a people who have taken the marriage rites too lightly. As in Swinburne's poem, "the marriage-garment, seeming fair Was dyed in sin and woven of jealousy To turn their seed to poison." Hence:

> I, Tiresias the prophet, seeing in Thebes
>   Much evil, and the misery of men's hands
>   Who sow with fruitless wheat the stones and sands,
> With fruitful thorns the fallows and warm glebes,
>   Bade their hands hold lest worse hap come to pass,
>   But which of you had heed of Tiresias?

And so to such a situation comes our poet-hero. He mourns the burned and decayed land. The nymphs of true love are departed, the last vegetation is drying up. Sweet Thames, that inspired a true nuptial song in Spenser's day, run softly till our poet ends his dirge, for he sings not loud or long.

By the waters of Leman—or Babylon, or London—I sat down and wept—an exile in a strange land, remembering Zion, for they that carried us away captive required of us mirth, saying, Sing us a song of Zion; but how shall we sing the Lord's song in a strange land? On the personal plane, is the lost Zion New England, the poet's own native habitat? We do not know. But then we have the passages about the "cold blast" the poet feels at his back, which I have already quoted, and which seem to say that Zion, if such were Zion, was well left behind. There is the same question here of the "profit and the loss," that is continually weighed, but never measured, and it is not measured here. We do not know whether we have a lost son of New England or a rejected messenger to Old England.

What we do have is Tiresias, a seared seer in a sere land, who resumes the theme of the broken tradition. Twit, twit, twit, the last twitters of the nightingale; jug, jug, jug—inspiration out of jugs, or perhaps the jugular vein severed and spurting. Tereu . . . Tereus and his murdered son.

And then the squalid love scene of "the small house agent's clerk" and the typist. Love has come down to this, apparently, the low affair of the vulgar in a democratized and industrialized world. They are the crude inheritors. Moreover, it is only mechanical and indifferent, the love which Tiresias sees at the violet hour, when coming home from work is like going home to death. For love is death and death is love, according to Tiresias. Worse even, when lovely woman stoops to folly in these sad days, she cannot even hope to die because of it. In the eighteenth century, to cover her guilt and give repentance to her lover, she could at least die of shame. But now she only smooths her hair with automatic hand and puts a record on the gramophone.

O City, city, which might have been built on righteousness,

like the eternal City of God of which Augustine wrote. The poet catches a few echoes of holiness in certain out-of-the-way spots of modern London. But these echoes are scattered and feeble in the pagan city.

Again we have some English history to explain what has happened to our lovely ladies. We go back to the rude king, Henry the Eighth. Henry had no son, but only a daughter, Elizabeth, herself barren, and we have a picture of her drifting down the Thames in a gilded shell—not the true bark of faith—with a frivolous wooer, Leicester. The boats of pagan love have been drifting down the Thames to the sea ever since, Highbury to Richmond, Richmond to Kew, Kew to Moorgate, Moorgate to Margate Sands, the Coney Island of England, and the end of the land. Every stage has meant the debauching of some Thames daughter, from upper down to the lowest classes, to the accompaniment of the wailing of the Thames nymphs.

So the modern river of life sweats oil and tar—like the oily river Styx—instead of the dews of holy love; and the pagan barges are only drifting—past the Isle of Dogs, or cynic animalism, with Marxist materialism off perhaps to leeward—down to the sea of death.

To this sort of Carthage, then, came our hero, or "I character," or knight, or exile, or prophet, or sailor: "where a cauldron of unholy loves sang about his ears." The rivers of individual lives and loves are polluted and the land is burning with a self-destroying fire; God the Destroyer is over the land. Hence the fire sermon of Tiresias, or better, perhaps, of Jonathan Edwards, "Sinners in the Hands of an Angry God." But our hero's destiny is peculiar. His card is the drowned sailor, and he is plucked like a brand out of the burning land, burning, to be dropped in the deep sea.

Part IV is the quenching of the "I character," "Death by Water," which takes only eight lines. Phlebas, or Palinurus, the young Phoenician pilot, full of the blood of life, and handsome, was demanded as a sacrifice. On the open sea of God's eternal will, on a calm night, his eyes on the stars, he was overcome by sleep, and fell overboard, carrying the helm of the boat with him. Some say he got to shore on a near-by cape and was killed by the natives; others, that he was simply drowned.

Now, anyway, he is as a body unburied, and his soul flits like a shadow on the shore of the living, and must wait perhaps a hundred years to be accepted by Charon and taken over to the abode of the dead. He therefore has no middle life, but only the memory of his early youth and flowering, and the thought and hope of death—which is always present. There is perhaps the consolation of Mother Church, herself a current undersea as it were—the garden where all love ends, the single rose of forgetfulness. There is some discrepancy here, once more. Mother Church is supposed to be the way of life, the true spouse for whose abandonment the Waste Land is suffering. But again, here she is not life, but death—the hope only of empty men, as we learn in "The Hollow Men." It is hard to reconcile these two views.

But finally there is the last part, "What the Thunder said," or the voice of God, and in spite of the drowning of Phlebas, the burying of Adonis, the failure of the questing knight in the garden, and the blinding of Tiresias, we still have an "I character" in the poem, a prophet prophesying, and a hero questing. Who are they? The prophet speaks Sanskrit. Possibly he is Mithra, the Far Eastern storm-and-sun-god, though it is uncertain here whether he brings storm or sunshine.

The part begins with a summary of the other parts, and seems to leave the vegetation god still underground and the questing knight on the last difficult part of his journey toward the Grail Castle; while "we," or the Lost Generation, are now dying, with a little patience, but not too much apparently.

Here comes the test of the Dry Mountains, or suffering in the desert of doubt—the soul separate from God—where there is rock and no water, a road winding in the sand, over the mountains, with God's voice heard, but no grace, and no place either to stand or lie or sit. There is not even solitude in this desert—as there was, say, for a John the Baptist—but in the crowded modern world people are everywhere; red sullen faces sneer and snarl from mud-cracked houses: the vulgar masses again, who are such a threatening factor in modern life, according to our poet.

If there were only a little water, rock but a little water, such as the pilgrim had found on the rocky puritan coast of New England where he heard the hermit thrush sing, as we have noted earlier in this chapter. But here there is no water, or grace, at all.

This recollection seems to bring back the memory of the Hyacinth Girl, or the Lady of Lilacs of New England—the true love of our knight who had been left in the garden. Addressed here as "you," she remains the one memory of grace, the one faithful person who had once blessed the pilgrim on his way. She probably figures at this point as the Grail Messenger, "who directs the hero on his road to the Grail Castle," according to Miss Weston, "or reproaches him for his failure there." She may also be the medieval Lady of Grace, like Dante's Beatrice, who helps lead the intellect toward the divine truth.

It is worth pausing to note here, as any reader of Eliot will have noted, the place occupied in his poems both before and after "The Waste Land" by the image of this lady of the lilac garden. It is an important place, and the reader observes how the treatment of the image has steadily been raised from a sort of troubled mockery, as in *"La Figlia Che Piange,"* to respectfulness, and finally, as in "Ash Wednesday," to something like adoration, such as one would accord the medieval "Lady of Grace." This Lady of the Lilacs undergoes a sort of gradual beatification.

The theme of the designing female—the Lady of Situations—runs through all the poems too. Nor is she wholly disassociated, it seems, from the good lady of the garden. All the lovely ladies, apparently, are designers and temptresses! But, as the poems go on, the two ladies tend to separate. The lady of the garden is more and more granted the virtue of sincerity. In fact, in all the poems she is the one good person you can find, the one saved soul.

All this is borne out by the present passage of "The Waste Land," which begins "Who is the third that walks beside you?" This "third" person is Jesus, as he appeared to the disciples on the road to Emmaus, or in other words, the risen Christ. He is wrapt in brown mantle, hooded from the view of our pilgrim, but visible possibly to the lady, who is now either urging the hero on or reproaching him for failure, we do not know which.

Now high in the air is heard the murmur of lamentation of Mother Church, seeing prophetically the hordes of "barbarians" coming out of the east—over the plains of Russia—with their purely materialistic philosophy, promising to engulf all Europe in chaos. There is little indication that this prophecy had in mind Nazism and Fascism as well as Russian Communism, as forces leading toward chaos in Europe. It looks as if it were Communism alone that it refers to. However, for those who would link all these systems in certain respects—as indeed they have shown certain common elements—this passage may be taken for the striking portent that it was later to appear.

There follows another prophecy, the doom of the "unreal cities" —Jerusalem, Athens, Vienna, London—falling towers of selfishness and materialism. The smoky "violet air" of the cities recalls the violet period of London, "violet" being the color of age, and also of Lesbianism and the decay of normal love; and I take it the reference is to the "fin de siecle" era of Beardsley, Whistler, Oscar Wilde, and the others. The passage is one of the most evocative of the poem:

> A woman drew her long black hair out tight
> And fiddled whispered music on those strings
> And bats with baby faces in the violet light
> Whistled, and beat their wings
> And crawled head downward down a blackened wall
> And upside down in air were towers
> Tolling reminiscent bells, that kept the hours
> And voices singing out empty cisterns and exhausted walls.

This applies also, I imagine, to the French Symbolists and Baudelaire, and to all the Black Mass ritual of making good be bad and bad good, and cultivating a precious aestheticism by upside-down religious formulas.

This also is the Black Chapel that the questing knight comes to before he reaches the Chapel Perilous, which we have next:

"the grass is singing over the tumbled graves, about the chapel, there is the empty chapel, only the wind's home. It has no windows, and the door swings, dry bones can harm no one." Well, I think this Chapel Perilous is the "Chapel" in the English sense, that is, the independent as distinguished from the Established Church. This is the house of the winds of doctrine, where the door swings freely, and anyone who pleases may come in or go out. It has no absolute magical ceremonies, no window of tradition into the past, and its "dry bones" of barren puritanism are neither harmful nor good. Now, perhaps, according to our poet, its weak faith is ready to hear the cockcrow and deny the Lord, as Peter heard and denied. We hear two of the three ominous cockcrows (if this is what they signify) in a flash of lightning, and then a "damp gust, bringing rain."

There seems to be a question whether this is a spring rain, bringing relief, or only the prelude to some greater catastrophe, perhaps a great storm brought about by the sun-god in his storm aspect, like the storm and earthquake at the Crucifixion, which was followed by the Harrowing of Hell according to medieval legend. This may be the meaning of the thunder that we now hear in Sanskrit, DA *datta*; DA *Dayadhvam*; and so on, with the sacred river Ganges sunken, to become like Lethe, the stream of death, and the voice speaking out of the high Himalayas, shaking the depths of Hades. Perhaps it is necessary to propitiate this thunder-god, who, according to some authorities, likes to be invoked in syllables of pure sound.

Translated, the thunder means Give, Sympathize, Control, excellent texts certainly, though one might question why it is necessary to go so far back as India and Sanskrit to find them. They seem to be directed as warnings to, and possibly as keys for release from, the Dark Tower which is the final scene of "The Waste Land" and the last trial of the questing hero.

The texts provide an opportunity for self-examination on the part of our "I character," who apparently has survived all the drought and disasters of the Waste Land to date. This self-examination appears to concern private decisions and personal or religious experience. We gather from it that grace has not been satisfactorily won, the Holy Grail has not been found, and the "I character" remains locked in the Dark Tower of the separate self. There are only distant rumors of a "broken Coriolanus," that is, a humbled and contrite spirit: rumors which point ahead apparently to the author's later poem "Coriolan," which is a treatment of the theme of arrogance and family pride—unfortunately, an unfinished work.

All this seems almost too personal to concern the reader. What does concern him, however, is the question of the chief character in the poem—the hero, if there is a hero. This question is especially raised by these commentaries on the three texts, and especially by that on the third text, "Control." The commentary is:

> . . . The boat responded
> Gaily, to the hand expert with sail and oar
> The sea was calm, your heart would have responded
> Gaily, when invited, beating obedient
> To controlling hands

I understand by this that the boat of marriage or love or faith might have sailed smoothly and happily down the river of life and out into the sea of eternity had the right question been asked at the right time: had there been true self-knowledge and control.

I am not quite sure what this "would-have" incident is, in terms of preceding events, but it seems to be the unsatisfactory incident in the Hyacinth Garden, followed by the hasty departure of the lover over the sea "—and the sea was waste." It is like Palinurus the Phoenician sailor sailing off in his ill-fated bark and falling out of the boat in a calm sea, like Adonis fleeing from love, like Aeneas leaving Dido burning, like Gawain failing to ask the question, like Prince Ferdinand losing his father in the storm. It may even be the same as Tiresias beating apart the serpents. Everything points indeed to the fact that this is the fundamental situation of the poem, from which drama should follow, and fate demand an accounting from the hero.

The disturbing thing is to find this incident still with us at the end of the poem, in the pathetic past tense of "would have." For "would have," in absolute fact, does not exist, never did exist, never will exist. It is the antithesis of the dramatic mood, which is always indicative. Drama always traces sequence, follows the logic of fate, and hence disposes of any given incident for good and all, one way or another, for better or worse. "Would have" is the failure to dispose of an incident, or the failure of drama.

We have been confused throughout the poem because of the ambiguity of the chief character. It seems there is an "I character" whose card of fate is "the drowned Phoenician sailor," but who does not have the fate of the drowned sailor, since we still have an "I character" after the drowning. It seems there is an "I character" who is Tiresias struck blind, but who still is not Tiresias struck blind since after Tiresias we still have an "I character." It seems there is an "I character" who is Ferdinand, or Gawain, or Adonis, or some other fated character, yet who never meets any of the fates of these characters, since we always have an "I character" left over and a fate still to be decided. Well, I think there is no need to make a mystery of this. The "I character" is no one else but the author, and there is a "would-have" incident and a fate left over because they have never actually been transferred to some character in the poem, but remain his, outside the poem. The poem itself thus lacks a hero, incident, action, and fate.

All this is to observe that the dramatic machinery of "The Waste Land" gives way to the personal, or confessional mode, the failure of dramatization being of course the same as the failure of impersonalization. It is interesting to note that Eliot's most truly dramatic poem is still the early "Love Song of J. Alfred Prufrock." We have much the same basic incident—the silence in the garden—that has so large a place in "The Waste Land," and also in other poems, "Portrait of a Lady," *"La Figlia Che Piange,"* Section IV of "Ash Wednesday." The difference in "Prufrock" is that the incident is disposed of, as it never really is in "The Waste Land," just as Prufrock himself is promptly recognized by the reader as a person and a type, complete in himself, and complete within the poem. Prufrock defines himself. He "is no prophet—and here's no great matter," even though he, too, had seen his head (grown slightly bald) brought in upon a platter. Perhaps the trouble with "The Waste Land" characters is that they all suppose themselves prophets. Prufrock, anyway, dismisses such pretensions, sadly defines his limits—shall he part his hair behind? does he dare to eat a peach? He had seen the moment of his greatness flicker; and "in short, he was afraid."

These are decisive strokes, and Prufrock's fate is decisive, too:

> We have lingered in the chambers of the sea
> By sea-girls wreathed with sea-weed red and brown
> Till human voices wake us, and we drown.

Here the Phoenician sailor is drowned and left drowned; and the character's doom is the victory of the author's imagination.

Sweeney, the other character of the earlier poems, and incidentally, like Prufrock, a New Englander, is also recognizable as a type and person. He is the opposite of Prufrock—all vulgar instinct to Prufrock's all finicky sensibility. Together they would make a man; apart they are each half a man; body without soul, soul without body. And the author keeps them apart.

The curious thing, as the poems go on, and as Sweeney ships with Prufrock overseas to live among the nightingales, is that the two characters begin to run together, though only to acquire each other's faults. Prufrock takes on a certain sensuality but without pleasure; Sweeney takes on Prufrock's introspection but without intellect. By the time of "The Waste Land" and "Sweeney Agonistes," it is hard to distinguish the one from the other.

"The Waste Land" puts Prufrock in a public house, while "Sweeney Agonistes" makes Sweeney conscious of sin. Indeed, Sweeney here comes to live in the same Dark Tower, wears the same mask as the other Lost Generation intellectuals, talks the same metaphysics of death being life and life being death, and is only waiting, like everybody else, for the knock on the door.

"Sweeney Agonistes," by the way, may be seen as "The Waste

Land" with its images and symbols simply degraded a few degrees more. The wasted kingdom has become a cannibal isle, and the sacred meal is now cannibalism. The Dark Tower is the bathroom of Sweeney's murder story, where the man kept the girl in a Lysol bath, and didn't know if he were alive and she dead or she alive and he dead. The incident that cannot be disposed of is now a hypothetical murder, just as it is in the still later play, *The Family Reunion*. Also, modern love and birth control are like murder; and men and women on the cannibal isle eat of each other under any old tree any old time, consuming their children in the process. And all wait in jittery suspense for the god, death, who will come and devour them all.

But already, in "The Waste Land," we have seen the merging and melting of individual characters, both men and women, until they are all subsumed in the hermaphrodite Tiresias, as we are told in a note. My point is that this merging of identities is the same as the failure to deal with a basic incident, the same as the failure of drama. True drama separates character and measures different fates. One is reminded here of Proust, another late-European introspective writer, whose characters all tended at last to have the same features. There can be no drama if everybody is the same person. There can be no difference if no one's actions are really accounted for.

The reader knows what action, or drama, in a dramatic poem is, for example, the incident of the Ancient Mariner and the sea creatures in Coleridge's fable, which offers comparison with "The Waste Land" in many ways. In both cases you have, apparently, a hero who has committed a fault; you have drought, suffering, and enchantment; you have the severe spiritual testing of the hero. In "The Ancient Mariner," however, unlike "The Waste Land," something happens: the mariner in his suffering becomes aware of the sea creatures, "O happy living things!" and after this unconscious act of sympathy his powers return, he prays, his burden falls. "And when I woke it rained."

That is redemption, or movement in the way of spiritual recovery. It did not rain in "The Waste Land," and there is no reason why it should have. There might be another sort of action, fatal or tragic. Almost any poem, say, of Robinson Jeffers, not to mention Shakespeare or the Greeks, would do to illustrate tragic action, how the chief character because of some fatal flaw of pride or corruptibility moves from error to unrepented error and so to final disaster. There is no "would have" about it; what happened happened and must be accounted for, and with an intractable character, the accounting is finally tragic.

The surprising fact about "The Waste Land," with all its dark threats and horrors, is that it is not tragic; nothing fatal really happens. The reason is that it is not dramatic. The fable, or epic, elements, as I have suggested, fall subordinate in the end to the confessional motive, and that is the note left with us. Hence that last tag end of the poem, which so far I have not mentioned:

> I sat upon the shore
> Fishing, with the arid plain behind me
> Shall I at least set my lands in order?
> London Bridge is falling down falling down falling down
> *Poi s'ascose nel foco che gli affina*
> *Quando fiam uti chelidon*—O swallow swallow
> *Le Prince d' Aquitaine à la tour abolie*

THE WIND BLEW FROM THE EAST

These fragments I have shored against my ruins
Why then Ile fit you. Hieronymo's mad againe.
Datta. Dayadhvam. Damyata.
    Shantih shantih shantih

Even after following through the poem, this passage will no
doubt look rather obscure, and lucidity is surely not a merit of
"The Waste Land." But we still have, as you see, our ever-
resurgent "I character," who now takes his place where he has
never really vacated it, as the author commenting on himself.
Our poet-hero-commentator sits on the shore fishing, is still cast-
ing for the holy fish of truth, as he was at the beginning. The
arid plain is behind him—perhaps this means that we have got
out of Dante's upper hell and are now only in purgatory. Shall
he not set his own lands in order? or in other words, they are
not in order yet. As for the old kingdom, there seems to be no
hope for that; London Bridge is falling down falling down falling down, my fair lady. Our hero-author-victim asks his good
lady to remember him as she climbs toward heaven, while he dives
back into the purgatorial fire that refines him.

When shall he be as the swallow, that is the true bird of poetry,
favored by Apollo, and with a body as well as a voice? O sister
swallow, when shall his spring come? The prospect is not good.
Our prince of the sea, wrecked voyageur, misguided knight,
blighted god—Ferdinand, Adonis, Phlebas, Palinurus, Gawain,
Parsifal, Rishyacringa, Tiresias, T. S. Eliot—came to the broken
tower, himself like a tower struck by lightning. He is incon-
solable. The only thing he can do is pick up the pieces. Still he
is glad to oblige. Like Hieronymo he will amuse the court for
an hour or two with his little make-believe tragedy. Hieronymo

has these hallucinations when he thinks of his lost son. But as a matter of fact, Hieronymo's never better than when he's mad! And again the warning Sanskrit thunder, and peace, peace where alas there is no peace.

There is one development here however. We have the reversal, or turnabout confession, that you can find in most of Eliot's poems —the author turning on the author. If the Prophet has struck too high a note, the Fool will take down the Prophet. It is Marsyas the rash flute player flaying himself. There is strength in this, and indeed this note of humor and self-mockery has been the strength of the poem throughout. The pathos, if it were pure pathos, would be intolerable. But even in the test of the Dry Mountains, pathos is saved by humor—if there were water we should stop and drink . . . here one can neither stand nor lie nor sit. What we can do is make even the worst situation look slightly ridiculous.

This gives a clue as to what has actually happened to the epic form as used by Eliot in "The Waste Land." Nothing could be more in the grand tradition than the models for Eliot's poem: *The Divine Comedy, The Aeneid,* the great myths of the Grail and the solar cycles, the spiritual epic of Calvary itself. But Eliot has not taken his own subject seriously enough to make an epic of it. He supposes, apparently, that the modern world is not important enough to deserve serious treatment. Dante might think enough of Florence and a local feud between Guelphs and Ghibellines to fit it into cosmic drama. Eliot reduces London and the fate of western Europe to mock tragedy.

As the poem turns from prophecy into confession so far as its spiritual content is concerned, so the form turns from epic to mock-epic. When humanity is not important enough for sympathy, a hero will not be serious enough for sacrifice. He may, however, be a mock hero, and it is a mock hero and mock-heroics that actually emerge from "The Waste Land." There has been every appearance of heroics, just as there has been every appearance of disaster and tribulation. Our hero has been buried alive in the underworld, fried in the lava of the burned-over land, tossed sizzling into the deepest sea, struck by a triple thunderbolt from the highest heaven. Still he neither succumbs nor triumphs. The heroics simply won't come off. At the end we still have the hero unchanged, fishing in the same pond, ready for more bolts, burning, burying, and drowning.

Our hero, in short, is a tough character. If he is sensitive and suffering, he is not suffering and sensitive enough either to melt into something better or crack into something worse. He survives as he is, because he is tough—and toughness is a quality that is good for comedy or burlesque, but useless for serious drama. As such, it is a perfectly legitimate quality; only it is not some other quality, such as daring, self-sacrifice, asceticism, humility, wisdom, or love. The tag end of "The Waste Land," with its "Hieronymo's mad againe," loses us our epic hero, but gains us a mock-epic one, and allows us to view the whole poem, in a sense, as a mock-epic or mock-heroic.

In the study of the author as a whole, we are left with the two alternating characters, much as in the case of Henry Adams. There is the prophet, or preacher (like Adams's "witty scholar") who admits no fallibility, and the fool, or errant soul (like Adams's "penitent child") who admits no consistency. The two characters, in various guises, go on and on, the one preaching a gospel that is supposed to be the only salvation (for example, the Witness in "The Rock"), the other telling of doubt and despair that no gospel can touch (for example the harried soul, Harry, in *The Family Reunion*).

Again, as with Henry Adams, there is the turning of the errant soul from the hard justice of the Fathers to the charity of the Sisters and Mothers:

> . . . Will the veiled sister pray
> For children at the gate
> Who will not go away and cannot pray. . . .

Yet I think this takes a somewhat different form from Adams's drastic rebellion from the stern law that he connected with the Fathers. Adams had taken the masculine God as Law without Love, just as he was to take the feminine God as Love without Law. But if there is alienation from a Father-God in Eliot, it is not in failure to have understood love as an attribute of divinity. Everything points to the fact that love and law had once been seen together, and then lost together. Our poet mourns the lost image of his father—full fathom five he lies—and we believe in the earlier vision:

> Looking into the heart of light, the silence.

But:

> I that was near your heart was removed therefrom
> To lose beauty in terror, terror in inquisition.

It is only after the alienation that divinity, or truth, separates into paternal wrath on the one hand and possible maternal charity on

[251]

the other, and the poet writes, "No place of grace for those who avoid the face."

Everything suggests the case of the son who had inherited the family blessing—and then somehow, through willfulness or pride, forfeited it. If we were to inquire in what manner, I think the Coriolanus story might be of help, the case of the aristocrat contemptuous of the "common people." Actually the missing relation, with Coriolanus, is the one to his fellow men—to the brothers. And it is through this failing that the other relation fails, the relation to truth, or God. Coriolanus, taught overweening pride by his mother, spurns the "voices" or opinion of his fellow citizens. He calls them curs, and says he prizes their love as he would the dead carcasses of unburied men. In fact, he prefers exile to any concession to the people, crying characteristically as he leaves, "Me banished? I banish you!" When his noble friend suggests that he repent and ask for reconciliation Coriolanus says, "For them! I cannot do it to the gods; Must I then do't to them?"

In Eliot's case, the significant point is the continued preoccupation with the lost image of the Father, and the general dissatisfaction with the Mother alone as a spiritual symbol. In terms of Mother Church, this disaffection amounts to a scandal, not only in "The Hollow Men," where she is called the hope only of empty men, but in "Ash Wednesday," where we read this ambiguous homage:

> Grace to the Mother
> For the Garden
> Where all love ends.

According to Dante's religious belief, or any other real faith in this mode of belief, this of course is where love begins. In Dante there is no conflict between a masculine and a feminine deity, any more than there is between love and law, history and God, or fate and nature. Eliot, like Henry Adams, separates truth and history; he turns to a past "period of unity" not for the present, or eternal, values in it, but for a historical situation that has actually disappeared. It is precisely what is gone that would have to be present to realize Eliot's demands. The same applies to the aristocratic political and social situation that would have to be conjured back from the past. Nothing is surer than that to value a past age for what belongs to it peculiarly is to miss in it what belongs to all ages. The recognition of this is our poet's despair.

"The Waste Land" is the picture of what is dying in the present, as it is of what is dead of the past. We must take this for its not always clarified truth. It tells of the decay of old modes as it does of the abuse of new ones. It tells of the remnants of the feudal in the commercial, the patriarchal in the agricultural, the imperial in the democratic. It reflects Pre-Raphaelite and Symbolist playing at religion for the color in it, and the effort to substitute the too-strong secular sciences for too-weak morals and religion. It reflects, in short, a society overburdened with traditional forms which are yet impotent to deal with a modern world —which leave, instead, a fatally widened chasm between form and morality, tradition and human needs. Our poet has eaten of this fruit. Henry James had circled around it, been fascinated by it, hinted at the phosphorescent gleams on its beautiful old surfaces. But James had kept himself apart, saved by innocence, to keep a precarious hold on enchantment. The poet of "The Waste Land" is not innocent, has partaken, and the fruit has been bitter.

Hence, after James's ambiguous children, child brides, and wide-eyed young provincials wandering bedazzled in the old palace gardens, we get Eliot's weary middle-aged lovers, lost sailors, haunted souls, bitter and evil old men: Prufrock, Phlebas, Harry, Gerontion, Tiresias. From James's adolescent dreams of union with the enchanted beauty of the past, we come to the nightmares of bondage in Eliot's dark towers of the Waste Land. Still there is no "middle life," no flow and continuity, no generation and reproduction for the sons of a new world committed to the forms of the old. With Eliot all is disenchantment and remorse, folly and despair. "The unread vision in the higher dream" recedes further and further into the mist, while the glittering pageantry of tradition in the mother kingdom has become a funeral procession:

> While jewelled unicorns draw by the gilded hearse.

The virtue of "The Waste Land" and Eliot's mordant and self-mocking verses is that it is knowledge, if partial and bitter. Here are James's blanks filled in—all those hints of evil and treachery, horror and perverted good, that James left so shadowy. For James they were all overlaid by glamour and glimpsed through innocence. With Eliot they are exposed in knowledge and chagrin. Not that we can take Eliot's knowledge whole, any more than we could take James's glamour pure. Eliot's hopelessness on one side is too complete, just as his grievance is unmeasured, his mockery unselected, and his insight undefined. The observer must decide for himself how much territory these states of mind actually cover, for Eliot has not put them in their place. Each one in turn con-

sumes the universe and, most unfortunate of all, the sense of irreparable wrong. The observer knows that all these states must
each represent but a limited content of fact and significance. Some
knowledge of this, indeed, seems to be present in the author's last
work (as this is written), the play, *The Family Reunion*.

It is a Puritan, Calvinist, New England hell that this Orpheus
sings: New England in its dry humor, Puritan in its fastidiousness,
Calvinist in its introspectiveness and terrible and wrong sense of
predestination. It is Calvinist, too, in a certain exclusiveness, as
if one should want to keep a conception of the Elect even in
Hades. Baudelaire is French, Latin, Catholic in contrast to our
poet.

But it is with Baudelaire that we are to compare Eliot and "The
Waste Land," rather than with Dante, or Virgil, or Milton. The
vision is of the underside, from the underside. This may be called,
not a vision of truth itself, but of truth as it looks from a false
position. From here, even good appears bad, because it seems
inaccessible, and all patient humanity, with its mixed faults and
virtues, becomes red faces sneering and snarling. The heavens
themselves seem veiled in all aspects except God the Destroyer—
who actually is not God, but only, again, a form of the opposed
self. We do not praise the failure of reconciliation and integration. We do respect the sensibility to the position.

CHAPTER IX

On New World Grounds

~~~~~~

THE culture-stream in the New World has the peculiarity of coming down through a great stretch of space as well as of time, as this book has frequently reminded the reader. This is a large, distinct, and altogether notable fact: in the first instance, nothing less than or different from the Atlantic Ocean. We are children of Europe, but with an ocean, another element, between ourselves and our Mother. Space is as great a mystery as time; together only they make existence. We are peculiarly the product of the most interesting segmentation of the earth's cover, and what we make of it inheres in it. No sign in the heavens could be as meaningful as the fact itself.

How to accommodate in our tradition the Atlantic Ocean! This book has tried to trace out the one way, the nostalgic, that is, in the mode of time as memory. American nostalgia has always diminished the factor of space toward zero, and tried to empty the Atlantic Ocean of its salt water. But this turns out to be the same as making it a minus quantity, a gap. The ocean remains but measures loss; the American, in the view of nostalgia, is a

European with the disadvantage of being cut off from the Mother nourishment. Hence the pathos, or the enchantment, the fascinated staring back across a gap, the yearning pull of the life cord over an emptiness. My story can be wound up quite quickly, how the day of enchantment for these our New World-fostered children of the old Mother, Europe—Henry James's day and the innocent wonder of the "grand tour"—was followed by the day of disillusion. It was not just like going back to the old family place and seeing the wonderful old things. It turned out that many of the old things were really old, or in other words broken, decayed, past their best use. Mother Europe, with her heavy burdens of the past, became a charnel house, and the children who had wandered enchanted into the old garden became the Lost Generation of the Waste Land. Cover them over light of leaves, the unfriended bodies of our children strayed!

It is the merit of T. S. Eliot that he tells the end of the story, or lets us read it between the lines. This is the way it ended. It is not good to keep things too long; they molder, they fall in a heap of dust. This is the burden of Eliot's poems, if his prose says something else. Matter is to be used and used again; then it stands up in fresh forms; then matter is eternal. But let us not hang on to a material form beyond its natural life, for we become bound only to the dead body. It turned out after all that the children of the New World had known new forms; the old did not answer their needs, and were a death to their spirit.

It is the virtue of T. S. Eliot to show that the one wrong reason for going back is to find security. There might be any number of good reasons: for knowledge, for comparison, for history, for pleasure, but the impossible end is spiritual certainty. Thomas

Aquinas or Whitman or possibly Einstein will tell you the same; the series is endless, and if you try to find a resting place somewhere back in the series, you are on an endless journey to no end, as T. S. Eliot came to say. Every alcove opens into another, and history is safe only as history. As a quest for the right time and the right place, it is a bottomless pit, a wilderness of mirrors, a succession of "time-coulisses," to use two of Thomas Mann's terms, and one, again, of T. S. Eliot's.

Security lies in knowing both the repetitions and the variations, for there is never life without both. Then the past comes to the present, the present leads into the future, and there is no gap to stare across transfixed with longing or fear.

Not to put the variations of life with its repetitions is much like the other way round, and the American children who stared back at the eastern horizon and Europe's encrusted Golden Bowl, were as romantic as those who always picked up to go further into the golden west. They were brothers under the skin, these New World children, bewitched in their different ways by the illusion of distance. Neither could leave in space as space, and time as time; they turned out to be equally bad at judging what is common and what is different simply because it is near or far away.

They are like the two kinds of provincials—the one who makes the local parish everything just because it is his, and the other who makes it nothing because it is—or was—his. Neither knows how to deal with the local—your intellectual snob nor your intellectual dub. It counts too much with both.

And so again with the American children of Europe, it was

naïveté and not knowledge of the world that led them on their backward pilgrimages. They were the bright youths brought up favoredly and too guardedly, and starting on their quests not knowing what the quest was. The initial question was the one they failed to ask. Who am I? What is my own? They lacked self-knowledge. They were not the gods but the half-gods of a new international era, like Woodrow Wilson, the great exemplar in action of this phase of American experience and tragic half-god of a possible internationalism.

The story of which Wilson was the chief figure and victim is much like the stories I have been telling: how the shining knight from the New World sought to redeem the evil Old World, and break the bad enchantment. He was neither quite pure enough nor wise enough to act the savior, though there was something of knowledge and something of purity in the impulse surely. But actually, the American was divided and confused by his half-knowledge and half-purity; for the other half was the old enchantment and the old evil. There was the question to ask at the very start of the journey, and the failure to ask it was the same as the failure of the quest. What did he know? What must he do? It was innocence of the conditions of the quest that was his downfall, and lack of knowledge of his own role.

What Wilson typified and drew out was the mixed adolescent nature of America, mixed, that is, on the international stage. Europe, and especially England, was still the Mother, even though now she was to stand for a mate, an equal, and a lady in distress. Presumably the young knight and prospective rescuer would act from his own virtue and truth, for redemption would depend on it. The rescuer must come from outside the bad enchantment in order to break it. His good word must be better than the bad charm. It was no good if it was merely innocent and eager.

But Europe was still the Mother, the center, to the romantic child that came to her rescue, and it was not really internationalism that urged his act, but filial sentiment. The grounds and laws of Mother Europe had caused the conflict. They were the flaw in the crystal, the break in the Golden Bowl, and you cannot heal a break by acting along it. You cannot change a cause by joining it. This is only to confuse the word and the act, in which case the act always wins, as it did at Versailles. Wilson found himself yielding bit by bit his own theoretical grounds (which actually he had never stood on) until he had to be satisfied with saving, like Maggie, only "the beauty of appearances."

Back in his own world the more local American felt a certain nausea at his first big international adventure, which measured roughly the difference between his own supposed grounds and those he found himself drawn on to. The native American might outlive the episode if it were understood; it could be thrown off, like adolescence, or better yet, learned from, like experience. But the European-American found it hard not to imagine that the empty word was still a deed, and the old charm could be saved somehow by a new charm.

The image broke again, and Mother Europe was farther than ever from the redemption dreamed of too innocently and not purely enough by her romantic child of the west. The trouble with the European-American was that he did not know either his Europe or his America well enough. The fact about the new international American was that he was not international enough. He was, in fact, but one kind of provincial, who found himself committed to the partial under the guise of the whole, and to the old under the guise of the new. Further away than ever, as Eliot confessed, was the unread vision in the higher dream.

Well, history has many cunning passages, as Eliot also observed, and this was only one of them. Nothing is harder than to distinguish between a saving remnant and a lost cause, between the permanent and the dead, between the new and the fashionable. For example, there is something wrong with the nineteenth-century business ideal and something beyond it, but it is hard to distinguish between going forward and going back from it. Criticism that seems to come from the vanguard often comes only from the rear, and there are strange bedfellows in every alcove.

Henry Adams, neglected by his own generation, was discovered by the succeeding one and looked something like a prophet to the disillusioned survivors of the first World War. He, too, appeared to be a victim of nineteenth-century business and materialism and too-optimistic liberty and progress, and his point of grievance seemed like a point of wisdom. But actually, Adams looked from a spot behind the nineteenth century and not in front of it, and his dismay at the materialism of commerce in a democratic world was really mourning for the vanished privileges of a hereditary "best people." Much of what passes for criticism of business, and even in supposedly advanced circles, has the Adams tone. It is a curious fact that the landed and leisured gentleman, "unsoiled by trade"—the predecessor of the businessman —still dominates much of the intellectual tradition. And from that point of view business is not wrong because it is too narrow an order. Business is wrong because it is "vulgar"; that is, it is too broad. It lets in too many people rather than too few.

Business and industry deserve their due, especially in a great country that has been knit together and nourished very much by business's idea that everybody's money is as good as anybody's, and trade need not inquire first about your name, family, religion, politics, or geography. You have to catch up with the business revolution before you can pass it.

On the left as well as right in America, it has been easier to catch ideas that come in the well-grooved currents of the East Wind than to work them from the history and thought of the New World. It remains a surprising fact that many bright American boys know instantly more about movements abroad than they do about life at home. It is not that they dislike their own history and culture; they do not know it. They have not learned its language, but instinctively understand a French, German, English, or Russian reference for the words they use. Their imaginations are still Old World, even as to new ideas. They, too, have kept the Atlantic Ocean empty of its water, and made a gap between the acts they hope to do and the grounds they have to stand on. Generally speaking, the grounds are much better than their acts. But that is why events both at home and abroad continually mystify our intellectuals, and every year or six months requires of them a new explanation, a new position, and a new hope.

Grounds are what you have to stand on. It is not that truth varies from place to place and time to time. On the contrary, it must be the same everywhere and always, or communication would be idle. But grounds, or your conditions along with your working principles, are the elements of truth you believe you can use for your good, you can establish with your fellows, you can make work. We like to make truth work for us and not against us. It is just as much a tribute to truth for me to get sick according to certain definite laws and sequences as to remain healthy; but I prefer, if I can, to illustrate the latter effect rather than the former.

Grounds, then, are the ideas you claim to believe along with the conditions in which they must operate, and hence are limited. True, there is always the one absolute unit, the person, the monad of consciousness, who in a sense can take absolute grounds if he wishes, since he has absolute jurisdiction over himself, if he is strong enough to exercise it. Hence the famous question of the philosophers, whether a man will not suffer and die more gladly upon his own grounds than live falsely on those others force him to take—a question that presupposes compulsion even to the point of death, and which might perhaps be answered yes, with the understanding that it would be better still if he could live to see his opponents take his better ground. A modern philosopher and hero, Gandhi, has I think seen this come to pass more than once. But anyway, the individual is the only unit with absolute choice about his grounds (up to and including death). After that your conditions multiply, you have to get some sort of consent from others about the principles you want to see in effect, or else have an apparatus of power to establish them and keep them established.

That is why smaller units can look more charming than larger units, so far as nice principles are concerned (providing outside compulsion does not end them altogether), and here and there a community or group or individual lives a fine and good life, while the state, the world, to which it belongs, looks gray with corruption. The larger the body, the more conditions to meet, the harder to establish jurisdiction for good principles; but the greater achievement if you manage to do it. So there is always a certain compensation about size of organization. It is a question of mass. The smaller the mass, the easier to influence a good way. But, the smaller, the more uncertain with respect to outside units, as many small nations in Europe have been discovering once again, with whom you must have some sort of working agreement or unworking disagreement. So there is always qualification, we each live by the sufferance of all, and no one can afford to be self-righteous.

Nothing is sillier than the kind of individualism that acts as if it were alone in the world, for it is not, and only has the choice of understanding its contingencies or running blindly on them. Equally silly is our demanding righteousness in others without respect to the conditions and jurisdictions which exist. What business is it of theirs or his or mine? On what lofty grounds do you stand when you tell me to be good? These are always proper questions, by which we recognize whether a person understands himself, that is, his own contingencies and powers, before he lays down the law to others. The subject matter of reason at any time is the set of conditions and powers that actually exist, and we recognize an appeal to reason only when we are convinced that arbitrary demands, or merely personal wishes, have been waived. This is true even for a man in an established office, however powerful, for in the end we measure the greatness of the officer by his use of the power lent him by the body that gave it, and we subtract both for underuse and overuse by the man. It is no accident that the favorite line of our greatest president was, "Why should the spirit of mortal be proud?"

Voluntary consent is the most precious form of order, in fact, the only secure form. But its essence is the appeal to nothing but what will be freely recognized by others as their own interest in common with yours. Dynamically it is the continual submission to that appeal of every interest felt by some to have become common with you and vital to them. In the end these interests and this feeling cannot be faked.

It is very nice to want voluntary co-operation rather than force, and high principle rather than low, in larger and larger areas of society, in more and more of life. The good society is always in that direction. But this is not anyone's to choose except so far as he is ready in good faith to risk letting others choose with him,— and "bad people" as well as good. The same goes for all sizes and kinds of social units, from families to continents, and all sorts of interests, from drinking water to sea power, with respect to those of the same sort in other hands, as far as you care to imagine, to the rounding of the globe. Until you are ready for a given risk, it is much better not to make confusion and noise by saying you and yours hold your own interests by sweet reason, while other bad people, or classes, or nations appeal only to un-reason and force.

Democracy is the risk of letting others choose with you, on the same terms, about a common vital interest. It is also faith in the nature given man to choose with. I do not think this latter part assumes some belief in the automatic or blind goodness of nature. I think it is only the assumption that a man, or perhaps even a radish, will choose what is good for him rather than bad, in the long run, with a little experience, provided he has the chance to choose freely, and later feel the effect of his choice.

Let no one suppose, if there is a margin for good choice, that it is likely a large one. I think it is likely very small—no more on the average, perhaps, than the power of a moment's consciousness compared to the inertia of a man's life! But if it exists at all, it must be very important, for it can be the means over time of almost infinite development.

Add that the chance for a man to choose from time to time about what looks good and bad for him, in his social policy and leadership, is a thing his own social institution can give him, if he and his fellows want to set up and keep up that kind of an institution.

If the above propositions have merit, I think our New World grounds may be described as especially favorable to their operation. In such a sense, I think you might say we have had the chance to make more of truth work for us, and less work against us, than have people in less fortunate times and places. Contingencies with us are not so many and unmanageable, both within and from without. Especially there has been the large margin in space—the human space inside and the salt-water, nonhuman margin outside—and this has allowed us to deliberate about our grounds with almost unprecedented freedom from pressure. Often we have not taken advantage of this freedom; we have not deliberated. But history never before, perhaps, offered a people such a chance to choose, both as to external and internal principles of association. It is no merit of the people that they have the grounds; their only merit is in their use of them.

We have been free to destroy as well as to improve our grounds, and often it has looked as if this were the freedom we have chiefly used. There is no magic in our idea if abused or not used. All depends on its use, for use is the only good of a principle, just as use is the only title that time recognizes to the earth and things of the earth. America has become the land of things in super-abundance; but their misuse is their destruction, or simply invites their appropriation by—or sacrifice to—other people who think they can use them to better advantage. And both within and without the national border the world teems with people who are in a position to think so vividly.

It needs no prophet to tell the triumph of better use over any mere theory of ownership. It is the only rule we can find to defend our taking of America from the Indians in the first place. And now in the day of the pre-emption of the land, and the multiplicity of its goods, whoever holds them beyond their good use has reason to know the weakness of his position. Things go dead in the very grasp, and all over America are people for whom the holding too long of too many things brings confusion, fear, and emptiness of the very meaning of things.

Yet American virtues have sprung from the same grounds—of good fortune—or rather, from the risking of good principles on good grounds. Our best principle has been risked, and on a widening scale. The colonies risked common choice as between themselves, in becoming a nation, and the world had hardly before seen a revolutionary group of men—Franklin, Washington, Adams, Jefferson, and the others—with so much good faith in their idea, and in each other. Again, in the time of Jefferson's administration, the nation risked using and abiding by its main principle when it chose between the party of the "superior few" of the Federalists and a new popular party—the first test of the sort. And again, after terrible conflict, and with whatever ill grace in part, the country risked return to its principle of common choice, South with North, under the extraordinary good faith of Lincoln. The very breath of life of the country is the faith that has been risked and to a degree won at such times, and we continue to live on the words that express the faith.

Less dramatic, because it was piecemeal and slow, there was the risk as each new state entered the Union and every new family took its place with the people already established. In the end, this was perhaps the broadest test the principles of the country underwent, for it actually carried them onto grounds the founders of the country had hardly visualized. Not until the latter half of the nineteenth century was there much comprehension of what it meant that America offered itself not only as a state of states, but as a nation of nations—to use a phrase of Whitman's used recently by Louis Adamic.

Yet it was the amount of risk run, the willingness to set up no test except the one of common interest with all, which measured the virtue of the thing being created, and made it truly a new thing under the sun. The United States could be glad that the risk was run, even though few people even yet understood what had been brought to pass during the great nineteenth century, when the fortune of the New World was offered to all comers. There were those who had begun to think that its virtues were its faults, and its faults its virtues: this period of open doors and openhandedness.

Though the risks were real, the strength of the country in the twentieth century lay more than anywhere else in the good will that had been created by its open doors of the nineteenth. This is the mystery of voluntary consent, working on the largest scale ever known, and is the most precious form of order—millions of soldiers and guns could not have requisitioned what was here given freely because it was received freely. And it has both a national and international meaning, the one as important as the other. There had never been anything like it before; never before had so large an area of land and so great a number of people, of so many different cultures, been welded together in so short a time—and this by no iron bonds, no compulsion, hardly even by a test of loyalty to their new country, or even a first quittance of loyalty to an old. It was truly a nation-beyond-the-national that was in process of creation, and the only possible bond strong enough to do it was the bond of no force at all.

The risks were real. There are always some people who will abuse such freedom as the last half of the nineteenth century gave people in the United States. These abuses were to require serious correction. Still, it will not do to assume that they mean, by themselves, a fundamental American lawlessness and weakness, as other peoples docile under heavy weights of usage or discipline have sometimes assumed. It is all a question of what sort of law, whether more outer or more inner, and only the security of a voluntary order can make such a degree of outer freedom safe. But so far as true solidarity is concerned, it has yet to be shown that the most voluntary does not make for the strongest order there is, and that the greater danger does not always lie with those who wish to substitute bonds of compulsion for bonds of good faith.

The most valuable possession of America, in the first half of the twentieth century, is its store of good faith. It is almost irreplaceable, for it is the transmutation of the original gift of fortune, during an unrepeatable period, into the character of a people. It will be harder and harder to add to this original store, as the nation grows older, though this is the only sound aim to follow. It is easy to waste it, in a hundred ways, and America in the twentieth century has managed to waste a great deal of it.

Good faith is wasted whenever a public official acts differently from a word given the people—for this is to cancel out the meaning and practice and virtue of common choice. Or again, good faith is wasted whenever some distinguishable group—by amount of property or kind of heredity or what—feels that through no fault of its own it has lost real choice about its common vital interests. The ballot is not the only medium through which the sense of equal choice is felt. There are many other subtle ways, social and economic, in which people sense participation or exclusion, and nothing is more important in a democracy than such inner states. It is not the prerogative of others to assume how anyone feels as to whether his choices have been restricted or his freedom arbitrarily limited. Only the group, the individuals affected, can feel, for this is the mystery of voluntary assent, and the only possible basis for good faith. It is always a risk to let others choose with you about a common interest, but there is no good faith without it. And whenever a group knows itself somehow cut off, the strength of the whole body is weakened by exactly so much: by the size of the group and the degree of damage to its inner faith.

Of course, it works the other way too. Any group, small as

well as large, can draw the circle itself, and say it marks a peculiar line, leaving its own people inside and other people outside, so far as some real common interest is concerned. So-called "minority groups" who draw and keep such a line take the risk of their own exclusiveness. No group of any size or kind can expect in the long run to draw upon free choice one way while they reserve it another. For this means that they draw only on the surplus margin of general good will—a dubious and fluctuating quantity.

Responsibility is equal for equal units. The level of freedom is determined by the willingness, along with the opportunity, to accept responsibility for the whole, and the downward spiral is easier than the upward one. When any group is separated from a vital common interest—say, men unable to find work—there begins, very reasonably, a doubt as to their voluntary loyalty, and with this doubt, a fear of their right to help make common decisions. Then it looks necessary to restrict their various freedoms further, and add further conditions to such rights as they still have in the whole. Fear breeds compulsion, and compulsion more fear, and the whole machinery of state takes on a different character. America could quickly find knitting about itself those links of fate which by good fortune it has been able to throw off, and see every mean device of state, that it had thought left behind, return one by one.

Or take it in the cultural field, where America has promised the creation of something different, a nation beyond the national, a culture beyond the cult. The very essence of this is its mixture in terms of old cultures, not the domination of any given line or strain of inheritance, except as elements from it are freely chosen by the whole. So far as its international role is concerned, the genius·of America is this free mixture. We have proved that you can "put all kinds side by side" and they will get along—provided you really give them a chance to choose about what is common, and do not force the choice. The appeal here is to the over-all and under-all common interest. It is this and this alone which can dissolve inherited differences, and really substitute a new loyalty for an old. And so far as America's international meaning is concerned, the more international elements we have, the greater the meaning. The more kinds of differences from out of world chaos—religious, racial, national—we manage to attract and provide a ground for under and over their grounds, the more America becomes a model and presage of the whole.

Yet there have been those, especially after 1917, when America partly abandoned its own supernational grounds to choose national and kindred-national grounds, who have begun to think differently, that the danger is in variety and not in the accommodation of variety. To these it begins to appear that America's mission in the world is to support a certain form of blood-and-language culture. This thought comes from many points and in various guises, but most commonly it follows the "English-speaking union" idea. There is little serious likelihood that the United States will reduce itself to a copy say of Fascist or Nazi styles of culture, unless through that peculiar form of contagion by which people begin to reflect the traits of a counterimage they are fixed on with hate and fear. This is possible. Democracy can lose itself this way as well as another, by becoming authoritarian in the name of opposing authoritarianism. But it would mean it had really lost faith in and courage to use its own principle. However, there is more likelihood that in fear of the "aggressor nations" and the

ideas of their leaders, we will approach nearer the British overlordship idea, as if it were identical with our own, and inherit too
closely the British role in the world. This always looks like internationalism itself to many of our people.

But indeed, as this is written, the United States is still largely
untried internationally. There is little evidence that it knows its
own grounds, and how to use its own principles, when acting
external to itself. Its greatness is still mostly a national greatness,
or at best a greatness within the Western Hemisphere. So far as
the world as a whole is concerned, America has very little con-
tested the leadership of Europe, and especially of Great Britain.
So far as the world has a center, we cannot say it is not still the
small, brilliant, proud peninsula of Europe, with all its intense,
clashing cultures, its broken geography, and its belief in imposed
order rather than voluntary consent. Americans for the most part
do not understand state and empire, rule and glory, blood and
land, hereditary enemies and clannish loyalties, in the European
sense of the terms, and this is both their strength and their weakness. And Wilson, the American crusader who dreamed of making
over Europe and slaying the dragon that guarded its hoard, un-
happily left her dragon and world leadership just about where
they were, except in a more irritated state.

The future looks dark, and it will be harder than ever for the
United States to use its own best principles, domestically and
externally, and more than ever important that it does. International ways at best have had almost nothing to do with the democratic principle, not even our Monroe Doctrine. Its principle is
only "noblesse oblige," or in other words, benevolent overlordship, and no good can be served by pretending it is what it is not.

What powerful nation, the United States included, is ready to risk letting others choose with it on the same terms about vital interests common to each? Has England ever been ready to let others choose with her, on equal terms, about control of the seas? Is the United States ready, say, to internationalize the Panama Canal, or even Pan-Americanize it, and with no last word left quietly to our naval arm?

Yet these are the smallest and simplest of questions, the very beginning of question, if one wants to talk seriously about a democratic international order.

The future looks dark, and if it is true that England's long overlordship is beginning to break down, America will face many near practical questions about her international principles before she does anything important about far theoretical ones. There are points in our own New World where we are already called on to decide between following the Queen-Mother ways of England, or trying to work out our own destiny of the association of brothers and equals. So far, we have shown little willingness to bind ourselves to any common rule with others which in any way touches a "vital interest" of our own. We have insulted other races by discriminatory laws. We would like our cake of a brotherly international order while we eat our cake of complete national freedom.

Nemesis—Karma—is the real ruler of much of the world, and it looks as if much more pain will be piled on before the burden will be thought unbearable.

Yet, it is true, the New World has been able to break many links of the chain. Despite all its wasting of fortune and endangering its store of good faith, much remains, both of faith and fortune. It can act on better grounds, can refrain from acting on worse grounds. On the whole, the various nations, races, groups in the New World, with some sad one-way exceptions, wish each other well. They have less need either to fear or hate. On the whole, the New World has not, characteristically, wished ill for peoples elsewhere, and has not singled out particular nations as mortal enemies—though there are definite tendencies in that direction. If those tendencies grow, America will quickly enough forge its own links of fate, and bondage to the world's ancient chain of evil. The seed—even the plant—is present. There are Americans who have chosen the enemy. It does not matter who he is, inside or out, of what breed or nation or kind; if you have chosen your mortal enemy you are already in bondage to him. And America is nursing its own seeds of destruction.

Nevertheless the New World nations have proved within their own boundaries, and to some extent across them, the truth that it is not blood that breeds fear and hatred, but conditions and ideas. More favorable conditions, truer ideas, can work marvels, as both South and North America have shown. Americans of South and Central America have apparently gone much further than North Americans in proving the common blood of mankind. Some of these nations are already far advanced in creating a new race beyond the races. North Americans, while talking a great deal about the equality of mankind, actually cling to pride in blood and race and are laying up humiliation to come. But North Americans, perhaps, have gone further than their southern neighbors in political freedom, education, and mobility up and down economic levels. Southern and Northern Americans have much to learn from each other, just as they have little still to receive from their common motherlands of Europe.

But it is a terrible truth that Americans have more ground to know and understand than any other people in the history of the world: there are no born barbarians. It is a terrible truth, because Americans have no cause to misunderstand what keeps other people in bondage. They themselves, many of them, have come from such bondages. It is not innate viciousness. Americans have much either to give on their own grounds or lose on other grounds. They have less cause to fear, less cause to hate, and that is their fateful position. They are easily damned.

There is a new idea in the world, effective common choice in economic as well as political rule. There is no question of the power of this idea. It is written in the steel, the electricity, the machines of the times. Men who rule by economic power, and keep the last word with themselves, and fear to risk the common vital interest to the choices of all concerned—these men show by their fear and anger the certainty of their own downfall. None can stand and look easily at the future.

Yet it looked as if this idea had somehow got linked with another that has no necessary connection with it, and in fact, tends to cancel its natural power. Was the unhappy connection made in the mind of its most famous prophet, Karl Marx, and had he borrowed from history the evil he hoped to remove from history? I think it may be, for as I read Marx, I read a brilliant economist with ill-considered ethics and bad politics. In Marx's name, at any rate, the two ideas go on side by side, first that socialism can redeem the world from the present ruthless use of material force, and second, this can be brought about only by a more ruthless use of material force.

The first proposition is perhaps as hopeful and valid as the other is old and discredited. Together they simply make confusion, the ancient confusion about ends and means. And they have delivered many admirable people who hold them into the hands of their enemies.

So far as our New World grounds are concerned, this particular confusion was threshed out long ago. Good faith is impossible if you put anything above good faith, even party or organization loyalty, which is valuable in itself. That is why we separated Church and State. Orthodox communism seems to have united them again in the very respect that the New World believes most unfortunate. There is no recourse when mere orthodoxy is the highest law, it does not matter what sort of orthodoxy. This means the rule of the man who interprets the orthodoxy, and afterwards of his narrowly chosen successors. The New World values above all voluntary choice of all people concerned, in good faith. With this we can meet our problems; without it we only add worse problems to bad.

All this side of the new doctrine has an old and familiar look to the New World; it looks like the Old World at its unfortunate worst. And there is a curious resemblance between those of our own young people who look back for security to some earlier period of "perfect orthodoxy," and those who look forward as they suppose to security in this new "perfect orthodoxy." Neither seems to have reached New World grounds. Conformity is the last word with both, and this always means fear of the free judgment of men, and ultimately of one's own free will.

We can only choose the good aim while rejecting the bad way. But let no one who stands to lose personal advantage by the good idea suppose he can discredit it by pointing to the wrong means. The new idea is to be judged on its own merits. But indeed, our own grounds have already judged its equivalent to be good and necessary. Our democracy was established in the belief that economic power would be well distributed among the people. Only on that assumption, according to our most representative statesmen, will political democracy work. Now, if you can no longer assume the wide distribution of economic power, if you have seen power in our history continually move from the broadly held land to the narrowly held machine—or the capital that controls both machine and land—then we must make our original assumption good, if we want to stand by our original truth. This is our history and its own dialectics. The new *is* makes a new *ought*. But the capitalist who confuses the two and the politician who says the *ought* remains the same while the *is* has changed: these bad reasoners stand just where the Marxist stands on his worst side. American capitalism might make bad Marxism come true, and help shift our society from its best New World grounds.

All this is simply tit for tat, from whatever side. It is the ancient wrong way of taking the grounds of your opponents, or worse grounds, in order to gain victory for your better grounds. It has never happened. There has never been a single inch gained by this poor strategy, but many a one lost; for when you accept your opponents' grounds, you have already abandoned your own. But every inch that has been won has been won another and better way—by refusing to fight on your opponents' grounds, but standing on your own. Then it is your better grounds that may win for you, if they really are better, and win something better than a personal or party victory. They have the chance of winning your opponents too, instead of losing them.

Wherever vital interest goes, in the process of history, the people must be there too in all their strength. Jefferson, for example, knew and insisted on this in his time and in its terms of a crucial vital interest. The crucial interest was still political freedom and equality, theoretically given by the Constitution, but which had not yet met a serious test, for no second popular party had risen to challenge the power of the first.

Jefferson risked his case on our own new grounds, and disdained to use against his opponents the weapons (of coercion and old-style appeal to conformity: the alien and sedition laws) they had raised against him. The result was social evolution in its only true sense, since it carried our entire society to the new plane. On this particular issue, the opposition was better than defeated: it was disarmed. In this area of our life, we virtually abandoned those bad weapons, and no one afterwards cared to use them in the same way. We can actually begin on Jefferson's grounds, and with his better weapons. Let no man in our day underestimate his advantage. For to use worse weapons than your own society allows you, is to abuse the good faith that exists, and carry us all back toward the jungle.

We would meet Plato any time on our main principle, and confound anyone who still believes (as I fear some of us still do) in the superior rule of a superior few. The end we all agree on: the well-being of all the people. But we insist that anyone's well-being depends on a sense of participation, or responsibility, with respect to the good of all—or can you separate happiness and virtue? But here is Plato—and a strange man to find there—saying you can separate them so far as the majority of the people is concerned, so far as their government is concerned, and make them happy without their being responsible.

No, we say you will get a nation of children that way and not men and women. We suggest that is what our "economic guardians" would also get, if they had their way in industry.

Or take it from the other side. Responsibility makes for virtue, and the larger portion of the people given responsibility, the more you have drawn upon your available resources of good government. But here is Plato, and anyone else who thinks in terms of a small "elite" class, aiming to deprive most of the people of most of their share of responsibility, and the government of a large part of its own means of government.

We would not forgo using the talents of the more talented, not by any means. We only add that we would not give them special powers. We would call upon the virtues and powers of everyone, and so get the most for our money. That is what I understand by Lincoln's phrase, the government of, for, and by the people: simply the sound practice of making our end product, our material medium, and our immediate motive as nearly the same thing as possible—namely, the good of all of us.

They are quite right who make social ends a real concern of the individual. For the truth is, we are physically made that way, each made of the elements of all, and our human race is the one party we cannot resign from except by self-destruction. It is not just an ideal aim—the good society; it is emotional, practical, psychological—what you will.

Of course, there is always Hudson's Bay and the fur trade!— as Robert Frost says in the poem. There is always some chance to escape civilization for a cruder civilization. But like Frost's wearied talker, we'll generally decide to stay. Because really to go, as the poem says, is only an *empty threat*, or in other words, a choice of emptiness. "You and I off here with the dead race of the Great Auk!" Go, if you prefer emptiness.

But for the "Lost Generation" it looked rather a matter of returning, returning from the desert of faithlessness into which, from whatever cause, and guilty or innocent, they had wandered. It may have been science misread, or science used in place of ethics and religion, or Rousseau, or Freud, or Marx, or even Shakespeare, read or misread. It may have been back to nature with man's nature left out, or to the "glory of the past" with emphasis on the pastness, or the self by itself, or art by itself, or ahead to Utopia with the same empty band wagon. Let us save time and agree it was whatever it was, because we know where it led. It led first toward faithlessness in the nature of reality, and then in the nature of oneself.

They cannot be separated. Lack one lacks both, as Whitman said—for one reflects the other. Until you can place a thing outside of you, you have not got it in you. You cannot tell me even the smallest fact without also telling me a universal, nor can you tell me a universal without telling me some fact.

Well, the fathers often recited empty universals, so the children came telling their empty particulars.

The fathers had named God too easily and often, often meaning only a man that is not there. So the children's mouths were stopped concerning a great given that is.

The fathers insisted on duties whether they served anyone or not; so the children insisted on pleasures whether they pleased anyone or not.

The fathers and mothers went to the few places they could go as a family; so the children went off separately to all the unfamiliar places.

The parents had the children they deserved, and the children got what they asked for.

I may fix myself against some certain evil, fix myself toward some single good, until I am tired to death. There is no separate thing, however important in itself, that will not turn to ashes in the mouth if the whole desire is fixed on it. I can pick these pockets of the universe one after the other and have nothing to show for it but empty pockets. For every separate thing is most important only when put with everything else.

I did not make my world; still it made me, and what do I use for true and false except what I find in the world? Where do I stand to tell it off as a whole except somewhere in the world?

Well, there is the place-no-place, known as the rock of Prometheus, that we go to when too serious about our own seriousness. But instead of finding freedom, we find ourselves bound; and there we may last just so long as we can feed on our own hearts, and stand the tension in our own guts. And near by is the place where we are too light with our own levity, the hollow gorge known as mocking laughter. This is the place of semblance, irony, and all things seen in double focus. There we hold out so long as we have a taste or talent for playing, and not for fun, our own fool.

But I find after all it is absurd to imagine I rival what in no way rivals me. I see I only rival myself. Nor do I lack courage for taking the courage of my own heart stream, nor dignity for taking the dignity of my own grounds. And I see I may lessen what grieves me only by leaving the point of my grief.

Then there is the "glory of the past," meaning a time when people were happily in touch with great and permanent truths. Let us mourn for such and such a time, because of the passing of what must have come from what never passes! O the vanishing of the everlasting; O the everlasting of the vanishing!

Likewise there is that idea for the perfect society of the future, which when people understand it will make every man love his fellow man, and makes people who now understand it so angry with their fellow men.

Henry Adams was sure that energy was running downhill. He went back all of seven hundred years to show this sad condition, and how high it had been, and how low it had fallen. O energy to be so energetic to be so inert!

Here let us present the beetling brow and protruding lip of the great human male I Am, whether in forum or field, fireside, pulpit, studio or town; in uniform, robe, or neat business suit; saying in seventy languages quite often through a beard, Me for God and she for God in Me, and by his side, sure enough, patient Griselda, if not three or four.

And just across the way may we present a rival attraction, the goddess-queen with the secret smile in the corners of her lips, clothed in the fashion of the land, if in a taste just tending to opulence, saying, Me for Love and he for Love in Me, and likewise if less in words, Men will be boys and boys will be men, with examples of each about her skirts.

May we submit a revised billing for these two spectacles, but covering well enough the essential business, namely, the Old Adam and the Old Eve, and commend them henceforward, principals and cast, to the unsentimental offices of comedy.

Scientists speak of "impersonality," and many show what they mean. Others, however, and some of fame, ask to be thought impersonal in finding human life without the idea of the impersonal. And a good many artists and writers, following this lead in part perhaps, deal as they insist disinterestedly with people they insist cannot, in being people, have any notion of disinterestedness.

It is true, many people, and among them artists and scientists, fear impersonality as if it were death, and sheer loss of themselves, and altogether painful.

Yet all the while almost everyone, and by no means only scientists and artists, know at times what it is to be impersonal, and know at the same moment a sense of happiness and power.

The lover knows it when he sees that the well-being of his beloved is his own deepest desire. A craftsman feels it, feeling in his hands how the material is, or a mechanic when he has fitted the parts of the machine according to its own working principle.

The mother knowing she does the best for her child, whether or not the child knows. The congressman who hears the cheap jibe against him and returns quietly to his work; and the reporter writing from his own unspoken judgment of the facts. The engineer submitting the plans that are not anyone's mere wishes, but what the construction calls for. A minister or priest or rabbi who understands that his idea may be misunderstood and does what is needed anyway. The wife or husband during the quarrel late at night, letting go the livid giving and taking pain, and after a deathly moment feeling the life that flows back, bringing with it the other person.

The poet writing the lines of which he says to himself, these are true whether I live or die! The novelist, after looking with difficulty at the character least sympathetic to him, seeing suddenly how it takes its own living being. The talented young person sick with the question of his ability to live up to his hopes, as he puts even that question aside to make sure of life itself as a first step. The scientist at the moment of sure proof knowing with awe that it lies outside of him. The farmer knowing he has used all he knows and the rest is not up to him. The executive delegating the task, and with it the freedom to do it; and the man in the shop knowing his own worth, and proceeding only on that basis.

This sea of impersonality, or truth, that looks so much like death to anyone from outside, is as everyone knows from inside, from inside, life. Call it humanity or divinity, it is the ever-possible fulfillment of the nature of man.

Yet I shall not say, right or wrong the human race, unless I wish my kind ill, for I see it is with conditions. I think nature has been looking a long while for a species that thinks well enough of itself not to do ill by itself. I can easily spot the small-time politician speaking fatuously of his grea-a-a-at party or country; why then have a small-time politics for human beings, for myself?

If I am looking for people to stay by the party, the country, or even themselves, I will find them, I think, who put theirs and ours with everything and everybody else. Then they are likely to stay as long as necessary.

Our own grounds can rest only on this largest ground—the ground of reality—as indeed our principle assumes it. We can risk letting strangers choose with us about our common vital interests only if we have some confidence in a common truth for us all. There is no getting around it, a risk is a risk. It means letting go for the time being, and relying on an outside situation you cannot entirely control. It means, in short, faith. But what is the alternative? Never being sure of anything or anyone (unless it is our own little band of sworn blood brothers, and how far do we trust them?) we cannot keep our eyes and hands on all the time, and that comes down to very little.

We are not content with such small grounds, and such little freedom and fun. And why should I think myself essentially different from other people? I know when I do think so, instead of being happy about it, I soon feel only misunderstood. So I take it it is a false idea. Rather, I think the laws must be true for others which I have found true for myself, myself being an illustration and not the law; and I know I am uncomfortable in a false position; and anger leaves me worse off; and I dislike being mistrusted, but respond rather to good faith; and I imagine it is not greatly different with other people.

[286]

This at any rate is the assumption we have taken as the best to work on. We have rested our institution on our faith in the nature given us as men, which is a thing beyond us and beyond our institution. Anyone who looked very long at the matter was bound to come to the conclusion of Whitman, that "the real and permanent grandeur of the States must be their religion, otherwise there is no real and permanent grandeur." Yet we believe it wise to leave our state uncapped by the appearance of perfection, or specific divine sanction, knowing this is as it may be, and something to work at; and we have trusted men to be truest when given freedom to be true. All these things we believe good grounds for a good institution, but with the grounds always larger and more substantial than the institution. For a creation of man for his own use may be quite imperfect, and still survive and even be made better, as long as he believes in the grounds it stands on; but when he mistrusts its grounds, then no elaboration of the structure can keep it from breaking to pieces.

How has it worked with us? It is clear, the losses we have taken from our risks: that men have misused their liberty; that because their institution does not tell them they must be good, some have thought there is no reason for goodness; and because they are not required to believe anything at all, some have felt this left them with nothing either to count on or account for. No one can deny the ill results that have actually occurred, and that men have done themselves all kinds of harm, and others too, by their freedom to believe or disbelieve what they will. Let the actual facts here be rated for just what they are.

Still I rate at a high level the grounds we have actually won by use of our principle, taking into account the extent of the grounds, the size of our mass. The whole secret of this matter lies in the assumptions which people have come to act on and do not dispute, because they are convinced of their merits, which is the same as the level of good faith which actually exists. I say this has been carried high, as good faith goes in history, over similar areas. I know when I am well off in the freedom of my body and mind, and can only marvel, for example, at my ready access—except when "national interest" is threatened!—to almost any knowledge or opinion that has been recorded or divulged anywhere, anytime, with little physical trouble to me, in fact with the general co-operation and consideration of the society of which I am some part. I put this and things like it at the extraordinary place they should have, realizing that in history my circumstance has been duplicated only for narrow circles of society, often uncertain, in danger, and qualified by compelling intangible forces. I think my situation in this respect is not much better or much worse than that of most of my fellow countrymen, and on absolute grounds is more privileged than that of Erasmus or Aristotle.

I reserve again the real obstacle that exists for a large portion of my countrymen in their access to materials which are abundantly present for their own livelihood. I repeat, this is not the sort of loss we can take as part of the natural risk of our principle, but must see as a violation of our essential principle. Can there be freedom of choice that leaves out choice of making a living? The best new and old grounds call for the use of our principle to extend it, and so keep on our course, realizing that in our failure men of opposed position, agreeing only in a worse will, will try the whole matter by a different principle altogether, to the great real loss of every one of us.

Yet, much of the fortune of our conditions has been translated and remains with us as a social attitude; and this is something to build with as well as on. I think it is no flimsy structure, likely to vanish in a few years under a cloud or be demolished suddenly by some opposing idea, any more than it was built up in a few years of favor. I think it is a matter of actual nerve-and-brain set in the people, as it is also a mechanism in our institution. I think you might find a definite power of tolerance or accommodation for a given society as for an individual. I look about at my fellow countrymen, and I think I know good humor when I see it, reserve power, and willingness to listen to another's opinion, provided it is presented in good faith. I like the man on the street who tells me of course I may see it another way, but this is his angle. I think he is a good metaphysician. I think these qualities exist especially in those who produce or actually handle the real wealth of the country, in both town and country, in the shops and on the land; and I see it too in many of our associations of business and professional men, and in other organizations of women and men.

No one can leave out the innocence and ignorance in many places, the false optimism, contempt, anger, and arrogance in others. Let the presence of all these qualities be measured for what they are, neither greater or less. Whoever counts too much on the fund of good will among his fellows only digs a pit for himself and his friends; yet who does not call on what there is, in good faith himself, leads us only toward destruction.

When we look at what is possible, given our conditions, we are all shamed. The most fortunate of us knows his failure. Every token of wealth not used is not used somewhere else; we take a double loss for every useless gain. In deep vaults in our cities are the many pits we have dug for ourselves of sterile wealth, and who cannot see, in Kentucky, the great pit we have been digging wide and deep enough to engulf a nation, if long left unfilled and unfulfilled?

Who will find us a truer measure of man's economy? For Adam Smith and after him Karl Marx proposed only the crude measure of things, or labor spent producing things; as if yours and my good varied directly with our massing up of potatoes or wool or lumber, and afterwards a man still could not do better to measure his gain than by the quantity of his eating and wearing and owning of things and more things!

Well, some of us know the emptiness of hunger without things, and some the emptiness of things got beyond hunger, and got and consumed past love, and these are two sides of the same bad coin. But all of us know that the goods we get out of life are not told either by our bushels of produce, nor by our hours of work, nor what we can exchange these for, nor any token of them, though it certainly involves all of them. But not as if our labor were all time lost, and our consumption all time saved!

I say this is not man's economy, and that we shall measure all these things more truly on another scale, not merely in our minds, but in our society, and reduce the errors both of too much and too little by the same truing of the standard.

We can be glad for the path already marked, for in 1776, when Adam Smith published his *Wealth of Nations*, a document of our own took quite another tack, and declared for a different set of human goals, however much some of us since have tried to read property for happiness, privilege for liberty, and greed for life!

I see the same way pointed out by other hands, and by our best, and the road ahead very much lighted by men in back of us. By Emerson, with his shrewd sense of the best gifts of our hours and days; by Thoreau, personally testing what is worth a man's time; by Whitman on a dozen levels freeing the good of life from ancient indignity and dirt; by Lincoln, master by the hardest road in the darkest day of the means and motives of men. Nothing in our circumstance keeps us from building further on this plan. Everything shames us rather, to build with and for the good of men and women, with care for feeling and motive, without malice toward peoples in or out of our borders, but in good faith.

In our daylight history we have been given grounds to see well beyond a blood-and-earth patrimony. We know too many bloods to think blood more than one, and know and remember too many plots of ground to think earth is not the same the earth over. There is even a kind of portent in the not-enough earthiness of our Woodrow Wilson and the naïve unnativeness of our Henry James! We are a mobile people, and do not propose to become set in our ways if we can help it. Man, after all, is an animate creature. We do not like walls and being walled in, and do not want to let our roots harden into chains, or a local air grow thick about us to the point of suffocation. Most of us, I think, feel uncomfortable when someone waves a flag, even our own. We want to say let the thing wave itself, if it has something to wave.

And our globe-trotters, exiles, restless children, are a kind of portent too.

True, there are particulars everywhere, as perhaps some of our romantic wanderers have come to know to their grief. No one yet has got anywhere that was not somewhere, or left a set of circumstances without finding a set of circumstances. Be sure they are just as good or better and not worse!

The wind blew from the East, we came from the East, most of our words, much of our light, perhaps human life itself spread on this earth from the East, and comes down to us from time. But all comes to us where we are, in our time. The world spirit, I think, shrinks only from confinement and flees only from flight. I think it never fails to make itself free to people who free themselves, and is at home anywhere, any time, where people make a home of the world.

Index

INDEX

Boone, Daniel, 4, 5
Borah, Senator, 17
British imperialism, 272-274
Bunyan, Paul, 2
"Business ideal," the, and democracy, 261-262

Calvin, John, 28; theory of "elect," 66-67
Calvinism, in T. S. Eliot, 255
Carlyle, Thomas, 94, 95
Castiglione, *The Perfect Courtier*, 59
"Causa," verse by Ezra Pound, quoted, 72
Channing, William E., 94
Christianity, movement to New World, 31, 32
Church and State, Separation of, 40
Cicero, 60, 63
City of God, The, by St. Augustine, 224, 236
Civilization, ideal of in Henry James, 110-113, 131
Clemens, Samuel, see Mark Twain
Cliffton, William, verse quoted, 10
Coleridge, S. T., "The Ancient Mariner," 247
Commager, Henry Steele, on Henry Adams's *Democracy*, 183
"Common man, the," 5, 57
Communism and democracy, 276-278
Confessions, of St. Augustine, 223
Conrad, Joseph, quoted, 163
Contrast, The, by Royall Tyler, example of the "international situation," 79
Cooper, Gary, 5
Cooper, James Fenimore, 5
Copernicus, 28
"Coriolan," by T. S. Eliot, 242
Coriolanus, story of, and T. S. Eliot, 252
"Cousin Nancy," by T. S. Eliot, 205
Crevecoeur, J. Hector St. John, quoted, 5; and the American "natural," 6

Dante, 178, 188; in criticism of T. S. Eliot, 206-209; 213; in "The Waste Land," 222, 224
Daumier, 102
Democracy, a novel by Henry Adams, 183
Democracy, evolution of in America, 35-41; Whitman's oath of, 55; "type-ideal" in, 56-59; compared to aristocracy, 62-64; imagination in, 59, 71; theory of, 265-266; American grounds of, 266-276; economic, 276-279; and religion, 286, 287
"Descent into Hell," tradition of, 222
"Dialogue on Dramatic Poetry," by T. S. Eliot, 209
Dickinson, Emily, 198
"Diffusionism," 4
Disney, Walt, 49
Divine Comedy, The, by Dante, 207; and method of "The Waste Land," 222, 224
Donne, John, 210
Dreiser, Theodore, 85
"Dynamo," Henry Adams's symbol of the, 192-194

Eakins, Thomas, 2
East-West conflict, 16-20
"East Wind," message of, 14; as "racial memory," 14, 15; children of, 21; current of, 22; 97, 262
Economic democracy, 276-279
Economy, measures of, 13, 290
Edison, Thomas, 49
Education of Henry Adams, The, 166, 169-174
Einstein, Albert, 41, 258
"Elder gods," 3
"Elect," the, 65-69

INDEX

Eliot, Charlotte Stearns, mother of T. S. Eliot, 201, 202, 205

Eliot, Thomas Stearns, 86, 97, 168, 169, 189, 191; role of, 195-197; New England heritage, 197-199; birthplace and background, 199-203; American inheritance, an unsettled account, 203-205; question of the essays, 205-209; insight of, 209-211; validity of poetry, 212-215; difficulty of, 215-221; method of "The Waste Land," 221-226; its meaning, 226-244; confessional element, 212-215, 244-250; failure of drama, 244-250; "The Waste Land" as a mock-heroic, 249-250; divided character, 250-253; significance of, 253-255, 257-258; compared with Henry Adams, 251, 253; compared with Henry James, 203-204, 253-254; 261

Eliot, William Greenleaf, grandfather of T. S. Eliot, 201-203

"Elite class," 56-58, 279-280

Emerson, Ralph Waldo, 4, 11, 189, 190; in T. S. Eliot's poetry, 205; 218, 291

Enchantment, nature of, 87-88; of Henry James, 88-89

"Endymion," by John Keats, in "The Waste Land," 231

Erasmus, 28, 34, 288

Ericson, Leif, 32

Essays, Emerson, 190

Esther, a novel by Henry Adams, 74, 169, 176

Eucharist, the, in symbolism of "The Waste Land," 224, 225

"European-American," the, in James, 152-153; 260-261

"European element," in James's "international situation," 106-108

Evil, American innocence of, 78, 85, 275

Family Reunion, The, play by T. S. Eliot, 246, 251, 255

Fascism, 272

Federalists, the New England, 69

Fertility rites, in symbolism of "The Waste Land," 224, 225

Feudalism, decay of in America, 50, 51

Fink, Mike, 2

"Flickerbridge," story by Henry James, 150

Folk gods, American, 2, 7, 8

Ford, Henry, 49, 79

"Forgetting," as a creative factor, 44-47

Fortune, in the New World, 27, 30, 44; changes in style of, 28 ff; part of New World mystery, 54; translation into good will, 266, 275, 289

Founding of Massachusetts, The, by Brooks Adams, 187

Fox, George, 28, 38

Franciscans, the, 28

Franklin, Benjamin, 2, 6, 11, 63

Frazer, J. G., quoted, 230

Freedom, level of, 271, 288

Free land, influence of, 17, 39

Freneau, Philip, quoted, 10

Frontier, "oral tradition" of, 2

Frost, Robert, "Empty Threat," quoted from, 281

Functionalism, and pioneering, 45

Galileo, 28

Gandhi, 263

Garland, Hamlin, as example of "interregional" conflict, 79-86; background, 80-82; literary influence on, 82-84; conflict of, 83-84; contribution of, 84

"Genteel tradition," 83, 212

Glamour, in Henry James, 145, 150, 151, 163

Golden Bowl, The, by Henry James,

INDEX

INDEX

"Rights of man," element in American democracy, 35-37

Rockefeller, John D., 51

Roderick Hudson, by Henry James, 81, 107, 127

Rogers, Will, and the American "natural," 6

Roman Empire, make-up of the, 56

Romanticism, left and right, 9-11, 258; of Henry James, 89-92

Rossetti, Dante Gabriel, in allusion of "The Waste Land," note, 231

Rousseau, question of influence on American "naturals," 4-7; his mysterious "Law-giver," 64-65

Rule of Phase, The, by Henry Adams, 170, 183, 194

Sacred and secular truth, problem to Henry Adams, 191-192

Sandburg, Carl, 48, 85

Sargent, portrait of Henry James, 105

"Saving remnant," the, 65-69

Science, movement to New World, 31

"Session" articles, by Henry Adams, 171-174

Shakespeare, 43, 152; comparison with Dante by T. S. Eliot, 206-209; Hamlet question, 210-211

"Sinners in the Hands of an Angry God," by Jonathan Edwards, 236

Smith, Adam, "leisure-class ideal," 13; measure of value, 290

Son of the Middle Border, A, by Hamlin Garland, 80-84

Social question, in *The Princess Casamassima,* 111-112

Socialism, and democracy, 276-279

South America, 30; and racial democracy, 275

Space, influence in American culture, 3, 4, 11, 47, 266

Spiller, Robert, introduction to *Esther,* 177

Spinoza, 195

Sterility, of life in the "enchanted kingdom," 151-153

Sterling, John, 94

Sumner, Charles, 75

"Superior few," the, Plato's theory of rule by, 59-64; idea of in New England, 69-70; in the South, 70; lack of imagination of, 59, 71-72

"Sweeney Agonistes," by T. S. Eliot, 245

"Sweeney Erect," by T. S. Eliot, 205

Swinburne, Algernon Charles, "Tiresias," in "The Waste Land," quoted, 228, 234

Tempest, The, by Shakespeare, quotation, 208; 229

Tennyson, "Maud," conflict in, 210

Thackeray, 94

Theocracy, in New England, 65-69

Thomas Aquinas, on the intellect, 218; 258

Thoreau, Henry, 198; on man's economy, 291

"Tiresias," by Swinburne, in "The Waste Land," quoted, 228, 234

Tradition, American, 11-12, 27-28

Turn of the Screw, The, by Henry James, "evil" in, 138

Twain, Mark, 7-8, 58, 152

Tyler, Royall, *The Contrast,* 79

Use, principle of, 13, 267

Variety, accommodation of in American culture, 43, 272

Vegetation god, in "The Waste Land," 224, 229, 230, 238

Versailles, treaty of, 160, 260

Virgil, 207, 222

Virgin Mary, the, as viewed by Henry Adams, 178, 180, 184, 186

Virginia, contribution to democracy, 34-36

INDEX